PRAISE FOR PASSPORTS & PACIFIERS

"...Jain shares amusing anecdotes and things she's learned during her journeys with her kids in the United States and abroad in a blend of engaging remembrance and practical travel manual. She advocates traveling with kids as a means to instill in them a sense of compassion and a love of new experiences, but the key goal is to have fun together as a family...She effectively stresses that both children and travel can be unpredictable, so resourcefulness and flexibility are essential. The author has a flair for apt descriptions: She compares a crowd in the Sistine Chapel to "four-year-olds clustered around a soccer ball" and bikes in Copenhagen at rush hour to "the mosquitos of Belize," and she muses about mountains "capping the earth like meringue on a pie." Her voice is down-to-earth and her sense of humor and commitment to environmental sustainability are evident throughout."

Kirkus Reviews

"Reading Kaitlyn Jain's very funny stories made me feel regret for not traveling more when my children were young . . . but also huge relief I didn't."

George Mahood, author of *Free Country: A Penniless Adventure the Length of Britain*

"Passports and Pacifiers is an impossible-to-put-down book that is part travelogue, part advice column for would-be jet setting parents. Jain is a talented storyteller who takes us on journeys from the gelato shops of Italy to the beaches of San Diego, from Mayan ruins in Guatemala to cruises to Helsinki. For parents wanting to raise their kids with memories and meaningful encounters with cultures from around the world, this is a must-read."

Jason Farman, author of *Delayed Response: The Art of Waiting from the Ancient to the Instant World*

PASSPORTS
AND
Pacifiers

PASSPORTS AND *Pacifiers*

Traveling the World,
One Tantrum at a Time

Kaitlyn Jain

ISBN 978-1-7359600-0-5

First paperback edition February 2021.

Jain, Kaitlyn.

   Passports and pacifiers: traveling the world, one tantrum at a time / Kaitlyn Jain.

Library of Congress Control Number: 2020921925

For more information and permissions, www.kaitlynjain.com.

Cover and interior design by Kingdom Covers, www.kingdomcovers.com.

 BOSTON BELS PUBLISHING

Olney, MD

These are my memories, from my perspective, and I have tried to represent events as faithfully as possible.

Printed in the United States of America.

In memory of Artie, who was there at the beginning,
and there faithfully whenever we returned.

CONTENTS

PASSPORTS

AND

Pacifiers

First Trimester

PREPARATION IS KEY

MY THREE-YEAR-OLD MIDDLE daughter lay prone on the floor of João Paulo II Airport, her feet thrashing the air in the throes of an epic meltdown. I braced myself to avoid the impact from her Minnie Mouse tennis shoes, violently lighting up with each kick. She still wore her sheer-sleeved Cinderella pajamas and hand-me-down-thin pink cotton socks she had carefully selected for our red-eye flight from Washington, D.C. to the Azores off the coast of Portugal. Her matted hair mixed with the grime of the floor where hundreds, if not thousands, of people walked each day in filthy shoes from around the globe.

I had no sustenance to appease her, no pacifier to calm her. At that moment, her salve lay buried deep in a bag on the other side of the x-ray machine amid the diapers, toys, and snacks. I couldn't even offer her my arms since they held her angelically sleeping baby brother. She had made it so many hours but had been broken by my placing her suitcase on the scanner. Apparently, she wanted to do it herself. Her face shone red with frustration as she screamed and cried, a huge production lacking any true tears. Walking through that final metal detector on her own two feet to that short flight was her final step.

This wasn't our first challenge of the trip, and I was pretty certain it wouldn't be our last. Our oldest had thrown up on the airplane. After discovering my fourth pregnancy just three days earlier on my son's first birthday,

3

those tingles of excitement I felt in my belly were beginning to morph into nausea. What would be next? I wondered. What had we forgotten?

"Can you imagine if we had another?" my husband joked to my unknowing, but horrified, parents who had joined us.

We were traveling the world, one tantrum at a time.

Chapter One

AM I AN IDIOT? OR JUST A WEIRDO?

*G*ROWING UP MIDDLE class in middle America, travel to me meant days of driving to get anywhere. Crossing a river was exciting. Seeing a license plate from Alaska, unreal.

As my family's youngest, I fell under the shadows of the others—my super-athletic, likable sister; my bulldozer of a brainy brother; even my dad, a former semi-professional athlete who returned to his small town. I could relate to my middle daughter crying out for attention with a tantrum. As a child, it had taken everything I had to keep up.

My sister, Kylie, was my hero, a She-Ra in my eyes. I wrote odes to her basketball skills and used the tracks she etched in the snow as my guidepost. To avoid direct comparisons, I focused on a different sport, volleyball. I liked a game where I could rise to the challenge with a well-timed ace but also float under the radar of complex team dynamics. At least after some practice. As the youngest child, I wanted attention—but not all eyes on me.

I still vividly remember when my high school coach, at one point the country's winningest, thrust me into the spotlight. He was an intimidating bear of a man and probably reveled in allowing that University of Michigan-bound senior to humiliate me, a lowly freshman, by serving me off the court. She directed ball after unreturnable ball at me, at least a half-dozen times in a game to fifteen. I single-handedly lost that game, aided by my coach's refusal to sub me out. Since I was ghostly quiet, he called me Casper, but he knew the threat of negative feedback on my performance would drive me to work harder. I quickly improved since I hated (and still do hate) failing or letting others down.

Then, three years later as a senior, I demonstrated that fear in front of an entire auditorium of athletes and their parents—though not my own since they were, fittingly, at one of my sister's college games. I was smart but oblivious, a strong but painfully naïve girl who had moved from a small town to a larger school, a pebble in the larger stream of life.

At an end-of-season sports banquet, I got up to speak about our amazing basketball season with my teammate, Kim. My friend was tall and well-liked, gorgeous, homecoming court material. Kim either had fantastic confidence or faked it really well.

After she shared thoughtful team anecdotes, I edged over to the microphone to thank our fans. For that, I turned to the guys on the football team in the second row. They weren't like the stereotypical football team. Oh sure, they were a bunch of jocks, but we were no *Friday Night Lights*. They had one of the worst records of any of the teams at the event, but the seniors supported us and came to every game, home and away. They made signs and wore homemade t-shirts bearing our names. Perhaps one or two were fond of me, but all seemed to be head-over-cleats for my friend. They, and a few others, were our Super Fans.

As I went in for the close of my speech, I talked with the unnecessary confidence of a senior at the top of my high school game.

"I would ESPECIALLY—(pause for effect)—like to spank the football team."

Spank the football team? Spank. The. Football. Team. Like my three-year-old stuck on one side of the x-ray machine in the Azores, the "th" sound remained trapped behind my treasonous teeth.

Howls erupted throughout the packed auditorium, echoing across the stage, spanking me in the face with each guffaw. Mortified, I attempted to bumble through a correction, but in her shock, Kim had moved in front of me, cackling loudly into the microphone. Now people were laughing with her distinct chortle, and the auditorium felt like a comedy club, hooting at my expense. The soccer boys fell on the floor, slapping their knees with laughter. The football guys blushed in appreciation, and standing center stage, I burned red.

Thankfully, the guttural aspects of the memory would fade with time and would become just a funny story in my life. "Ha, let me tell you about a time from high school…"

That is until I relived it through my oldest child, second-grader Brooklyn. At her school's International Night, I learned how parenting could influence our memories.

Brooklyn stood on the stage in the midst of a Parade of Nations with her kindergarten-aged sister, Ella. They shone in fire engine red and glistening gold lehenga, gifted from their paternal Indian aunt.

"What country are you from?" the emcee had asked.

"Brooklyn," my daughter replied in her trademark, loud monotone voice. A moment of silence hung in the air before the crowd laughed. Loudly. I felt myself flush for my daughter's misstep as my own memory bubbled up.

The moderator asked again. "Norway," my daughter tried. We had brought Norwegian smoked salmon to share in reference to my heritage. The crowd laughed a second time. I noticed the strong odor of Bangladeshi curries punctuating the still air. Looking at my daughter's smiling, flustered face, I felt the diversity of food churning in my stomach. The salmon clashed with the Scottish shortbreads, and the samosas battled the bulgogi. As my breathing shallowed, my youngest, Baby Sienna, pulled my long hair—and me—back to the present. Lucas, my third child, smiled at me with hints of Swiss chocolate on his lips.

I had transposed myself onto my daughter, reliving my most embarrassing moment in her beloved elementary school. As parents, we experience life again through the eyes of our children. Sometimes that may involve ghastly moments, but I have found that, like a perpetual 90's throwback party, more often, we get to relive the highlights.

New experiences evoke that innate curiosity shown daily in the eyes of my kids. In the morning, as I open the nursery blinds, my baby girl stares admiringly at the sun's brilliance. My son's jaw drops in wonder whenever he sees a train zooming down the track. His older sister's face lights up like a jack o' lantern when the unexpected occurs—*Wow, this plastic horse outside the grocery store gallops.* My oldest reveals it when an idea clicks—*There are 3,600 seconds in an hour!*—and she grasps a new concept. I feel it with travel.

The journeys I had crossing cow country for tournaments showed me that I love seeing new places. My first time away from my family came at seventeen when I grudgingly let my parents send me away to the Appalachian Trail for an optional college orientation. Coming from a small town in Michigan, I quickly realized I didn't know much about the wider world.

That was my mindset as I arrived a day early in Charlotte, North Carolina and met Jessica, a short, plucky girl in platform shoes and funky jeans who spoke with a thick Long Island accent and clipped her hair in a unique, trendy style. I was sure she wondered how she'd gotten stuck with a country bumpkin like me. My idea of culture was the 'hors d'oeuvres' my mom made me. Basically, that was a Buddig turkey and butter sandwich, smooshed until the white bread lost all of its volume, and then cut into sixteen pieces—something you'd see in the Kalamazoo edition of *Bon Appetit*. I discovered later that though Jessica and I dressed differently, we both came from working-class families who shipped us down a day early to save on airfare.

My camping group had an abnormal number of geniuses, even exceeding the standards of my school. Perhaps they were all overachievers and came the first available week. I just needed to fit it in before volleyball preseason. I was a jock among academics; my ability to dig a volleyball had secured my acceptance. Of the seven of us, one person has since started an innovative health company, another is an attorney with the Justice Department, and one is a tenured professor. Jessica, the Long Islander, is now a psychiatrist and one of my dearest friends. For my part, I demonstrate a unique ability to birth children in rapid succession. That is a feat in and of itself.

In the woods, though they were smarter, I showed strength. I carried a heavy load and led the pace for hikes. I also unintentionally (but thankfully) scared a bear on my solo hike. I persevered precisely because I was willing to try new things and excel outside my element. The experience accomplished its goals; I learned about myself, and I bonded with future classmates. It also set the course for my future travels.

While there, I picked up a camping party trick: how to avoid a lightning strike while stuck in the woods. Members of the group should disperse along the path and crouch to make themselves as small as possible. That way, if one person gets hit, the electrical current will not pass to the others, leaving them able to tend to the injured. But don't lie down since you want to minimize contact with the ground. With two feet firmly on the ground, the circuit may pass through you without hitting your heart.

That's the theory anyway. After thirty minutes of squatting in the cold rain, I bailed to the tent with one of the guys. He looked at me grimly and said, "This is hell." I reached back to my Catholic roots, said the Hail Mary, and prayed we wouldn't get struck.

A few months after my college camping adventures, my team qualified for the NCAA tournament for the first time in school history. The NCAA committee matched us with Nebraska, a team with more wins than any other program and five national championships.

"Where *are* we?" my teammates asked. I felt at home, flying over the quartered corn fields. My home state had more water, trees, and let's be truthful, appeal, but Nebraska held a certain charm with its Fazoli's restaurants and fervent fans led by their cornhusking mascot, Herbie Husker.

The next year, we repeated the feat, but instead drew Hawaii, winner of only four national championships and arguably the country's most idyllic state. My teammates groaned. We'd be taking the longest flight in NCAA history across five time zones the week before exams. I was thrilled—free trip to Hawaii! At sunrise, a few teammates and I snuck out to warm ourselves and study on Waikiki Beach. No Fazoli's there; I ate exotic sushi and snorkeled for the first time.

In hindsight, perhaps I should have been a little more concerned, like the upperclassmen. I did suffer on my Macroeconomics exam, but no long-term effects beyond seeing that third letter of the alphabet for the first time, and a professor who suggested I change my major. I just worked harder. I really don't like being told what to do.

Two years later, I left the continent for the first time to study in Australia, branching out from my American classmates to immerse myself in the culture. I met my foreign neighbors, joined a netball league, and experienced life as a local. (Netball ≈ basketball with no dribbling or backboard. I felt like I had gone back in time to the original rules of the sport.) Although I did travel extensively using the outrageously strong U.S. dollar on semester breaks and long weekends—to Sydney, the Great Barrier Reef, Melbourne, and New Zealand—my typical weeks revolved around barbeques and the Brisbane Lions, the local Aussie Rules Football team.

I extended my stay after the program ended to organize a daunting trip with three Aussie friends to Uluru, a giant monolith smack in the middle of the country. Those seventy-hours of car time one-way gave me just a glimpse into the real Australia, the red dirt and the Aboriginals, the poverty and the—remote towns. The path was easy—a straight line into the heart of the continent. Finding a car company that would rent to college students traveling to the Northern Territory proved most troublesome, though. It did serve as an impetus, teaching me I could find a way to do what I wanted and see what I could.

After that, I scraped my money together for annual trips to Europe, allocating a portion of my meager paychecks for travel. Living in expensive Washington, D.C., that meant meticulous planning to keep the costs manageable. I shared a tiny hotel room with my parents in Europe, chaperoned a trip with my brother, Bryn, for his high school students cruising the Greek Isles, and flew to Paris when the airlines practically pay you to go. Walking the Seine River is quite chilly in February, but I ate croissants with the locals in warm cafés, and the Louvre was inexplicably less crowded.

In business school, I co-led a service trip to Morocco, negotiating an itinerary to get us the maximum exposure for the minimal price. Among the open-air markets in Marrakesh, I glimpsed my future. Eating baklava while my classmates were debating whether to try lamb brains or stick with mutton, I spotted a family with three children under six sauntering into the tent. The kids were a little cranky and hungry, but pretty well-behaved.

"Wow," I commented. "That's so cool." Six months later, I would see my own blue line.

Before business school, I had grandiose visions of working abroad for an innovative consumer products company and segueing into corporate responsibility. But that was before I emerged from business school six figures in debt with a watermelon under my cap and gown. In an instant (if your definition of instant is nine months) my goals shifted.

I discovered my first recruit in the team that would win any competition I entered—my own squad of six including a husband and four little ones. Like a gumball machine, I popped them out in a row. Boom. Boom. Boom. Boom. All within five-and-a-half years.

I slowed down and settled in a modest, suburban lifestyle as a working mom and wife, just basically trying to keep it all together. But it didn't stop my desire to see new places and things. I still craved travel. What was a new mom to do?

Bring them along!

It's still challenging to know, truly know, how easy travel would be with kids. Heck, it's hard to know how difficult getting a baby to sleep night after night or soothing a temper tantrum is before having your own. I searched for travel books but found them targeted to singles or couples. I wondered, do kids travel? Would they enjoy Italy? Belize? Sweden? Was I an idiot for considering this?

People see pictures from our travels or they hear my stories about globe-trotting and say things like, "I can't believe you did that," or, "I can't imagine doing that with my two children and you did it with four."

Yes, sometimes there are tantrums and things don't go according to plan. That stress may seem inevitable to those who fear the unknown, but like raising kids, travel with them is rewarding. It is entertaining. It is memorable and awe-inspiring. I will take those occasional meltdowns for the opportunity to see my kids' raw reactions to a wild monkey or a real-life castle that may possibly be Elsa's.

Travel exposes kids to so many intangible benefits—seeing and trying new things, expanding their perspective, learning compassion, and experiencing different cultures. But before those kids could come along and I could take them overseas, I had to find a partner. Someone as weird as me.

Chapter Two

BEFORE BABIES, THERE WERE PECCARIES

"**I** NEED YOUR HELP!" I shouted out the restroom door to my husband, AJ. I was in a desperate situation and didn't know what to do.

"I can't come in," he responded. I could hear his breathing from behind the door.

"Of course you can," I cried. "Get in here!" I heaved my hip against the door, pushing it open as I held my fifteen-month daughter under my arm like a football. AJ peered in, shifting his eyes around before entering.

"Are you sure I can go in?"

"Yes! I'm not doing this by myself," I responded matter-of-factly. He locked the door, sealing off the three stalls to half of the other patrons at the restaurant. I hadn't been to another Fazoli's since that Nebraska trip so many years before, and I'd been happy to find a homey green circle logo with a giant red tomato among the gas stations and Walmarts.

My daughter had her first official blow-out in the middle of nowhere.

It seemed to be everywhere—her pants, legs, feet, and, if she didn't stop creeping that hand, soon to be in her hair. We efficiently worked together for our first two-person diaper change since leaving the hospital. One person held her, and the other rinsed her, peeling off her clothes to wash—or better yet, burn.

Why was I here? AJ had somehow convinced me to fly to Cincinnati, then drive three hours across rural southern Indiana to crew for him as he ran a fifty-mile race. I was seven months pregnant, showing, and feeling it much earlier than I had with my first.

AJ had turned into a traveler, seemingly overnight. After taking up running three years prior, he had set a goal of running a marathon in each state. He had just run back-to-back races in Rhode Island and Connecticut and had left me pregnant and alone with my parents and a mutant Never-Sleep one-year-old while he checked off Vermont. To be fair, he did drive fifteen hours straight after running to relieve my tired and cranky body.

AJ wasn't always this way. I may have planted the seed, but he nurtured and fertilized it. He was no longer just along for ride. Now he knew how my uterus felt.

Our first months together were a whirlwind. A first date that lasted eight hours and then him traveling across the Maryland/Virginia border to see me almost every day. He was smitten, if I do say so myself.

When we met, AJ asked if I had any deal breakers. "Smoking," I admitted. "I absolutely cannot date someone who smokes." Then, realizing I may have overstepped as I tend to do, I glanced at him sideways. "You don't smoke, do you?" I awkwardly asked. I had never tried a cigarette.

"Oh no," he proclaimed. I slowly released the breath I didn't realize I had been holding. "Well, only when I drink," he confessed.

"Well, not with me," I announced. And that was that from my point of view. His lungs would thank me later.

My puppy, Artie, had fallen hard too. My family has owned Boston Terriers starting with my grandfather's childhood dog, Billy Boy. We had some growing up, my sister adored her two, and Artie joined me shortly after I graduated college. Like a moderate justice, he held the swing vote for any future relationship. With his stub tail, Artie shook his entire body to show his pleasure. His frame would curl in on itself to form a C when he wriggled with happiness.

Artie literally leapt into AJ's arms when they met. In fact, Artie set us up—indirectly of course since he's a dog. I met my neighbors through him, including AJ's high school friend, Mario, who would then play the matchmaker. Mario and I attended dog 'happy hours' together in the building. Basically, residents letting our dogs play for an hour on the rooftop. That sounds way more yuppyish than it seemed, but looking back, maybe the Manhattans gave it away.

For me, as much as AJ made me laugh and as dedicated as he was, I knew that I would thrive best with a life partner who shared an innate love of travel. AJ liked it but not necessarily in a ridiculous, adventurous way. But I did know that he was driven by food; he was Ever-Hungry. His list of loves includes the kids, me, his parents, running, and eating out. That's about it. Maybe some friends. I appealed to his stomach to draw him in, integrating travel with food. We dined at probably the world's only Icelandic/Indian fusion in Reykjavik, sampled fish and chips in London, and topped it off with Italian gelato.

In our first year together, I found a rock-bottom weekend deal to the Dominican Republic that offered a dash of romance on the beach at an all-inclusive resort. We could lay on the beach, lounge by the pool, and eat tasty meals. We swam among colorful schools of fish being hand fed by our guide. The fish drew to him like ants to the lollipop left on the counter for the long Thanksgiving weekend away.

Before getting engaged, I wanted a true adventure—for the least amount of money possible—to convince me AJ and I were truly compatible. A travel adventure to induce relaxed exhilaration. The relaxation of a vacation and the freedom of a new place with few expectations. I could use this to explore different places—beaches, deserts, and the jungle—while experiencing camel rides, snorkeling, or hikes. Costa Rica.

And, somehow, AJ went along even though the planned stop at the lovely Manuel Antonio beach was scuttled by unending rain. He wondered what he was getting into.

LESSON LEARNED

Planning forms the basis for all of my travels, whether with little ones or not. Methodical organization serves as a key to a) Getting us out of the house, b) Doing and seeing what we want, and c) Staying within budget. At work and at home, I have rarely met a spreadsheet I didn't like and enjoy inputting dates, figures, and places into their rows and columns.

Boring. Yeah, I know. As my husband will attest, formulas and equations are not for everyone. They really aren't for much of anyone. An outline on a sheet of paper works. I ask myself the following:

What is the trip goal? To see someplace new, have fun, experience wildlife, relax, have an adventure, fit in romance? A trip can (and I believe should) have multiple goals, but relaxation is hard to balance with 'see everything possible.' Relaxation can be mixed with hiking or one activity a day if you manage your pace.

What are the landmarks or activities you do not want to miss? In Paris, it's the Eiffel Tour, the Colosseum in Rome, the Great Barrier Reef in Australia. It's not just the sites you feel obligated to see; adding your own personal list makes it yours. In Costa Rica, I knew I wanted to see monkeys and volcanos so Corcovado and Arenal were on my must-dos.

What are other options? With our trips a week or two long, we can't nearly see it all. Therefore, I make a nice-to-do list of things we'd like to do if we find the time. It is interchangeable and modifiable based on the pace of the day. The beach or zoo if the weather is beautiful, the aquarium if it rains. With children, we keep this long since we never know who or how many kids will be napping and when we'll have a spare hour or two. That's how we end up at some fun, but bizarre, places.

When traveling with kids, it's important to go in with moderate expectations. See or do the things you really want. However, have a good A and B list, and realize you must go MUCH slower than you'd prefer. That's okay—the rewards are still there.

Are you looking for a specific hotel or location? Depending on your flexibility and budget, discount sites can be a solution, especially if just looking for a nice room in a good location. If you have specific needs (like a suite for your four children), those sites can be challenging. I personally prefer to pre-book lodging, so I don't have to worry about it onsite with kids in tow.

Are there any specific places we want to eat? I'm no restaurant connoisseur, but I do like to try the local specialties. Langoustine soup in Iceland, milk-brewed coffee in Costa Rica, crepes everywhere. A friend visited Barcelona for a milestone birthday and shared that he had a list of fifty (no joke) restaurants that appealed to him.

I use many sources for research. After determining my budget, I pick a destination, choose a hotel, then fill in the details of the itinerary. I read blogs and visit travel sites, gleaning facts from guidebooks. It's not challenging as it seems. For this trip, I had virtually befriended the resort owner. Through him, in one of the wildest places in Central America, I coordinated logistics. That laid-back, chill guy served as ambassador with his wealth of knowledge.

AJ and I flew into San Jose, Costa Rica and stayed that first night at the aptly named Hotel Villa Bonita in Alajuela, three minutes from the airport. I hadn't expected such a quaint—read: cheap—hotel surrounded by a terrace of large, colorful flowers in the city. Alajuela was also regarded as safer than the capital city. My guidebook had directed us to a hidden gem—one complete with the aroma of early-morning fresh, creamy coffee.

We wandered around the local park, Aguela Mingo, grabbing chicken and plantains for dinner and an Imperial beer for Ever-Hungry. At seven o'clock, dozens of people spanning all ages packed the park, milling around under the large mango trees. It contrasted dramatically with the empty parks back home, those striking green spaces void of chatter.

Corcovado National Park sits in the southwest corner of the Osa Peninsula, a one-and-a-half-hour flight from the capital. I was drawn there by an article in National Geographic describing it as "the most intense in the world, biologically speaking." The park hosts two-and-a-half percent of the world's biodiversity and is listed as one of the ten best national parks in the world. Five-hundred species of trees, 367 of birds, 140 of mammals, and 117 of amphibians call it home. All in a place about the size of Detroit.

There are two main entries to the park: isolated Drake Bay on the Pacific Ocean and slightly more touristy Puerto Jimenez on the Sweet Gulf. We chose Drake Bay, an outpost that consisted of just a few hotels, some homes, and maybe, maybe, a couple of shops. Our plane, seat-wise the size of a Honda Odyssey, approached the runway, a small dirt strip among dense trees. The spot looked hardly long or wide enough for our tiny plane. As the pilot nosed down the plane, we saw goats grazing on the runway. The pilot pulled back up. We circled again as men ran around trying to contain those goats. On our third try, we eased down, and the goats were again free to roam.

In that empty field among the plush mountains, the smell of the day's heat coming in and a dense moisture in the air, we realized we had literally been dropped in the middle of the jungle. Our jeep crossed a stream en route to our hotel. Jinetes de Osa was tidy, a small and charming bungalow on the water, backing to the forest. It sat along the main road, if you could call it that.

Departing a few days later, a torrential rain would transform that narrow, formerly dusty street into a river. Our return taxi would hydroplane out of town, water shooting five feet in the air as we plowed through. Additional streams would appear, and the initial one had become a full-fledged river. With no bridges, we would have to switch to an even larger, tank-like SUV to cross. At the airport, we would learn that our Sansa Air flight would not be coming since the plane had run out of gas, and we would cross our fingers for standby on their competitor, Nature Air.

But that would come later. First, we had our jungle expedition. After leaving our luggage at the hotel, we jumped into a small boat for a night of camping.

My gut loses all strength while on the sea. Some people have iron stomachs—mine is like a blender, churning with every wave. It's somewhat ironic since my grandfather was a Norwegian sailor who served in the South Pacific, but I inherited my dad's lack of sea legs, and I am successfully passing that along as well. At five years old, I threw up on the discount family trip to Cancun while crossing a channel. Though, looking back, perhaps the discount part played a larger role. The most extreme example occurred while on a Great White Shark diving trip as a newlywed, getting sick in the shark tank. We took a modest-sized boat out to a reef to see them through a cage in the water. It is quite an absurd escapade, making it appealing to a twenty-something. I hopped in the boat after taking Dramamine just a little too late.

I sat outside in the back of the boat, feeling the breeze pass over my clammy skin. It was miserable, but I felt okay once we stopped. After donning my wetsuit, I entered the cage with a few others. Our predator had been spotted! I bit down on the snorkel, lowered my head under the water, and watched as the shark passed within a few feet. It felt terrifyingly exhilarating. I protectively moved my fingers away from the open bars—just in case. But then, my stomach began to rumble. A clammy feeling washed over me.

I looked to evacuate as quickly as possible so I wouldn't throw up on my cage mates. That would have made an impression. "Yeah, this idiot American threw up all over us, which drew the shark even closer."

The next time the shark passed, as his tail was receding from sight, I moved as quickly as I could. I used my minimal strength to keep my mouth closed as I pulled myself up, exposing myself for those few moments. I rushed past my incredulous husband—AJ had volunteered to let me go first, out of fear or gentility. "What's going on?" he asked.

I shot past, ran to the other side of the boat, and offered my breakfast to the fish on the other side.

"I didn't want to throw up in the cage," I responded when I was through. He gave me a sympathetic look before he took his turn, marching like a man to the gallows. I was bummed to be relegated to watching from the breezy deck while AJ experienced the adventure up-close.

I had researched a three-day diving trip to see hundreds of hammerhead sharks near Coco Island, but my stomach vetoed that idea. Or perhaps it was AJ's deathly fear of sharks and our lack of diving experience. Instead, we took a nearly-hour long boat ride along the coast to Corcovado. I suffered silently, trying to enjoy the dolphins swimming alongside us in the deep blue water. As we arrived, a loud, scary howling emanated through the air and shook the jungle. It was AJ's turn for regret.

Our guide, Javier, hopped off the boat and onto dry land. "Do you know what that is?" he cheerfully asked. Javier exemplified Costa Rica, a sprite man with boundless energy and great knowledge of the flora and fauna of the park. For our trip, he would be the jack-of-all-trades. Beyond this excursion, where he knew every bird and how to track large mammals, he later guided us on a snorkeling excursion in the Caño Island Biological Reserves. He even tracked a sloth for me, cradled in the upper branches of a tree at the fancy hotel next door, a baby clinging to her fur while I watched in ecstasy. This guy did it all.

"A jaguar?" I guessed. AJ looked back at the boat, regretting the endeavor.

"That's a howler monkey," Javier explained, all business as he set about on our tours. He aimed to surprise and delight us with what we may encounter next.

Into the jungle we walked, following the roaring sounds of those howler monkeys. Even though we knew it wasn't dangerous, it still felt ominous. There were still plenty of creatures out there that could kill us—jaguars, crocodiles, peccaries, and poisonous snakes, spiders, and frogs.

We arrived at the Sirena Station, a central depot with cabins, a kitchen, and severely limited electricity. Javier pointed out a large lizard lounging on the wall. Named the Jesus Christ lizard because it could walk on water, its common name is actually the Green Basilisk Lizard. It grows up to thirty inches long but weighs only seven ounces—hence the large surface area to mass ratio that allows it to run fast enough to be supported by water. Pretty cool to see; we got to witness it later during a hike. But for now, the lizard lazed in the sun painted on the cabin walls. I eyed the open windows and wondered how often he and his friends frequented the rooms.

The answer revealed itself when Javier showed us to our digs, a sparse room with two twin beds. Large nets hung from the ceiling and tightly skirted the beds. Javier instructed us to stash our bags underneath the nets on the mattresses so nothing would get on (or in) them. He warned us not to leave anything on the floor, especially at night, or we may find a friend in the morning. We quickly obliged.

The Sirena Station has a network of eight local trails, over twelve miles total. We set out in one direction for one of the most amazing hikes of my life. Javier had the eyes of an eagle and the nose of a bloodhound as he scoped out our path and determined where to go. He led us through magical rain forest along a meandering small creek. The sweet smell of orchid wafted by. Every few yards, Javier would stop, whip out his binoculars, and point to a unique bird or large insect. Eventually we came to the mouth of the Sirena River.

"Don't go near the water," Javier said after we spotted two large crocodiles lounging on the beach. Not large by Costa Rican standards, but large by 'don't eat me' ones. "There might be another in the water." Noting my expression that a hiding crocodile wasn't a bigger concern than the ones on the shore, he continued, "Those two are harmless. They don't want to move while they're taking in energy from the sun." A sly grin formed at his mouth. "Want me to touch one?"

"No!" we shouted in unison. He was probably pulling my leg, but I couldn't be sure.

"You don't want to come back at sunset," he warned. "That's when they'll be looking for food. Sometimes you can also see bull sharks here, too."

We saw all four species of monkeys in Costa Rica—the howlers barreling through the trees with babies on their back, the capuchins making faces at us, the spider monkeys swinging gracefully with their long arms high in the trees, and the tiny squirrel monkeys bouncing quickly about. At one point, Javier stopped and sniffed at the air. "I smell peccaries," he announced.

AJ looked at me. "Peccaries?" he mouthed. But our guide was already off, tearing down the trail toward the overwhelming stench of a latrine. Then, as quick as Javier had moved, he stopped. He put his hand to his lips, though we were already silent.

Suddenly, we heard a crash through the underbrush. The scraggly, wire-haired face of the white-lipped peccary appeared. His tusks were short, straight, and looked quite sharp. Another rounded the corner and then more until two dozen peccaries blocked our path. They seemed to surround us, like the limbs of our future children would when sharing our bed. A few piglets were among the herd, looking timid as they stuck close to their mamas.

As Javier moved, we heard a chattering noise. "Be still. That's the Alpha warning us," Javier advised. "He's rubbing his tusks together." Apparently, they will chase humans and can injure or kill us if we give them a reason. We slowly backed away as Javier shared scary true stories. I didn't know it at the time, but AJ was terrified. Moments in life alarm us before they excite us. Before there were babies in our lives, there were peccaries.

That night, I saw cockroaches clinging to the other side of our bed nets and crawling on the floor. As I tucked the net around my mattress, I felt as if in a cage. At least no one could join me in my mausoleum.

We hiked before breakfast the next day, making our way beneath dense branches and trees to a hidden jungle hideaway. Underneath the forest canopy, within a low roof of thick limbs and powerful roots, we saw a couple of tapirs. Just a few feet away, Central America's largest land animals were frolicking in the mud to keep the insects at bay. I wanted to join them.

In his off-handed, understated way, Javier said, "Don't make a sudden or abrupt move. They are incredibly powerful and can break through the roots and branches like a sledgehammer." Noted.

Then there were more monkeys, more peccaries, and baby coatimundis. I loved it all. But then we learned the sea was getting rough and we had to go. Our return trip took two hours on huge, angry, bumpy waves, as we clung tight to our life vests. As nauseous as I was, I was grateful to be safe.

Back at our hotel, we visited the rooftop overlooking the bay and lay in the hammocks eating fresh bean dip and watching squirrel monkeys chattering between the trees. Since snorkeling had been postponed, we heeded the advice of another couple to hike to a beautiful waterfall in the middle of the jungle. We followed their sketchy directions out of town, two stray dogs in tow. The half dozen or so dogs in town rotated around us like a pinwheel, alternatively accompanying us before leaving as we passed a school of uniformed kids on the road out of town. After asking some locals for directions, we turned off, following the path to the river and walking along for another hour. The original dogs would run off and reappear every ten minutes or so, like my kids popping out of their rooms right after bedtime.

We followed the forested path, wading in as necessary as we crossed knee-deep water back and forth. When we finally heard the waterfall in the distance, the water had reached chest-deep and I had to carry my brand-new camera above my head. The dogs refused to swim and looped far from the cliffs.

The waterfall was indeed quite secluded and picture-perfect. Though not all that high, it appeared out of nowhere like that sticky spot on the table nobody made. At the pool, the apex of the hike, deep in the forest with no real concept of time or weather, suddenly the air felt heavy and still. We hurried back as rain began to fall. Then thunder. The water that had been chest-deep now came to our necks. At the original fork in the river, I felt my heart pound. The path entrance had disappeared.

When we had vacationed in the Dominican Republic a year earlier, with so much spare time, we bickered more than my kids do now. However, on our last night, we had an issue that tested our ability to handle stress. In that bad situation, we turned toward each other, resolving it together. Neither pointed a finger nor blamed the other. That was huge, early in our budding relationship. At that moment, I knew this man would help me get through the toils of day-to-day life. AJ aced that most important test. He would pull me through job and child anxieties, and he now helps me get through the stresses of traveling with small children.

Therefore, in Costa Rica, when we wandered around in the storm with the cowering dogs for what seemed like an hour, I didn't panic. Eventually we spotted something. A branch? A rock? A neon sign that said 'This way'? Whatever it was, it grounded us so the four of us could jog back.

The other guests warmly welcomed us as we emerged from the pouring rain. We scarfed fresh pasta, family-style at a big table, sharing our adventures amid deep conversations with our friends—the fun couple, the pair from Michigan, the man with a mustache like a walrus, the French Canadians, and Javier. Petrichor permeated through the windows into the open-air dining area.

My AJ, who had never camped, showed his good nature as he shared stories from our time in Corcovado. "And there were cockroaches covering the net to my bed and on my shoes in the morning," he recounted.

"Did you like it?" the only other twenty-something, Michael, asked. He was big and rowdy, hanging on to every word.

"I loved it," AJ returned dryly. "Just like you love the bugs in your room." The color of Michael's face altered to match the dozens of red welts covering his body. He had spent the night sparring with the army of mosquitos that had breached the window. He also returned a loud, surprisingly high-pitched hoot. It sounded like a fox crying.

That got AJ going. "The only thing better than that were the hundreds of crabs she made me see. They made a game of trying to pinch me on our night hike on the beach. It was delightful." The stories stretched into the night. I proudly sat next to AJ, laughing alongside the fox. I didn't know it at the time, but I had started the countdown to bringing my future kids.

AJ and I rented a car for the remainder of our trip. Outside the capital city, the unpaved mountain roads to Monteverde were painfully slow and in terrible condition. Large rocks littered the path and would ding the car if we drove too fast. (And by too fast, I mean about forty kilometers-per-hour.) But the views were arresting. Vibrant mountain flowers, sheep, and stray dogs dotted the countryside. For an hour at a time, we would rise up on the dark green mountains before falling into the grassy valleys. We could see dozens of mountain peaks in the distance, capping the earth like meringue on a pie.

We eventually ascended to our hotel, Arco Iris, in the spooky-looking yet charming Santa Elena for our tour at Monteverde Cloud Forest Reserve. After losing his watch, AJ awoke the next morning with the paranoia and the sun to get us there as the gates opened. Looking back now with small kids, I'm impressed with how we could actually get somewhere before seven.

For the next three hours, we wandered among the tidy, well-marked, peaceful trails of the 26,000-acre reserve. The silence was deafening among the virgin forest, our footsteps muffled by the thick canopy of trees and misty air. The only time I hear that now is when a kid is being quite naughty behind closed doors. The clouds enveloped us, and I felt them squeeze us tighter as we climbed the dirt paths up the mountain. We were so high, and the air was so dense, there were no views. At one point, we crossed the Continental Divide. It was astonishing to think we could follow it to Canada.

Though the park boasts over a hundred species of mammal—mostly bats—I'm not sure we even spotted a squirrel. We didn't see many of the ninety-one species of migratory birds or fifty-eight amphibians. We may have gone for the serenity, but all we glimpsed were quiet, creepy, massive black birds. (This is where my birder brother would correct me and say, "It's a Black Guan, Katie, not a black bird.")

Near the park exit, we did happen upon a tour group. Looking high up into the trees, we saw the famed and rare Resplendent Quetzal, one of the most beautiful birds in the world, with iridescent greens and reds. Most remarkably, the males grow two tail feathers up to a meter long each. They struggle against aerodynamics with those proportions. People travel to this park just to see him, including a college teammate of mine on honeymoon with her zoologist husband. My friends stayed at the park from dawn to dusk without a sighting. Finding that bird is like spotting Mickey Mouse walking around Disney—as true a find as any.

Our last stop, the Arenal Observatory Lodge, was well off the beaten path, miles out of La Fortuna on a dirt road. There was literally nothing there—except a great view of an active volcano and scattered boulders that had been thrown out eons ago. The cone was mystically cloaked in clouds. A local teenager at the hotel offered to take us for a hike.

"Chestnut mandible toucans," Christian said, pointing up in the trees. Brown toucans, an oxymoron to me. "There's a keel-billed one." That's the multicolored-bill Froot Loop one I expected. "And look, a parrot!" We were off to a fast start. After seeing some other birds—I'm not a birder so I can't recall what kind—I noticed a log to the side of the path. It looked pretty comfortable and sat at the perfect height for a rest.

"Don't sit there," Christian said. "Look carefully." I did. There was nothing there. He pointed with his walking stick.

"Oh my gosh, there's a snake."

"Hog-nosed Pit Viper," he said. "It's highly venomous."

"That little guy?" I remarked incredulously. He was about a foot long and resting.

"Yes. Don't sit on any logs." Got it.

"What about the coral snakes? I heard those are dangerous." Our crying fox friend had seen one when diving in Corcovado and was beyond thrilled.

"Oh yes. There's no anti-venom for those." I was back in Australia, land of a million unknown dangers. And so, we continued our walk to the base of an active volcano. After a few minutes, we arrived at rocks from lava flow younger than my oldest is now.

"Can I sit here?" I joked to Christian before I dared sit down.

"Yes, that's fine," he responded. "But first, scratch this." He was pointing at a large orange rock a couple of yards away. Termite mound. I can only imagine how high I would have jumped if I had obliged that one.

We sat on the boulders thrown about like food from my toddler's tray and watched the sun set over the lake to the west. In the distance, about a mile away, the volcano loomed. The car-sized lava rocks spewed red against the dark sky.

"Barbacoa!" Christian would shout with each massive fireball. It was one of the most incredible things I'd ever seen. He shared that less than forty years prior, people had deemed it dormant and campers would sleep in the cone. We stayed for a while, reflecting on this on our hike back to the lodge. I felt insignificant that night, a single Lego in a houseful of toys.

The volcano had motivated us to explode into action. We started with river kayaking nearby. Our guide, Carlos, took us and a British couple. Although the river was calm, we could not navigate. AJ and I argued as we lodged on a rock or a log or a crocodile. And then the Brits filmed us with a camcorder while Carlos came to our aid. Then I remembered—my guy had never truly kayaked.

Oh sure, in the Dominican Republic, we tried kayaking to a shipwreck off the shore. We could see snorkelers and divers at the fifty-two feet deep site, so it seemed a manageable, if far, trip. Still within spitting distance of shore, my guy shared his lack of experience. I wasn't eager to swim with sharks, so I reluctantly agreed to turn around. The 400-foot-long boat now seems to be quickly disappearing and is only barely visible from shore. I'm sure the sharks are still there.

Remembering that, I changed my tact from just shouting, "No! Go straight! Stop!"

That shift came at the right time. As we entered the crocodile-infested area, Carlos said, "Oh look, baby croc footprints." I am not joking. Thankfully we only got stuck there once.

Jacked up on animal adrenaline, we impulsively soared through the rainforest on a canopy tour. Zip-lining occurs stateside, of course, but there's no chance of seeing monkeys while doing it. We didn't spot anything like the howler monkeys we had seen kayaking but did enjoy the quite high, fast, and fun flying.

Since Arenal was active with hot liquid just beneath the earth, there was surprisingly not a shortage of options to finish our day. We skipped over the breathtaking, crowded, expensive Tabacon to see the cheaper, but still amazing,

Baldi Hot Springs. It had about ten pools with varying temperatures, caves, and less people—all with a distinct view of the volcano.

After eating locally and getting our obligatory gifts of coffee, we settled on the lodge deck. The clouds were finally clearing. AJ and I leaned back, watching the volcano appear little by little as the night wore on. We must have been out there for hours—I can't recall. We watched nature's fireworks as we talked about our hopes and dreams, how one day we'd return with future children and explore anew.

Every once in a while, we'd hear an enormous boom and get a little spooked. To settle my nerves, I'd remind myself that it's like a thunderstorm—once you hear the noise, the danger has already passed. By the end of the evening, the entire cone had exposed itself, just as I had in baring my heart to my future husband.

Chapter Three

NEW VIEWS OF NEW ENGLAND

PARENTS LOSE FORTY-FOUR days, or over a thousand hours, of sleep in the first year of an infant's life. That's according to a top mattress company at least, and I would imagine they love their sleep studies. That statistic is incredible, considering the world record holder can sail around the world in less time (just under 43 days). I vowed to do everything possible to avoid that fate. Whereas my husband's favorite bottom rung of the Maslow triangle is food, mine is sleep. I nap in the car, doze on planes, and, in college, would catnap after my morning classes before lunch in the mess hall.

Then, I had every new mother's dream: my own Never-Sleep baby.

Each evening, around seven o'clock, Baby Brooklyn would transform from a perfect, angelic baby into a demon. It's amazing how you can find someone so utterly charming and perfect yet also feel like they're moonlighting with the devil. My nights consisted of cluster-feeding, rocking, and attempting to transfer her to the crib. On good days, she would sleep for a bit. Most nights, she would not. One night involved walking her around our tiny apartment from two until seven, both of us collapsing as the sun rose.

I read every sleep book I could find in my waking hours. I put her to bed at different hours. We structured a strict napping schedule, cloistering ourselves in the house during those hours or putting her in the carrier if we weren't home. I begged her babysitter, a sweet girl full of energy, drama, and craft ideas, to share how she managed nap times when I was at work.

She wrote down three tediously detailed pages describing the hour-long process in a daily journal. It included things like, "First, I fed Brooklyn a large snack. Then I rubbed her tummy to get her to go to the bathroom. After changing her diaper, I massaged her back. Then I put her in the sleep sack. I put on the sound machine. Rock her for five minutes. Pat her butt for ten minutes. When that didn't work, I…" Pages and pages of this. Little did I know, we had hired my daughter a personal masseuse.

Still, Brooklyn fought sleep like a gladiator with us, waving her hands and chatting more than Elmo. We tried to swaddle; she broke free like Houdini. When she was older, she would strip off all of her clothes—including her diaper—to attract our attention. I resorted to putting her sleep sack on backwards and inside out. My parents called it her straitjacket. I called it success.

Then one night, after a year or so, I handed her to AJ and said, "She can have cow milk now. I will feed her during the day, but she's yours at night." They both protested that arrangement, but I needed my eight hours. I was pregnant again.

When the others came along, the routine resumed. Using the one aid I'd learned from Brooklyn, I co-slept from day one with Ella. Being wakened during the night can impact the deepest sleep, affecting the mind and body, and my kids needed my best self. With Ella, I meticulously timed naps so I could also rest, putting Brooklyn to sleep first, struggling through the convincing and patting. Baby Ella would sleep through anything; there could have been a gorilla in the room and she'd peacefully sleep. But with my first, my breast was my only salvation. She would latch, and we'd go to bed together—a sow with her baby piglet. We avoided her 'crying it out,' but on some nights, I'll admit I cried myself to sleep.

Brooklyn's inability to sleep impacted every element of our lives, including vacation planning. As a result, we scheduled our adventures in tidy morning and afternoon increments sandwiching a two-hour nap break. While driving, conversations would abruptly end when we'd see her open-jawed and softly snoring in the back seat.

We're not the only ones with challenges—not every baby likes to fly and not every kid will eat whatever they're given. However, we find that when our kids get three essential things—sleep, food, and exercise—they tend to behave. Even while traveling.

With regards to sleeping, the only silver bullet we found was the passage of time. After her first long day of kindergarten, Brooklyn finally fell asleep.

Being from Michigan, I was accustomed to it taking hours or days to get anywhere. But residing in quaint Connecticut for the first few years of parenthood, I learned that new doesn't have to be far. The ocean was two hours east. Even remote, rustic Maine was a mere six hours away—the same distance from my parent's home to the bridge connecting the two halves of my home state.

For day trips or overnights, we marched the kids down Boston's Freedom Trail, hit the Massachusetts hardwood at Springfield's Basketball Hall of Fame for my daughter's first shots, and visited the Mark Twain and Noah Webster homes down the street. The kids ran around the vast lawns of the mansions in Providence, Rhode Island. The charming New England towns preserved perfect little homes with white picket or stone fences. Old trees full of green foliage stood amid fragrant flowers blooming in a rainbow of colors.

That was exemplified in Burlington, Vermont where we toured Lake Champlain. The 435-square mile lake was long and thin, a striking ribbon of blue among the Green Mountains. It had been designated a Great Lake in 1998, quite an honor that lasted a full eighteen days (fewer days than the summer camp pass I purchased for my kids). The lake also served as a fun boat ride for the kids and its shore hosted a tasty namesake chocolate shop.

Among the dairy farms in the nearby emerald hills dotted with purple flowers, my kids became excuses for random stops.

"Ella wants her first ice cream cone," I said, pulling over for the Ben & Jerry's factory tour.

Then, "Brooklyn would love the waterfalls," when we approached Quechee Gorge near the Cabot Cheese factory. We hiked along grand vistas before walking down to touch the water.

We did gorge ourselves on cheese there, Brooklyn especially. My three-year-old sampled nearly twenty types, trying all but the habanero. "Should we get ten pounds or twenty?" I asked AJ as Baby Ella began to fade and I gave her the pacifier. "It's not all one kind," I defended as he rolled his eyes. Considering how much he spends on running shoes, I can splurge on some ridiculous things as well. Especially at wholesale prices. Twenty it was.

We planned to visit Martha's Vineyard a few months later, a trip nearly aborted due to a skipped nap. The night before our ferry, in Falmouth, Massachusetts, Brooklyn had her first temper tantrum. It traumatized us. Since then, I have seen tempers in all shapes and forms. Long tempers and loud tempers, ones due to exhaustion, others from frustration, and sad ones caused by a bite or the tearing of pristine schoolwork. My kids have screamed for hours at a time. We'll get two kids at a time, and we've gotten the rare trifecta. I don't think we've had all four yet but it's always good to have a goal.

That night, my daughter was screaming bloody murder amid our insufficient comfort. Brooklyn flailed her arms, kicked her feet, became non-verbal. We did not know what to do.

"I'm done," AJ announced at ten after hearing angry voices in the room next door, items shifting, and a door slam. Baby Ella had fallen asleep and the hotel was settling down, but the Exorcism screaming continued. We were not even to our destination.

"She's almost asleep," I wished. "And look at Ella."

He looked at our little angel, who earlier had gazed up at us with her wide eyes in a moment of oasis. "I'm done after this," he repeated. "We are never traveling again."

On that trip, we learned that pacifiers aren't just the physical object a baby puts in her mouth to suckle. They are those things that soothe us, our comforts of home. Not always an actual pacifier, it can be a cherished stuffed animal, a toy, a blankie. They are the things we turn to while under duress. Now that I have four, I see how different they can be. The baby's is her thumb. My son's is a truck. Mine (and now Brooklyn's!) is a good book while my husband's is a long run.

After an hour-long ferry ride, we arrived in Oak Bluff, a pretty little town with beautiful homes and pseudo-celebrities. The Clarion Edgartown thankfully offered an early check-in. After Brooklyn's nap, she reverted back to a Mogwai from her earlier hours as a Gremlin. The rest of the trip was dinners on the water, ice cream, pushing sleeping kids during long walks in Vineyard Haven, and walking hand-in-hand with my daughter by the Edgartown Lighthouse. It was enchanting and refreshing.

Cognizant of our stressful bus ride there, I sought out another way to get our car parked a few miles inland. We had skipped bringing it since the island has good public transportation. That, and the fact that the ferry was quite expensive and hard to book. But I had no desire to take another bus loaded down with our luggage.

As we approached the port, with Ella asleep on me, I approached an empty-nester in the passenger seat of a car. "Pardon me, do you happen to be going toward Falmouth?"

I knew the answer. It is an out-and-back road.

"As you can see, our baby is sleeping," I continued. "And we have another little one. Could you drop my husband at the ferry parking lot, so we don't have to all take the bus?" The friendly couple, fresh off a relaxing weekend, could not think of a real reason why to turn down a young mother.

"Are you okay with dogs?" the man asked, pointing at the large canine in the backseat. AJ nodded his head. "Then have a seat. Just watch out for Fluffy." Hitchhiking for the first time in his life, AJ shot me one last look as if heading off to battle. I blew him a kiss in appreciation. I was relieved to see him a short time later, thankfully not kidnapped by the poodle family.

"Who in the world will want to drive to D.C. with me tonight?" I asked my husband after scoring free tickets for a weeknight game to watch my alma mater in the NCAA basketball play-offs.

"You should ask Jenny," AJ suggested. Most of my friends were like me, cooking dinner and putting the kids to bed before curling up with a book. But Jenny is that person who is up for anything. Impromptu poker tournament? Jenny is game. PTA Secretary? Convince Jenny. Need a last-minute sitter during the day? The baby will be in good hands with Jenny. She is that person who gravitates toward new experiences. She also has great stories. When Jenny slid open the passenger door to join me, I noticed her red shirt and black pants—perfect colors to root on my team.

I possess neither Jenny's carefree spirit nor easy laugh. I organize, plan, and follow a strict schedule. However, recently I received a text message from Jessica of Davidson Odyssey fame: "We are driving to DW now. Going to be there through Monday. I doubt you are up to it but if so, we would obviously love to see you!"

"D.C.?" I responded, a little dense. "Do you want to stay with us?" Her only son loves my gaggle of kids. "Ooohhh…" came a minute later. "Dutch Wonderland." The small, cheap, easy theme park targeted to small children in Lancaster County, Pennsylvania. From atop the dragon roller coaster, you may spot a horse and buggy.

Thirty-six hours later, my three little ones were buckled up in the back of my Ford Flex, singing along to Moana. I generally lack flexibility (that's pretty obvious from the kids' strict nap schedules), but I do recognize it's important to sometimes *Be the Jenny*. Say yes. See a friend. Changing plans may feel like trekking through thick sludge but trying something new can be the beautiful waterfall at the end of the hike.

Acadia National Park, Maine

A year after Martha's Vineyard, I was ecstatic to show my kids a new state and explore the matrix of hikes through the trails known as Acadia National Park in late August. Our two dogs scored seats since we could not, in good conscience, go to the country's most dog-friendly National Park and leave them home.

On the way, we perused the L.L. Bean headquarters in Freeport, Maine. A whole town with adorable shops and cafes that came from one hard-working man's idea for a reputable clothing company. I had studied the company's history, their founder, and their return policy in business school strategy courses. That meant, of course, that I had to see the origins. "Nerd," AJ coughed as we arrived. The kids scurried to climb on the size 410 Bean boot while AJ held Artie back to avoid him raising his leg on it.

We overnighted in New Brunswick, Canada because Portland, our intended stay, didn't have anything for under $1,000. "This is crazy," I stated to AJ, asking, "Why is Portland so expensive?" When we drove through the city, I discovered the reason for the overpriced rooms—an Alanis Morrissette concert. I last attended a concert over ten years earlier, but she's still highly sought after. Isn't it ironic?

Searching for a place within a couple hours of Portland led me to St. John's on the Bay of Fundy. The dramatic bay tides act like a long funnel to pull in an extraordinary 160 billion tons of seawater, more than the combined flow of the world's freshwater rivers. A typical tide is about two to three feet. However, two hours north of where we visited, at Hopewell Rocks, these tides reach a phenomenal fifty-six-feet. Among the forty to seventy-foot-tall pillars of rock, people navigate deep water in kayaks. Then, just a few hours later, they walk along the pebbly shore. Perception tells you whether it's paradise for a surfer or a shell collector.

Although the drive was long, my kids didn't seem to mind. At nineteen months, Ella achieved a life milestone with the ceremonious swapping of the car seat. Facing-forward, she could now see the clock and stare at the back of Mommy's head. Brooklyn discovered that one of her books included a CD of nursery rhymes, giving us hours of listening pleasure, including a soothing version of *Twinkle, Twinkle Little Star* that put me to sleep a few times.

Of bigger concern was feeding my Ever-Hungry husband. Since he cared more about the food than the tides, he worried about Canadian cuisine. It may seem that it's just poutine on top of an American diet, but once you cross an international border, all bets are off. Canadian KFC's don't even sell biscuits, I'm afraid, and Tim Hortons is not a beloved grandfather on *Days of our Lives*. AJ searched high and low for enticing food along our scenic coastal drive.

The morning after our drive, we watched the water rushing into the bay at high tide in Irving Nature Park. We hiked through the amazingly lush forest, watched the dogs swim after sticks, and walked high on the coast and saw seals sunbathing on the little islands of rocks. Ella insisted on walking and rewarded our patience with a nice, long nap.

Low tide came that evening, right at the witching hour of peak naughtiness. After an eight-hour drive, we would not be deterred, and the splendor did not disappoint. With the stories of water gone, we walked as if on the ocean floor. Massive seaweed-covered boulders littered the sticky sand, as if they had been thrown by Poseidon. The kids became gods themselves, heaving their pebbles just as erratically into the depths.

After the Bay of Fundy, we drove south to Acadia National Park in Bar Harbor, Maine. With over a hundred-fifty miles of hiking trails, forty-five miles of carriage roads, and sixteen stone bridges, the park fulfilled our expectations. It offers kayaking, biking, and ranger-led tours. You can explore the miles of coastline, swimming or studying the tidepools. For those without small children, the brave and/or foolhardy, a few of the seven 1,000-foot plus peaks offer an outdoor ClimbZone.

Ella woke me at the crack of dawn on our first day and no amount of cajoling, changing, or nursing could get her back to sleep. We were staying at the Chilltern Inn, a hidden hotel with a one-bedroom apartment in the back. I had proudly sectioned us into separate sleeping quarters—the dogs in the living room, Ella in a crib in the hallway, and Brooklyn in another crib in the large bathroom adjoining our room.

I snuck Ella and my younger, chubbier dog, Chloe, out for a hike. If I couldn't beat her, I'd join her. We were out the door at 5:30. Entering Acadia National Park, I spotted a placard for a name I recognized from the guidebook: Precipice, or, according to the Oxford Dictionary, "a very steep rock face or cliff, especially a tall one."

I climbed out of the car and approached a fit couple walking toward the trailhead. "Hey, do you guys know if I can bring my dog here?" From the car window, Chloe looked at them with her goofy grin.

The woman looked at the craggy mountain through the dim light and back at me. She didn't say anything. Her judging eyes gave me the response I needed.

I backed away awkwardly. "I'll just try the next one." Thank goodness I hadn't told them Chloe liked to pull at the leash or that I'd also have a baby riding on my back.

Instead, I strapped Ella to me at the modest, 525-foot-high Gorham Mountain. As we climbed the challenging, but not scary peak, we watched the sunrise over the water. The sun appeared slowly, transforming the horizon from ash to pink to orange. At the peak, still before seven, the sun blazed down as I took some shots of my two hiking buddies. It was probably the first intentional photo I'd taken of my dog in three years.

"Walk," said Ella. I grasped her warm pudgy hand tightly as she toddled down. We followed a sign at the bottom that read, 'Otter Point, .5 mile' to a small inlet. No otters. Since I loathe backtracking, we cut across. We'd make it back eventually since a one-way circular road skirts the park. For two miles with no cell service, I kept thinking it was just around the next peaceful green, beautiful bend. Four hours later, we eventually joined my worried husband. I now leave a note and estimate of when I will return. And a reminder that cell service may be spotty.

LESSON LEARNED

Hotel selection can be key to making or (more likely) breaking a trip. Though we don't plan to spend a lot of time in the room, a bad experience can affect everything. And with kids, our needs have changed. With a terrible sleeper, other assorted children and dogs, a standard room can be quite challenging. Starting with our second, and nearly always with three or more, that has meant booking a suite or connecting rooms. A suite does not always include a door separating the sleeping area from the living area. Some chains quantify it as a slightly larger room.

I always call or email to ask, "Do you actually have a door?" Unfortunately, I get "no" way too much. Embassy Suites and Residence Inn are always a good bet with free breakfast and hot appetizers that can be reapportioned as dinner for the kids. When traveling abroad, we typically reserve two rooms since reasonably priced suites are rarer overseas. We like the Radisson Blu resorts for their over-the-top delicious breakfasts featuring local flair (lingonberry crepes in Sweden) in a clean, consistent atmosphere.

I search around before booking. Sites like TripAdvisor offer great user reviews, guidebooks share trusted selections, and the hotel website displays the hotel specifics and room options once you've chosen a place. Depending on the hotel, booking through a discount site may be cheaper since those sites reserve rooms in advance and may have received a better exchange rate, or may throw in breakfast or rewards points to incentivize you to book.

Renting out someone's home, through AirBnB, HomeAway, Wimdu, or others can offer a good-sized space and may save a lot of money. We mix up our selection so that we can have the best of both worlds—I use the hotel for ease and reliability, free breakfast, and a hotel pool in a premiere location. The rental sites are great when driving through the countryside to get a feel for the culture, to see how people live, and for the space and comforts of home. (Laundry day!) Meeting locals is part of the fun and people who live in a quaint village halfway between two cities are usually excited for guests.

Good customer service also plays a role, especially with kids. We received memorable service at the Marriott Courtyard Burlington, Vermont when I tried my luck at our late afternoon arrival by asking for a cheap upgrade. The superhero clerk took a look at the clock and my young family, upgrading us for free. That gave our baby a separate sleeping area while we shared with her sister. That front-line person knew just the right thing to do for us when we needed it. To me, with two little ones, I needed a good night sleep. And I got it.

We had a picnic the night we crossed the land bridge that appears between Bar Harbor and Bar Island during low tide, spotting barnacles, snails, and tiny crabs. We also ate a cheap, delicious lobster dinner, the girls laughing as the crustacean exploded on their bib-less mom. We watched a sunset from Cadillac Mountain, wrapping the girls in towels to keep them warm. Our dogs enjoyed their time too, hiking up the short-but-somewhat-steep Triad, barking at carriage horses, and swimming at a leash-free park at Long Lake.

We set off for the coastal drive around the rest of the park, stopping at Sand Beach for Brooklyn to play in the (yes) sand before finding another hike, 1,000-foot Mount Bernard. She wanted to do it all herself, to prove her dad right and me wrong. ("Honey, you need to carry her in the backpack. She just turned three, she can't make it herself.") He goaded her along with a game of finding the blue route markers. Turning things into a game is a sure-fire way to pull along a kid on the verge of becoming bored.

We hiked through dense forests up the mountain, a path padded with moss that muffled our steps and a crisp cool stillness in the air, the setting a mixture of the *Anne of Green Gables* and the Brothers Grimm. The other peaks had rewarded us with views, but Mount Bernard had no precipice above the tree line, just an elevation sign for the kids to climb and request a photo at.

"Bummer," I said. "I guess there's no view." We continued on, trudging to the next mountain summit, ever hopeful it'd be just around that next gloomy tree. And then two things happened: a gorgeous panorama emerged, showing an emerald green forest rolling to the glimmering sea, and we realized we had no clue where we were. We walked carefully along the exposed granite boulders the size of trucks, feeling a momentary break from the forest that had embraced us like a hug from the Hulk. We had walked much further than planned for this view, and since we had not left any breadcrumbs, we had no desire to return on that same densely forested path.

Luckily, this also happened about the time we found other hikers who knew where we were since they carried an actual map. "So, we go down this way and turn right at the sign," I said aloud to AJ, memorizing their map. "Can you remember that?"

"Why don't you just take a photo?" the woman responded, holding the map. And so began one of my biggest hacks while traveling.

We followed those directions down the mountain, across a small river, and to a parking lot. Looking at the trailers nearby, we realized we'd never seen this place. Our car sat along some dirt road near a different entrance. After much goading from his charming wife (ahem, me) AJ went to the nearest home. Though he really did not want to ask for help, actually knocking on a stranger's door and asking to hitchhike to find our car was not the hardest part for AJ. He was mortified by his poor sense of direction, a weakness that led to an ambling, nearly fruitless drive through the woods with a good-natured yokel.

"Let's find some place with a view," AJ commented the next morning. That would be the picturesque South Bubble Mountain. The 766-foot South Bubble overlooks the gleaming Jordan Pond, thin and long, like my oldest felt in the womb. According to multiple sources, the trail was "dog friendly" and the trail was "moderate." I'm pretty adventurous, but I was happy a few minutes later we had left the dogs for this one. The descent was quite scary with tight passes of giant boulders on cliffs. We probably wouldn't let small children do the hike alone, but with my two cocooned against us, it felt safe. Upon descent, I walked hand-in-hand with Brooklyn along the boardwalk that spanned much of the three-and-a-half-mile shoreline.

A delectable aroma from the 125-year-old Jordan Pond House permeated the path to greet us. I could practically taste the butter, eggs, and sugar of their famous popovers melting in my mouth. And that's all we got to do since we arrived an hour too early for the popovers (starting at eleven) and were holding two hungry and tired kids. Instead, we grabbed cocoa, whoopie pies, cookies, and blueberry crisp. After that small New England snack, we went back to the car to sleep off the calories.

For my birthday, AJ encouraged me to have a whale watching date with Brooklyn. The whole family had attempted the venture already, but the whales won that game of hide-and-seek. Instead, we spent those three-and-a-half-hours on the boat entertaining the baby with visits to the concession stand. Every hour we'd find them something new—M&Ms, cheese crackers, hot chocolate, popcorn. It was draining. (Though possibly worth it as the rocking knocked them out for two-hour naps.)

"Cancelled," said the good-natured operator when Brooklyn and I arrived for Round Two. "There's a hurricane brewing off the coast." Back we walked to our hotel, two miles roundtrip. Then we went for another hike with the others.

One of the drawbacks to planning on a budget in a highly sought-after destination is the risk that the hotel only has availability for part of the stay. This can mean switching hotels partway through the trip. In Acadia, we exchanged compartmentalized rooms and privacy for the quirky Seabreeze Hotel with ocean views and a pool. The bizarrely configured studio could fit half of our home and included a bed tucked deep into the corner, a large kitchen, carpeted bathrooms, a couch, and open floor suited for gymnastics tumbling. AJ graciously stayed back with the napping kids so I could read poolside while the dogs bathed in the sun.

AJ did not want to give the whale cruise a third shot. Luckily, like asking the other parent, birthdays turn noes into yeses. AJ made it an event for me, bringing pizza, lobster rolls, and a blueberry pie. Then, the long-awaited humpback whales made it a party. They didn't just appear; the mother and her baby who came performed. Brooklyn exuded pure joy for the near hour they lunge-fed with us, their large mouths and backs surfacing every five to ten minutes. At show's end, they blew one last breath and flipped their tales as they entered the depths. We were leaving the next day, so it was the end of our journey.

In both college and business school, I studied a Selective Attention Test by Simons and Chabris. In the experiment, participants watch two groups of people—half in white shirts, the other half in black—passing a basketball. They are asked to silently count the passes between those in white shirts. (Take a moment to test yourself if you want.) About half of viewers miss a gorilla who walks in and thumps his chest. People can be blind to the unexpected, even when right in front of them.

That happens to us, of course. Even when I conducted the experiment on my family (further validation that I'm a nerd), I saw the same results as Simons and Chabris. I do feel, I know, that when we travel with kids, it happens less frequently. With their perspectives, we witness things we otherwise may have missed.

On our way south to Portland to search for Alanis Morrissette on Old Orchard Beach, we started our last day with a drive to the Schoodic Peninsula off the mainland. Schoodic is a relatively unknown portion of the park separate from the rest of Acadia we found as a quiet alternative for the dogs. To get there, we left the park, drove along the water, and reentered the park via Big Moose Road. Then we navigated a one-way six-mile loop of the peninsula, parking at Blueberry Hill.

The kids and dogs navigated the rocky coastal terrain among the sea gulls and terns before we hiked the 1,000-foot mountain with 360-degree views of the peninsula and the rest of Acadia across the water. Walking back to the car, I noticed a black raspberry bush. Another was just ahead. And another. My toes tingled in excitement, a microcosm of that moment before seeing the blue line on a pregnancy test. I hesitated a moment, wondering if the local bear population frequented the site.

Suddenly, my two little ravenous locusts buzzed, snatching the procured fruit from me. Since I had no means to carry it, we stuffed ourselves like Build-A-Bears. Worried they may be poisonous, my city-born husband refused a taste. I prodded Brooklyn along the trail for the last half mile with the berries, like a donkey after a carrot. Each new bush tasted like Christmas morning.

Acadia National Park had appealed to our five senses—the taste of fresh-picked berries, the smells of the sea and baking popovers, the sounds of the birds and children laughing, the feel of the path beneath our feet, and of course the abundant sights surrounding us. An adventure that captures all of the senses sticks the longest. Start small with your escapes if you have to. Just try something new. See life through a new perspective. Or at least keep your eyes open for the gorilla.

Second Trimester

EXPANDING OUR PERSPECTIVES

"IT LOOKS AS if you have been chewed on by rats," my nurse midwife announced bluntly at my two-week post-partum appointment. Since leaving the New York City hospital after delivery, my dedication to nursing had resulted in bits of skin being slowly nibbled away by my firstborn. "Why didn't you come in sooner?"

"My professor told me it hurts," I shared. No one ever tells you breast-feeding is painful, she warned me. I had taken her advice a little too seriously, nursing through lip-biting, fingernails in the palm pain.

"In your uterus," my midwife explained. "And only for a few days." She continued, "And just so you know, it will be worse with each one."

I left with a prescription for my MRSA infection and some tips on latch-ing, positioning, and healing. My first bout of mastitis. I'd get it a few more times. By the time I got it with my fourth, I recognized the symptoms with a new cough. I diagnosed a friend over a text message when she complained of a fever in July.

"How long do I do this thing?" I asked my lactation consultant once my infection subsided. I could remove the nipple guards, and my body had become a milking machine. "Three months? Six? A year?"

"Go as long as you like," she replied. Though I would have preferred a suggestion, she excelled at neutrality. "Some people go until three or four. The

World Health Organization recommends at least two years." That seemed like an eternity to a new mom living in shifts between naptimes.

My babies and my body took to it like a moss-lichen symbiotic relationship. I didn't broadcast that my kids nursed well into toddlerhood, but all except one were potty-trained before they weaned. And by the third or fourth child, I didn't care who judged me.

However, when Brooklyn turned six months, I was restless for international travel. The last trip had been Turks and Caicos for a babymoon, waddling around the pool and beaches and eating small portions ten times a day. "Clearly, I'm not the only one who thought to do this," I mentioned to AJ as we witnessed seven other pregnant women in line to board the flight home.

Like every new step with a new child, I couldn't be sure how to do it and had so many questions. Can babies fly on airplanes? How long could she sit still? Would it be safe?

I had traveled home to Michigan to show off my newborn. We flew to Texas, a five-hour journey, when she was nine months. Neither seemed too hard, though I did have family to help at both places. Years earlier when I was still young, fit, and debating a marathon, I had heard that you can do twice your perceived ability (i.e. since I could comfortably run thirteen miles, I could finish a marathon). I extrapolated that to set my flight goal at ten hours. It made sense to me.

Brooklyn's doctor, clearly more chill than me, quickly cleared us for travel. "After one may be best since she'll have gotten most of her shots." He paused before adding, "It will also give her more time to mature in her sleeping." As suspected, that did not occur.

Since she wasn't walking, Brooklyn could contentedly sit in my arms for hours. And since she was not in school, we could save money by flying off-peak. I booked us for late May, just before her birthday.

With regards to safety… this was my first baby and my entire heart in one breathing, crying, creature outside myself. I needed to make sure if anything went wrong, we had access to first-rate medical care. Of course, having prevalent crime and so forth were deal-breakers, but considering her attachment to me, going beyond that wasn't a pressing concern.

For our first destination, I desired a relatively straightforward flight to a safe place for a baby, one that was easy to get around. I resigned myself to Never-Sleep's poor sleeping, and since she was still nursing, food posed no concern. No formula to worry about, she had natural immunities, and she could eat what and whenever she liked. Although we ended up going to a foodie country, we could have gone to the land of peanuts and shellfish with my milk her sole nutrition.

Once AJ and I decided on Europe, I scoured the sites to find the easiest and most direct flights, ruling out any places I had already been. As the adage proclaims, all roads led to Rome. It came to fruition after reading, "Italians love babies."

"Everyone knows Italians love children."

My favorite: "Italians are, as far as I know, the only people on earth who worship a baby." Italy did have the lowest birthrate in the European Union and one of the lowest in the world. (A source from 2013, close to when we traveled, says only eight babies are born for every 1,000 residents.) Italians don't see enough babies.

Ciao bella! We were going to the home of Michelangelo and a birthplace of Western society, flying into Venice via Philadelphia and Frankfurt for three nights and out of Rome after another three. In between, we planned to see Florence and the countryside for four nights by train. My parents quickly decided to join us. They certainly wanted to witness Brooklyn's first international trip.

LESSON LEARNED

It can be challenging to know when to get passports for your family. Since one is required for international flights, and helpful for cruises, it is good to have. However, children's passports are only good for five years so it can be a costly endeavor if you don't actually use them. For our children, we submitted applications after booking our flights. That usually gave us the six to eight weeks of lead time needed to receive the passport. It didn't actually take that long, but those are the published lead times. With Lucas, we had to expedite with overnight service so we could have a passport for a funeral in less than two weeks.

Getting a passport may seem daunting but it's pretty straightforward. First, you complete a DS-11 application form. When submitting it, include two passport photos, proof of citizenship (typically a birth certificate), evidence that you are the parent (i.e. driver's licenses for both parents), and a passport fee. The fee for a child's passport is actually lower than that for an adult, but there's also an execution fee for the in-person review.

You can get passport photos at many photo shops or you can take it yourself. No hands or adults can be in the photo so baby headshots can be challenging to capture. If the baby won't sit still or can't support his head, you can lay him on a white sheet for the shot. Applications can be submitted at many post offices, some motor vehicle offices, or county offices. We lucked out in discovering that a nearby library offers the service. When we needed one for our baby, we loaded up the kids and let them pick out books while we waited our turn.

My advice: wait to get them until you need it unless you love booking travel just a few weeks before a trip. Expediting a passport can be expensive—especially for multiple people. And cherish those photos. Baby passport photos—and their outtakes—are adorable.

Chapter Four

DIAPERS AND GELATOS IN ITALY

"WELL THAT WAS awkward," my dad announced as he entered our hotel room holding a baby wearing only one shoe.

"What happened this time?" my mom asked. It was hard to even guess.

"It's not my fault," he started. "The people next door left their door open."

"So, what did you do?" my mom pressed.

"The rooms look all the same," he continued. "I didn't realize I was in the wrong room until I was all the way in. A man watching TV asked why I was there." My mom and I started laughing.

"Then what happened?"

"Well, I left," he admitted. "But then I noticed she had no shoe." He pointed at the bare pink foot full of soft, pudgy baby toes. "I had to go back in and find it. She kicked it under the bed."

My dad tends to involve himself in peculiar or even dangerous situations. He'll find the strangest ways to hurt himself. After hard runs, he's passed out. He collapsed while biking two hundred miles to my sister's house and broke a few ribs. He was hit by a car on his bike while picking up my prom photos. Thankfully, the photos were not damaged.

And those all take place in a country where people drive on the right side of the street, speak our language, and have our etiquette. Abroad, it's even worse. One time, after washing his hands in a WC in Barcelona, he wasn't sure which way to avoid an approaching man. He dodged right to avoid a full collision. Unfortunately, the man went the same direction. My dad quickly adjusted and went the other way. The man did, too. My dad's nose smashed into a mirror.

This is who we chose to help arrange the trip to Italy. Our options were limited, granted, since I was working full-time and holding a Never-Sleep baby until she collapsed. I plotted an adventurous itinerary, AJ offered input, and my newly retired dad found bed and breakfasts. He had discovered the Internet, only fifteen years late, and was happy to find deals. Helpful parents are the best.

Never-Sleep shocked us by passing more than half of the eight-hour flight in dreamland and dozing the entire third flight. Some people drive their kids around the neighborhood to get them to sleep; we just had to take ours on a transatlantic flight.

Thanks to that surprise, we felt refreshed when we met my parents (who were beyond excited to see Brooklyn) at the apartment. They took us to the Rialto Bridge, the oldest and one of only four bridges spanning the Grand Canal. Brooklyn traveled in her carrier, napping when tired, peering eagerly at the crowds when awake. It amazed us that the city worked with no cars, just boats, ferries, and man's oldest form of transportation, *a piedi*. I felt the history and tasted the city's romance. Everything was as beautiful as I had hoped—and I carry unrealistic expectations, to the chagrin of my husband.

Eventually, jetlag found us, like my kids do when I'm in the shower. After fourteen hours of sleep, her longest on record, my daughter returned to her usual pokerfaced self (excluding, of course, the multiple times she nursed throughout the night). She was ready to eat and sleep her way through Italy.

We started by venturing beyond the Rialto toward St. Mark's Square and Cathedral. The piazza serves as the heart of the city for social, religious, and political activities. Or for my baby, as a community center of sorts. I had no shame in nursing in the wide space and was only slightly embarrassed to change her diaper among the crowds with no restrooms in sight.

We wandered through Doge's Palace and crossed the majestic wood bridge, Ponte dell' Accademia, over the Grand Canal. We walked through the University and passed yet another cathedral. Venice has 139 churches over 160 square miles—nearly one per square mile. Ninety-six percent of them are, or were at some point, Catholic. Finally, we reached a triangular piece of land between the Grand and Giudecca canals. There, we had a breathtaking view of the St. Mark's Square and water on three sides. We rambled among the islands, crossing bridge after bridge as we explored.

Then, an authentic Venetian gondola ride through the narrow canals! Music flowed via the deep baritone of our gondolier and was echoed by Brooklyn singing along in jilted baby garble. My bargain-focused parents even joined us once AJ paid and they realized they were free.

After a while, our gondolier's son found us. He followed our boat through the narrow canals for ten minutes or so, demanding spare cash or asking his father to borrow the keys to the gondola, reappearing like whack-a-mole when bridges impeded his path. The fighting in Italian flowed through our ears like the song did before.

We began to feel the comfort of home that second day, like the ease of new shoes as they begin to break in, and we hit the point of relaxed exhilaration. The bridge near the apartment felt familiar, and the deli at the fork in the road announced we were just a few doors away.

53

LESSON LEARNED

The biggest question I hear from other parents is, how do you carry all their stuff?

My answer? We don't. We've found that we don't need as much as we think. Like creating a baby registry, determining what makes the cut can be overwhelming. So, here's my take:

Try not to overpack clothing, especially bulky items like sweatshirts and jeans. For us, six times too much stuff equals an extra pile of clothes that rivals the inside of my daughters' tiny, shared closet. We pack enough clothes to get us to our midpoint laundry day, plus an extra set for an accident and an extra sweatshirt and pair of pants. That's generally four or five shirts, pants, socks, and underwear, in a style that supports the weather. Then we give the baby a couple extra sets since her compressible clothes take up less space than her. And yes, we typically do laundry at least once. Bring your own laundry detergent and do it in a bathtub or sink if necessary.

Good shoes are imperative. We take two pairs each of trusted, well-worn shoes, wearing one pair and packing another in case those get wet. And that somehow always seems to happen, even when there is no rain. My daughters beg to wear sandals but, with travel, I am far too practical.

We always brought diapers, especially when traveling abroad. Although you can usually purchase there, we prefer doing what we can in advance. Plus, you never know what the pricing will be or if your destination will offer your child's preferred brand, concerning if your child has a sensitive bum.

We take minimal equipment: just a baby carrier, and once we had multiple kids, a compact stroller. When traveling by air, we leave the portable crib at home. We traveled sans stroller in Italy. However, for Disney, I purchased an excellent condition sit-n-stand stroller secondhand for cheap. That investment was nearly covered in one visit to the park; future trips and lending to friends paid dividends. While traveling, the stroller functions like many foreign busses—two, three, even four kids can hop on, some hanging out at strange angles or sitting on the roof. Well, not the roof… I do draw the line somewhere!

For peace of mind, find the closest big box store in advance to get anything you may have forgotten. Or, when traveling domestically, use the store to get your snacks, diapers, and toiletries.

We carry snacks, lots of them, with four little cups and a few spoons. We bring a MacBook with adaptor, a rechargeable or battery-operated sound machine, and an iPad with headphones. Since our Mac doesn't need a converter, we can plug all of my other gadgets in to charge.

We also let each kid pick out a specific number of items—three to five toys, books, blanket—that they can fit in their own personal suitcase or backpack. I encourage including a cozy or stuffed item since that also serves another purpose. Lastly, we always pack our swimsuits. Even if it's not a beach vacation, you will not want to turn your kids down when the hotel (or adjoining fitness club) has an unexpected pool. Geronimo!

Baby Brooklyn went straight to bed that night, and we finally relaxed with my parents. We were thrilled to have nine uninterrupted days with them. Living a twelve-hour drive away makes it hard to see them more than a few times a year. That made the time even more special.

The next morning, we took the two-hour train to Florence before walking to our hotel. We had packed as light as we could with a baby—no stroller—but the uneven cobblestone neighborhood streets still disagreed with our heavy rolling suitcase topped with a duffel bag. Without elevator access at Hotel Sole, we tromped up to the third level, eight flights of stairs. I was fortunate to just be transporting a baby and a backpack, but poor AJ had to lug the fifty-pound roller.

My father had not booked this one-star hotel for the ambience or customer service. It was a safe and central location. Period. In that compact space with one simple bed and no curtains, we discovered that standard European rooms don't necessarily accommodate larger families (or Never-Sleep babies accustomed to room darkeners). Thankfully we had just one baby. Dreading the sleeping arrangements, we headed out for our day in Florence.

Like the peddler in the children's book, *Caps for Sale,* Florence wears many hats. As the capital of the Tuscany region, it governs over a beautiful and wide expanse of vineyards, coastline, and farms. It also serves as a birthplace of Renaissance art and architecture. Within a ten-minute walk of our hotel, we reached the massive Duomo with its terracotta-tile dome. The cathedral took nearly 200 years to complete, started in 1296, with the dome designed by Filippo Brunelleschi.

Tucked tight in her carrier, Brooklyn quickly fell asleep. I felt twenty-months pregnant, my belly jutting out and carrying an extra twenty pounds, as we climbed up the narrow 463 steps. Little did I know that I was actually a few weeks pregnant with Ella! We walked along the inside of the massive dome, viewing Vasari and Zuccari's Last Judgment frescoes at eye level. The frescoes span the variance of life, from angels and saints to regions of Hell. Wow! It was huge at 4,500 square meters, and old, started in 1572.

"She's awake!" my mom chimed outside at the top, pleased for the photos to include the baby's face. My mom served as photographer extraordinaire on trips. She captured every moment, every laugh, and every cry in Italy. While I watched my baby's cheeks curl back in delight while trying cool, creamy gelato, my mom snapped a photo. My mom taught me the importance of taking photos when traveling—documenting to reinforce the memories for the kids and to decorate the walls. The albums from the trips she's joined us on are outstanding. That trip is as documented as Curious George's adventures.

The women in my family love to bake, and everyone does their best to eat. Our holidays consist of pie and cookie tastings, along with a lick-the-plate pudding topped with cream. My aunts create their pies from scratch, my mom makes the oh-so-buttery sugar cookies, and my young niece crafts fondant. I'm respectable with my skills; I have the genes and appreciate a good stick of Irish butter, but I don't have their presentation skills. My mom has a lot of specialties—I could name a list a mile long—but my favorite has always been her strawberry shortcake.

When I was young, she would make it as a regular summer treat. Bake the shortcake and let the strawberries soak into the warm cake during dinner. It was scrumptious. After my grandpa died and my siblings dispersed from our house like dandelion seeds, my father's mom came to live with us. As she was older, she had the nags that age brings, slightly blind and hard of hearing.

"Mom, do you want me to make you a dish?" my mother shouted gently to her good ear as she scooped out portions for my dad and me.

"No," she replied. "I don't want any today." She loved my mom's baking, but she also put on false airs about watching her figure.

"I'll play that game," my mom must have thought, leaving out the last piece for later.

As much as we can bake, we aren't the best cooks, though I do like my mom's lasagna. As a teenager, it was best when served with store-bought garlic bread, the kind caked with a thick layer of fake lard and about five hundred calories a slice. Then, out came the dessert. My dad and I wolfed it down while my mom delicately chomped through, mindful before it was a thing. Then we set about watching our daily Jeopardy.

"What is pi?" I'd respond or "Who is Janet Jackson?" as I read ahead and proudly answered (asked?) first. I really was a nerd. Grandma got up partway through and buzzed around in the kitchen, getting her piece of strawberry shortcake.

Grandma ate in silence, somewhat grumpy and unlike herself. About halfway through, she stopped and took her plate to the kitchen sink. It was odd, but she was old, and she might not have been feeling well. As the hungry teen, I gladly went for seconds of the garlic bread.

"Mom!" I shouted in my annoyingly self-centered adolescent voice. "Where did you put the bread? I'm so hungry." My mom came out to investigate. The bread was clearly gone. We searched the kitchen counters, looked in the fridge, and then I found it. It was half eaten, covered in strawberries in the trash. My poor grandmother, the epitome of a Catholic martyr, had just consumed her strawberry shortcake on garlic bread. And true to her character, she didn't complain in the least.

Brooklyn did not experience bad food in Italy. I imagine few do. AJ and I had saved many firsts for her—pasta, pizza, sandwich, ice cream. Not even ice cream. Gelato.

At Piazza Sant'Elisabetta, we introduced my baby to the wonders of Italy. She ate her first salmon and tried fresh spinach lasagna. She ate like a former castaway tasting these flavors. She loved the shells and the bread. I should have known Brooklyn would be picky after tasting foods in the culinary capital of the world; I had wrongly hoped she'd also develop a future palette. Over a thousand boxes of Annie's Mac and Cheese later, that has not come to fruition.

That night, we eagerly packed our bags for an overnight adventure. My parents had identified Cinque Terre, a portion of coast on the Italian Riviera, just three hours away. At the time, it wasn't nearly as popular as it is today. As with all of the cities, I checked with a college friend who had studied in Florence. She had not seen Cinque Terre but said it was supposed to be great. "Lots of hiking. Lots of steps." I could see her think through the airwaves. "That's definitely something you guys would enjoy." She knew my family too well.

Although Florence oozed culture, and I could see how my friend, a southerner with good taste and a penchant for languages, fell in love, I was ready to escape. Our hotel room was tiny, cramped, and as lit up as Vegas at night. When the claustrophobia-inducing elevator doors squeezed my camera and popped the lens cap off into the crevasse between the doors and to the bottom of the abyss, I'd had enough. The allure of the sea and hiking in the mountains called.

Cinque Terre literally means the Five Lands. The towns sit on a rugged portion of the Italian Riviera overlooking the Liguria Sea. We planned to use the walking paths to hike between them, starting in Monterossa al Mare, then Vernazza, Corniglia, Manarola, and finishing in Riomaggiore. The villages are accessible solely by train or trail. Terraces built into the steep cliffs cultivate grapes and olives. It felt as if an island, cut off from the last century.

After a rough night sleeping in the bright room, with a husband who couldn't sleep who woke our baby who woke me, we felt validated about our plans and the excitement ahead. Our train route included a changeover in Pisa, so we joined the crowds for the perfect shot of the Leaning Tower, either pretending to hold it up or leaning to the side to make it appear straight. Although she had slept through the train ride, Brooklyn woke on arrival, and scowled grumpily at her Nana's camera.

I had found our room in Monterosso, with a view of the sea in the distance as long as you stood in the far corner of the large balcony and turned your head at just the right angle, at a small family-run place, Hotel La Spiaggia.

"Have some wine," the owner, Andrea, offered. "It comes from a winery nearby. Relax," he continued as he served us chips. It was fantastic, the antithesis of busy Pisa.

We meandered through the village, exploring at the pleasant pace of and with the wonder of a baby. My dad pushed Brooklyn in a swing on the sandy beach.

I removed my shoes, feeling the cool sand between my toes, and walked with Brooklyn toward the water. When I reached the shore, I gently unwrapped her from my hip. She deftly avoided my attempt at putting her feet in the nippy water by instinctively raising her legs parallel to the ground. I tried lowering her a second and then a third time, but her feet maintained that gap, a repelling magnet of baby above the sea.

"Can you take her?" I asked AJ so I could walk into the sea. Seeing me knee-deep a few feet away, Brooklyn allowed her daddy to splash some water on her and slowly straightened her legs to relax her toes into the gritty, wet sand.

After a few moments, Brooklyn became fascinated by the sand and the water, seeing and feeling it for the first time in her short life. She wiggled her toes and giggled at the sensation. Then she placed her hand in the shallow water and splashed it a few times like she had when she discovered the dogs' water bowl. Before we realized what was happening, she had plopped into the frigid water under the warm breeze, feeling and sensing the water's vastness.

Back at the hotel, Andrea commanded us, "Get the pesto." He had recommended a truly authentic restaurant nearby.

"Yuck," I thought.

'Don't yuck someone else's yum,' my kids' future kindergarten teacher would have admonished.

And it's good advice. I had yet to try true Italian Riviera pesto from its region of origin. Basil, the base of pesto, thrives in the mild climate of the region. Authentic pesto is ground with cheese, garlic, olive oil, and pine nuts. That combination poured over handmade pasta made that morning melted in my mouth. For good measure, we ordered freshly caught lobster mixed into a risotto and a large plate of buttered pasta. The pasta pleased my daughter so much she plopped her clean, bare foot on the table in appreciation as she ate.

Being on a cliff, Cinque Terre is prone to the whims of God and weather patterns. Rain had washed out much of the path during our stay. My parents accommodated by waking early and adding a sixth town to the trip, Levanto to the north, before meeting us for breakfast. I declined on principle. It was Cinque Terre, not Sei Terre. My baby also slept like a baby—a real one, not a Never-Sleep one—in Monterossa. Yet another fix to our sleep problems—just move to a bungalow with a calming sea breeze.

Physical fitness bleeds through my family, my dad especially. Bike to my sister's house in Ohio from southwest Michigan? Sure. He once ran sixteen miles to AJ's office. AJ looked out into the dark sky, long after his coworkers had left, waiting for the man, the legend. My dad came hobbling up thirty minutes later than promised; after getting lost, he had to run partway along the freeway. My siblings are Ironman finishers.

I'm nowhere near that hard core, but I do try to incorporate exercise into my busy life. My college roommate, Elizabeth, reflects on the time I ran over five miles from Georgetown to Reagan National Airport to greet her. In my defense, I thought the subway opened earlier than it did. I was a volleyball player, not a runner; I had only meant to run half of it but didn't have money for a cab.

Inevitably, an exercise adventure pops up on every trip. On Martha's Vineyard, AJ pushed Baby Ella twenty miles while I biked with Brooklyn. While I pedaled the trails toward Oak Bluffs visive the beach, he took a wrong turn and ran through the town beforehand—clocking in thirteen miles to my three or four. Baby Ella completed a near marathon in the stroller that day. With no Gatorade.

We planned to leave our larger items in Florence, but my mom convinced us they would shuttle back to Monterosso and retrieve the bags. I was skeptical, but I went along with bringing a half-packed duffel bag beyond the backpack we had originally planned. Upon arrival, my parents realized their error and that we had too much stuff. My mother held her oversized bright red purse, AJ brought the backpack, and I caddied the baby. My dad grudgingly carried the extra (thankfully light) bag he'd convinced us to take along with his own gym bag. We looked ridiculous.

At just over two miles, the trail from Monterossa to Vernazza is considered the hardest and took us more than two hours. We climbed hundreds of stairs through the narrow path. The views made up for the hardships, though. We saw vineyards and orchards, and the sea sparkled for miles in the distance. I felt like a beast of burden, carrying a baby on my back. Brooklyn didn't mind; she loved being next to her mom and seemed to enjoy the breathtaking views. At one point, high on a cliff, we stopped for a proper break. As she nursed and dozed off, I felt more at peace and relaxed than I had the whole trip, exhilarated and tired from the strenuous part of the hike but strong from carrying my body and baby through.

The colorful houses, old church, and breathtaking view of Vernazza's bay appeared on the horizon. It was much livelier and populated than cozy

Monterossa with a fun vibe and active bar scene that appeals to singles and young couples.

From there, we trained in and out of Corniglia, since rain had washed out both trails. We'd still see all five cities, if not by foot. The vertical ascent up the picturesque mountain seemed imposing, making it the quietest and most remote of the Cinque Terre, 300 steps up from the train station. We ate more pesto at Cantina da Manana, a large outdoor space with fragrant, beautiful flowers. We gorged on dessert and the panoramic views of the sea underneath the clear blue skies.

We said *addio* to my parents and continued on to the last *due* (two) of the Cinque Terre. Before we set out from Manarola, though, I discovered a path to a rocky beach. Like the sirens of the Odyssey, the water seduced AJ to jump in and swim with the locals. He crossed the small, shallow channel and stretched out on some large black boulders.

Brooklyn and I navigated the pier-like area. "Dada!" she called, saying one of her three words as she pointed across the water. We met other babies, one her age from York, England and a local six-month-old. Brooklyn squealed with delight when I let her dip her feet in, part of the crowd but also in her own world. The York baby's ears perked up, and she joined us. My baby had started an international trend.

A bag and a hundred years lighter, we hiked to Riomaggiore, a twenty-minute stroll along Via dell'Amore, Lover's Lane, a paved promenade that hugs the coastline. Though the most crowded, the rocks overhanging the sea and benches built into the rocks charmed us. There were strollers and grandmothers out in the late afternoon sun. AJ and I ambled hand and hand down the path as Brooklyn waved to everyone. Perhaps I made that up, but with memories, you can add that glean.

Riomaggiore basically built itself into the side of a mountain. We climbed the steep brick path for our shopping—up, up, up. I would not want to chase a runaway stroller here. After my change of heart on pesto, I bought bottles for home and for the Italian American babysitter with the napping prose. We jumped on the train, got lucky with timing, and arrived back in Florence in just about two hours.

We finished our Florence adventure with the Accademia Gallery and arguably most famous sculpture of all, the Statue of David, along with other works of Michelangelo. Although I had seen photos and read about it, at fourteen feet of solid marble, it was much larger and more impressive in person. He's not the only artist with work there—Botticelli, del Sarto, and others are featured as well. Most of the work did come from the Medici family, donated to the Grand Duchy of Tuscany so they could be seen my a much larger audience. David himself had stood in front of Palazzo della Signoria until only 150 years ago to show devotion to the ideals of liberty and freedom. Perhaps he can make a trek across the Atlantic to remind our country of that.

To a baby, however, a large white stone didn't hold much appeal, so I took Brooklyn to a quiet bench outside to nurse. We sat in the garden under the watchful eye of a smaller replica of David in pink. Those colors were more her speed.

Earlier we had seen the famed Uffizi Gallery with some of the most famous paintings in the world—da Vinci's Birth of Venus and more paintings by Michelangelo. Brooklyn loved the frescoes on the ceiling from her perch. She gazed up, mesmerized by the intricacies, depth, and patterns. Never-Sleep dozed off with her head toward the ceiling, nursing and looking up, lulled to sleep by her multi-million-dollar mobile.

We left Florence after a charming walk to Ponte Vecchio, a beautiful medieval stone bridge known for the shops built on it since it is closed to car traffic. We scored delicious fresh cherries and strawberries and the best gelato so far. Finally, after five days of it, and probably a dozen servings, Brooklyn started asking for it.

We eased into the final stretch of the trip via train to Rome, the last destination in this madness. AJ and I handed off our baby to her Papa for a short break. All of a sudden, Brooklyn's hidden personality came to life, and she was a little ham. Those seated around her loved her and were drawn to her. Peering back, I saw the personality of an entertainer. She had a friendly smile and was interacting with the crowd.

We saw up close the baby loving I had read about. Older women wanted to hold her; men wanted to make her laugh. At the time, AJ and I patted ourselves on the back. We figured the no crying it out and constant closeness from our "baby wearing" was finally paying off. That day and subsequent ones would show the Roman gods were laughing in our face at that arrogance.

From the train, we cabbed to the apartment my father had found near Vatican City. Being a mother for just a short time, I was horrified at the lack of childproofing we saw. Live electric sockets littered the walls at eye level for a crawling baby. Brooklyn pulled herself to standing and opened the oven door. It was an open floor plan for the main floor—tiny kitchen, living room, and table.

"Where is the bedroom?" I asked my dad.

"Ask your baby," he said as he pointed at the spiral staircase in the center of the room. Sure enough, she was adjusting her footing to climb up this odd contraption.

I scooped her in my arms and wound around the staircase, greeted by an open loft with two beds. You couldn't stand up without hitting your head—well, Brooklyn could. I couldn't. My insides were churning at the emotions. Frustration at my lack of planning, anger at the situation, and panic at sleeping in a place like this with a baby.

"Where do you and the baby want to sleep?" my dad asked. "You can have the upstairs or the pull-out couch." He was cautious in his words, like a lion tamer entering the cage.

Mom hormones kicked into high gear, I tried to breathe deeply through my nose to avoid a confrontation. "I think we need to find another place." Silence. "It's not safe here for a baby." With Sienna, my fourth, I may have been convinced otherwise; she hasn't gotten the helicoptering that a first-born receives. But this was my baby, and I had all the time in the world to devote to her. "I'm sure there's a hotel around here. This isn't two bedrooms. We're not staying here."

My dad was not happy. He is an honest Midwestern; when he makes a promise, he keeps it. He's stubborn, and I inherited it. We were at a standstill.

Ever-Hungry, the peacemaker, stepped in. "Let's get some dinner and see what we can do."

The serenity of the picturesque Borgo Pio neighborhood embraced us. It was a quaint medieval neighborhood built next to the Passetto, a long wall

connecting the Vatican to Castel Sant Angelo. Restaurants lined the pedestrian road. As we ambled down the road, just a block away, I saw a modest
hotel, Hotel S Anna. I walked in to the former sixteenth century palace and
felt the air of comfort, the plush carpeting and dated stylish furniture of a
proper three-star hotel.

"Do you have any availability?" I asked the front clerk. "I'd like two rooms."
He showed me the large rooms, with a queen bed and two twins, and shared
the somewhat pricey, but reasonable rate. I offered to pay for both rooms. My
easy-going dad huffed the same way his ornery father had many times before
and turned on his heel to return to the apartment, skipping dinner with us.
He would stay at the apartment.

I felt terrible that I had upset my dad but at the end of the day, I had to do
what was best for my baby. We would be sleeping in a safe, comfortable hotel.

We ate with my mother, then walked her back. She wasn't quite sure
which building it was until she saw my father's bright yellow skeleton shirt
hanging out the window.

"I think this is it," she said. The neon shirt was drying on the line, waving
in unspoken apology for the earlier argument. My dad had washed the shirt
by hand and put it outside like generations before. Then my dad appeared in
the window.

"How was your run?" I asked. (Code for, I'm sorry.) The four-mile run
along the water had dragged out all of my dad's negative energy.

My dad made some jokes about AJ's running, I bantered back, and all was
forgotten and forgiven. We wouldn't speak of it again. This communication
style drives my husband crazy but sometimes differences are the best magnets.

In one of the most religious cities in the world, I couldn't imagine the karma
I would have by insisting on a room change. Sharing my bed, my baby awoke
to nurse whenever I moved or breathed. The 24-hour café was back open. At
least she wouldn't get electrocuted or fall down rickety stairs. Plus, we got free
coffee, breakfast, and fresh strawberries in the morning.

My parents picked us up for the long walk all over Rome, starting at nearby Castel Sant'Angelo, a towering fortress and castle built for the Emperor Hadrian. It is said that Rome wasn't built in a day, but we tried our best to see it in one. Brooklyn fell asleep on me as we crossed the St. Angelo Bridge over the Tiber River into central Rome. We echoed history on an ancient pedestrian bridge built a century before Christ, five arches in the water and decorated with travertine marble and angel statues.

"Which side do you think is better for running?" AJ mused, peering at the joggers beneath the bridge, following the course of the river and roadways on both sides.

On the opposite bank, past the runners, we approached Piazza Navona, known for the eclectic artists and unique and intricate fountains, before ambling to the Pantheon. Brooklyn woke inside from the overwhelming silence of the pious site.

We skipped over to Trevi Fountain, a 250-year-old aqueduct-fed fountain with sculpted figures. Though it was forbidden, my bumbling dad stuck Baby Brooklyn's feet in the cool water. We relaxed with the mass of people, comparable in size to a KIDZ BOP concert, but enjoying it all the same. From there, we wandered to the iconic baroque Spanish Steps, an elegant meeting place. I averted Brooklyn's gaze as we ascended the butterfly-shaped stairs since, though she couldn't yet walk, she could climb. I watched out for the infamous 'thieves'—women I envisioned as bejeweled Esméraldas. Instead, travel opened my eyes to misconceptions. The girls' poverty and youth surprised me, along with the babies in their arms and bellies. Rather than fear, I felt a longing to offer a hot meal and a hug.

We passed a behemoth, non-descript government building, Quirinal Palace, official residence of the president and one of the ten largest palaces in the world by area. We stood on the tallest of Rome's seven hills and, at certain angles, saw the city spread before us to St. Peter's Basilica. The stony silence of government buildings with muffled conversations, and muted civilians walking briskly, soothed my daughter. I appreciated that the massive walking tour lulled my baby into an extended afternoon nap, the cool breeze and dull murmur of the crowds replacing her sound machine.

The Monument of Victor Emmanuel II, a huge white marble edifice amidst statues, a staircase, and the Altar of the Fatherland, their unknown soldier memorial, loomed as we searched for the Forum. Then Circus Maximus, the oldest and largest public space in Rome, built during the reign of Julius Caesar for chariot races and the Roman Games. Passing the Forum and Palantine, we arrived at the Arch of Constantine, the largest Roman triumphal arch.

Brooklyn finally awoke at the ancient Colosseum. AJ changed her while I stretched for three luxurious baby-free minutes. Then my daughter joined the thousands of babies past who had nursed in that spot. Those babies got their sustenance during breaks in public executions and torture by wild animals. Mine did among hordes of tourists while her Ever-Hungry dad ate a hot dog and drank a beer, probably followed by a gelato.

Rome overwhelmed our senses—the rich smells, delectable tastes, foreign sounds, and sights for our raw eyes. I mirrored my daughter's awe at seeing buildings that witnessed thousands of years of history. Every street corner burst with something old, something new, something with sorrow, or something to do. It was illogical to see the Eternal City in a day, and we only got a taste, like a lick to the palm to sample the temperature of a baby's bottle. But that was enough to show us how minute our short lives are within the vast expanse of history.

My parents were sad to leave us (or rather, my daughter), so they came to our room to spend more time with us before their early morning flight. Brooklyn charmed them that last hour, making my parents laugh in that sad way you only can when you realize what you're about to miss. I cherish the video my mom captured that night of a ridiculously overtired but happy girl, chattering in her high-pitched baby voice.

AJ, Brooklyn, and I visited Vatican City on our last day. Since the cathedral was only a few blocks from our hotel, we had already seen it at night. Seeing the heart of my unfailingly Catholic grandmother's faith, St. Peter's Basilica, at night and lit up, took my breath away. My siblings and I had been baptized late in childhood after a near-death experience and some spooky coincidences. The magnitude of the cathedral and what it represented overwhelmed and humbled me.

The dome of St. Peter's Basilica, the world's largest at 448 feet, was astounding. The nave held more gold than I could have dreamed. Stopped upon entry, we saw Pope Benedict at the altar, 720 feet away. Pope Francis would ascend the next year and encourage public nursing. He stated, "You mothers give your children milk and even now, if they cry because they are hungry, breastfeed them, don't worry." I huddled with my baby on a chair I had dragged into the bathroom, one Pope too early and a baby before I learned not to care.

The Sistine Chapel was overloaded with people, like four-year-olds clustered around a soccer ball. Since the masterpiece covered the ceiling, however, its greatness was visible without barrier. Michelangelo's genius was impeccable, as if he envisioned future travelers admiring his work like we see the unencumbered moon above.

Holy people filled the streets of Vatican City. That's to be expected, sure, but I didn't anticipate nuns blessing my baby in the street or nodding to a priest wearing a cap from my sister's alma mater. My mom befriended another priest while in line at Old Bridge Gelateria, on the dividing line between Vatican City and Rome. Like my father, he came from the upper peninsula of Michigan, a bastion of 300,000 people and declining. We met a man across the world who could have lived next door.

For our last dinner, we grabbed pizza. What else? AJ and I reminisced on the joys of our trip, visiting Venice, Florence, and Rome. The highlights, however, were the little things: spending time with my parents, experiencing awe through a child's eyes, and meals in the sun. There's a lot to be said about seeing the sites, and with photos that give you the structure to make memories, but the best moments in life are those in between. We had done so much, and though she still refused to sleep, Brooklyn had excelled. We looked over at a table of nuns drinking a round of beer next to us and gave a salute.

Chapter Five

ROCKABYE REUNIONS

"H**I-IIII Y'ALL**," A sweet Southern voice beamed into the phone. My heart melted. "Bless your heart, I'm so delighted to meet you," my future roommate, Elizabeth, effused into the phone. Though I couldn't quite understand her through her accent, I wanted to bottle her warmth.

"Ope… hi. I have no culture, but I can talk about Lake Michigan's virtues, Petoskey stones, and the auto industry, you know?" I responded wholesomely in my plain Midwestern tone.

Although moving to the south had been quite the culture shock, I had been quite fortunate to find two great roommates at Davidson College. Elizabeth would become like a sister to me. We had been paired through a personality test and shared many quirks—introverted, hard-working, goofy, always believing the best in people, and her boyfriend's family owned Boston Terriers. I would also see a sweetness and genuine thoughtfulness in her. Her drive pushed her to become a partner at a law firm.

My second roommate, Erin, and I were quite different, though complementary as roommates. While I walked everywhere, she sped around in a fancy (to me) hunter green car. While I tried to tame my curls, her black hair shone naturally silky smooth. She was fun and wicked smart, becoming a doctor with seemingly hardly an effort. Erin brought me out of my shell, chatting into the night with gossip from our small school. She laughed at my jokes, shared in my ridiculous stories, and crushed on the tall basketball guys with me. Years later, on the night before my wedding, with my hands covered in Indian Henna, she transcribed a note to my future husband before dutifully removing my contact lenses.

I was their Northern roommate, the one who talked a little funny with o's that sound like a cow mooing and always wore shorts or skirts, even in the dead of winter. In my defense, that's around fifty degrees—late-May back home.

Since my Texas roommate didn't want to drive the eighteen hours to San Antonio by herself, I joined her over winter break. The deep south was as unknown to me as LOL dolls to my daughters. After my last volleyball game, my parents took most of my things, and I bundled the rest of my half of the dorm room into two suitcases. Erin and I drove 1,245 miles over two days, sleeping at a cheap roadside motel in Mobile, Alabama. As we settled in for the night, I quickly grabbed the bed near the bathroom and away from the door.

"But I wanted that bed," she complained.

"I don't want to sleep next to the window," I responded.

Two young, smart, single ladies. Not afraid to travel across the country or to leave home for college hundreds of miles from home, but terrified of sleeping by the window. I skooched over so we could share the double bed.

Her family welcomed me that week, showing me Texas Hill Country and a Spurs-Jazz NBA game when that meant Dennis Rodman, David Robinson, and Tim Duncan vs. Karl Malone and John Stockton. I watched my newly legal friend drink a mouth-watering margarita on the famed Riverwalk. Her family even brought me along to pick out their puppy.

We discovered that the rookie, Tony Parker, lived just a couple of streets from her parents. He was still new and fresh, surely underpaid. He didn't live in the mansions of Champions Ridge she had shown me a few days before.

"Why don't we stop by his house? We can bring him some cookies. Maybe he wants to grab frozen yogurt?" We thought we were the wittiest people alive. (Not much has changed.) And, based on some other stories in my life, that very well could have happened. A couple months later, on my way to study abroad, I agreed to go miniature golfing on Valentine's Day with a future NFL Pro-Bowler so my friend could have her romantic date. The next day, we scored free tickets for filming of America's Funniest Home Videos and got our fifteen seconds of airtime. Say yes to the adventure.

Other than trying to squeeze my dorm room into giant suitcases, the Texas visit went well. But of course, I had naively arrived at the airport only an hour early. And, since it was just months after 9/11, my overstuffed bags were hand searched. Of course, I had squished in two cans of tuna that set off alarms.

AJ, nearly-two-year-old Brooklyn, five-month-old Ella, and I were on our way to my college reunion. Then we were jet-setting to a wedding for my friend, Christine. Although I was only a couple years older than my business school classmates, my marriage put me a life stage ahead. That's why, when Christine shared that she was engaged, I was thrilled to be there for her special day—especially since it was at the beautiful Hotel Del Coronado near San Diego.

The timing could have been better. It was just two weeks after I planned to return to work after maternity with Ella and, of course, a week after the long-awaited reunion. But, like all unexpected things in life, I figured I'd make it work. I requested approval for a week without pay. I mean, what's another unpaid week after a four-month maternity break?

My family lucked out on the first flight. Although we were traveling with two lap babies, we somehow secured a row to ourselves and survived with no lasting damage. That didn't last for the drive; Baby Ella opened her mouth for thirty minutes of screaming and howling. The torrential rain slowing us didn't help. We quickly learned the trip theme: just say no to car seats!

Tempers in infants are challenging but usually easy to soothe. The mood begins with twitching in the fingers. She starts tensing up, shifting a little to show discontent. Pick her up right then, and you may avoid a cry.

For Ella, my sweet second one, the sucking on the pacifier picks up. At this point, she looks like Maggie Simpson with her succor in her mouth. Perhaps she's hungry and is mad it's not food, or perhaps she's tired and upset it hasn't put her to sleep. After a few seconds or even a minute of passionate sucking, the pacifier explodes out of her mouth. You know she is about to lose it.

Then there is that moment of calm, like the eye of a hurricane. Though she's in the back seat, I can sense her face turning red, pulled tight as she sucks in oxygen for a yell. And you wait. A couple of seconds, it's a minor misunderstanding that can be remedied by herself. Three seconds or so will require a hug or a kiss. Five needs a prolonged kiss and maybe some ice. The ice doesn't actually do anything, but the children like to feel like I'm doing something. If it's that dreaded ten seconds pause between the event and the cry, you know it's going to be bad. The one fifteen second pause, where I wondered if the cry actually was coming—that time she needed stitches.

This poor baby craved contact. Ella was as sweet as a lollipop, so long as she was being held. When in her car seat, she would scream, but hold her and she would sing like an angel. I'm a baby wearer, strapping them to my chest or back and proceeding on as before. I nurse on demand, co-sleep, just act a little crunchy as others may say. The fourth trimester. I trust that indulgence gives them more independence later. That has suited me well with my children's temperaments and with traveling, with this exception. The baby can't be near me in that dreaded car seat.

If she is that right amount of tired, the car seat can be tolerated. Just a little drowsy, content to go to sleep but not exhausted. Every parent knows that point of no return. Stick a pacifier in her mouth, and she'll fall right asleep. If overtired, she'll scream for an hour, lighting up ears miles away.

That is why, at just a few days old, maybe a week, I nicknamed her my Screech Owl. She could sleep—wow, this kid could sleep. After my struggles with my first, I was amazed to see an infant put herself to sleep and not wake during the night. At playdates, I would perform a party trick where I'd give her a pacifier, and Ella would hunch over my forearm, deep in dreamland. I needed a baby just like her at that point in my life.

Comparing Ella's temperament to Brooklyn's was like night and day. I told people that if I could combine those kids, it would be either the best kid ever or the worst, depending on which traits you procured. I'd seen both sides when Lucas came along. (Under the age of two, it was a great combination. Over two, not so much.) The two girls balanced each other. One easy-going, well-behaved kid who refused to sleep, and another who ran hot when not in physical contact with me but collapsed in her own bed at the end of the day.

Davidson College hosts an annual freshman tradition called the Cake Race. The cross-country coach started it to identify top runners. Local families would bake cakes, and the teenagers would run for first dibs. It has continued through the years, and there would be dozens of cakes for finishers. Although I wasn't a runner, I was physically fit and earned a top twenty pick after the track, soccer, and some of the field hockey and lacrosse girls.

The school held an alumni version for our reunion. Saturday morning, older alum showed up with their teenage children while the young alum slept off a night of partying with their friends. I took Brooklyn in her stroller. Just a dollop into my thirties, I could still compete when necessary, but was still not a runner. A peppy friend, a former cheerleader, appeared just as the race began.

"Hey Kaitlyn!" she exclaimed.

"Hi," I most likely heaved.

"So-and-so and you-know-who wanted to do this too, but they went out last night," she chattered.

Oh God, I thought. Am I going to have to run, push a stroller, and chat with this energetic former cheerleader I haven't seen in ten years? Yep—1.4 miles of jogging while making Southern pleasantries. The last hill up from the quad just about killed me. And for that, I earned not a cake but a melt-in-your-mouth Krispie Kreme doughnut.

At lunch, I saw friends I hadn't in years and met their children. That's why people go to reunions, not to run. Classmates cooed over Ella, calling her the Gerber baby. This kid could enchant and charm when she wanted. When in my arms, she carried a big smile with plump cheeks. I showed AJ my old digs since lunch was in the gym.

The head basketball coach, the ever-generous Coach McKillop, offered up his office for me to feed my baby. I knew him from my time fighting for playing time on the (former) one court gymnasium. AJ was thrilled to meet him, and I vowed to repay him with homemade chocolate chip cookies at a basketball game when they played Rhode Island a few months later. Davidson College is that type of school.

That night, I celebrated with my old roommates, reliving our lives of just a decade earlier. Yet, somehow, accustomed to being with my kids 24/7, during that three-hour break with my friends (friends I love dearly), I still missed my little ones.

The next morning, we were Los Angeles-bound. The six-hour flight breezed by for me as Ella slept like a pet rock. My poor husband wrangled the squirrel in his lap. Brooklyn bounced around, much like what you'd expect from a twenty-three-month-old seated in the lap of a man on a flight packed like sardines.

Minimizing baby-in-car time, we took a shuttle to the airport Embassy Suites. The hotel was surprisingly really nice in a 1970's sort of way. A massive atrium sat in the center, surrounded by the hotel rooms. Unlike similar hotels that seem drearily empty if not fully booked, this missed the creepy factor. The indoor fountains amused the kids, and the free dinners enticed my Ever-Hungry husband.

We also saved money by getting the car in the morning rather than paying for the extra day just to pay for garage parking at the hotel. I figured AJ could easily run to pick it up in the morning while I leisurely got the kids up and dressed. I didn't really factor in the ridiculousness of Los Angeles roads. Although we could see the airport from our hotel, just about half a mile away, with the matrix of highways and few sidewalks, it turned into a three and a half mile run for him. The poor guy grudgingly woke up early and came back just in time to devour fresh strawberries, pancakes, and made-to-order omelets with us. He and Brooklyn ate like there was no tomorrow.

Then we embarked on our southern California journey, stopping for a quick sojourn to beckoning Hollywood and Beverly Hills. We wandered for an hour among the Hollywood Stars Walk of Fame at the Chinese Theatre, just enough time to say we had been but departing before the crowds arrived. Brooklyn smiled broadly as she pressed her hands into Shirley Temple's prints, replicating a photo of me (coincidentally, down to the short shorts) my parents had taken thirty years prior.

Beverly Hills had dreamy weather, clear blue skies with the smell of jasmine in the warm California breeze. We passed vast mansions with perfectly coifed lawns and large gates. Brooklyn, AJ, and I walked hand-in-little-hand by Beverly Gardens Park, a quaint, well-maintained garden with an attractive, yet empty, playground. An enormous Morton Bay Fig tree cast a shadow, calling people to lounge in its vast shade. But like toddlers, we were drawn elsewhere, to the bright lights, the excitement, and the expensive shops.

We ambled Rodeo Drive for window shopping/peeking as the kids nodded off in our arms. Numerous plastic surgeon offices hid discretely in the alley, with clients hustling in beneath a scarf or hat. On a corner, we encountered the screen siren Raquel Welch. She looked just as I would have thought— older, beautiful, super-tan, not quite real. She smiled quite genuinely at our adorable sleeping babies.

Within the comforts of my home on the East Coast, I had mapped out an ideal drive, pausing for a stroll along the beach and eating cotton candy and funnel cakes on the boardwalk. However, I hadn't accounted for a Screech Owl in crushing rush hour traffic. We instead drove Sunset Boulevard, passing celebrity homes I had found in a guidebook—the haunted, pink Beverly Hills hotel and former homes of Madonna, Phil Collins, Marlon Brando, Jack Nicholson, and OJ Simpson in Brentwood.

LESSON LEARNED

With four expensive kids, we spend a lot of time in the car. When we want to see the countryside or coast, I like to rent one to see the sights at our pace. It works much better for us than an organized tour and gives more flexibility. That, and I prefer not to be trapped with other travelers. It also helps when either partner can drive a stick shift since it can save a lot of money. For car seats, we bring inexpensive, lightweight seats when renting a car. There are a few reasons for this:

1) We know what we're getting into—including the accident-history. There are also instances where the rental car company may not have much to choose from. We also know how to install it, saving time at car pick-up.

2) It's cheaper. A plethora of good car seats in all shapes and sizes are available at low prices. Six- or seven-pound rear or five-point harness car seats, blow up boosters, or light-as-can-be boosters. They may not have the bells and whistles of the 'tanks' in our Ford Flex, but they meet all safety standards and are at least as good as those you would rent. Additionally, unlike other baby items, car seats also fly free. Plus, they're portable to use in the babysitter's car.

3) They are easy. Excluding the Italy trip, we usually brought the infant's everyday seat since it was portable and quite comfortable. It fits with the stroller and could be gate-checked. Then, at the destination, it pops in the seat and off you go.

The car seats don't accompany us on trips with minimal car usage, i.e. when we have a car for less than half of the trip. Minimalism works best when traveling with kids, and it is not fun to lug around those extra items. Same with a stroller.

When in our own car, we make sure to pack a few things in addition to those essentials. Pillows and blankets—those occasionally make the international trips but not always since they're bulky. A portable toilet since my kids hate the auto-flush. At the age of three, my daughter held her pee the entire time at a theme park until I found a utility bathroom near the entrance that had not been upgraded. Stubborn like her mom, she didn't complain about holding it, she just soldiered on. Friends have recommended placing a disposable diaper in the portable toilet in case you don't have a place to dump it. A spare towel holds value in my car, thanks to my passing along the propensity to get carsick.

In late afternoon, we arrived at our dinner destination, the home of AJ's close friend from high school. I won't pretend to remember what we ate or how long we stayed. Those are the memories that disappear, replaced by the warm lingering feelings of a good night. I can say that AJ caught up with an old friend while I met his lovely wife. Their older girls carried around their young guests—since that's what five-year-old girls do—and dragged Brooklyn to the ground during ring-around-the-rosy.

I used to think about Disney, "There aren't nearly as many exciting rides as Cedar Point. There's no way it's as good." And it's true—Cedar Point has a record eighteen coasters to Disneyland's four. But visiting Disney as a parent, I saw the appeal. Disney is truly tailored to every age group. That's why some people swear by it, even choosing to honeymoon there. Dozens of books have been written on Disney, and I've analyzed Harvard Business School cases on the brand. It's an amazing proposition that I didn't quite get. But when I saw my kids' faces light up—even the five-month old—I finally understood.

We were literally across the street, watching the fireworks upon arrival. It seemed convenient, though like the Embassy Suites, with Southern California roads, the walk took twenty minutes. Leaving late for the park since my oldest slept in for possibly the first time in her life, Ella passed out by the time we reached the front of the line for our first ride, the Jungle Cruise. Then, while Brooklyn clung to me in fear during Pirates of the Caribbean, Ella woke up amused by the dog guarding the jail and the drunks on the bridge. Her favorite was the Pooh ride, basically a car gliding around a room that flashed brilliant lights and colors that illuminated my girls' impressed faces.

People walked by eating their giant turkey legs or Mickey Mouse-shaped pretzels while Brooklyn ate packed snacks and her baby sister nursed. We climbed the treehouse and rode Dumbo. After four hours, Ella threw her head back and screamed, her face transforming through darkening hues of red until we could get her to take the pacifier, her 'off' switch.

AJ and I each took a short break for some semblance of life without a baby crawling all over us. When he left, I pushed the stroller along the water, hoping Brooklyn would fall asleep. She didn't, of course. I tried putting her on my back, surrounding myself with kids like a baby sandwich. With another patron looking at me, horrified, I gave up.

For my break, I rode the Matterhorn. As a child, I had been so terrified of the monster at the top that, upon pulling down the lap bar, I would close my eyes and not reopen them until the ride had stopped. Seeing her as an adult, I wondered how the monster got so angry. Sleepless nights? Mastitis?

I rejoined my family in time for Small World, i.e. crack for kids. I have yet to meet a preschooler who says, "That was boring." In the same vein, nearly every single adult becomes nauseous by the third or fourth tour. At least that's what the YouTube comments lead me to believe. Even die-hards eventually will think, "Come on, Kangaroo. Can you do anything but rock back and forth? That joey is not falling asleep."

Brooklyn loved waving to all of the characters in the parade. "Mama! Mama!" she'd shout excitedly as each one rounded the bend. She pointed all them to make sure we didn't miss anything.

"Don't worry, we saw," we would respond.

Our last ride gave Brooklyn one last chance to kick off her shoe and set off a wild goose chase for us to find it, that needle in a Disney haystack. The day was quite draining for AJ and me, sucking us dry like left-out Playdoh, but Brooklyn was wild with happiness after a twelve-hour day with no sleep, and she collapsed at the hotel. She had the best day of her little life. And that made it worth it.

We used the next day to recover—well, for three of us. Ella was raring to go after her record five naps. That achievement will live in family lore, a record that has withstood four babies over eight years. In the morning, Brooklyn enjoyed the simple pleasures of jumping on the bed and tickling my feet to make the baby laugh.

Anaheim to San Diego is a nice short drive, just about a hundred miles. We attempted to minimize any fussiness by spreading out the journey. As we drove down the beautiful coast on Highway 5, both girls napped, and AJ and I reflected on how lucky we were. Most likely, we were actually debating our dogs' routines at my in-laws—sleeping or being fed what they weren't allowed at home.

We stopped for lunch in La Jolla to see the sea lions. Ella expressed fascination with the big creatures lazing on the beach while Brooklyn shunned them. The squirrels burrowing away near the rock wall held greater appeal. We ate sushi at a cute restaurant overlooking the coast. The sun shined down, but didn't overheat us, exemplifying the beauties of California living. No wonder it is the most populous and favorite state.

We skipped the highway to finish our drive via the scenic routes along the Pacific Coast overlooking deep blue crashing waves. We ended across the street from Hotel Del Coronado at the Glorietta Bay Inn. The fantastic location offered great views of the resort and beach, so we meandered down to check them out. Brooklyn immediately went to touch the water. As she frolicked in the soft sand, I breathed in a sigh of relief. We could finally relax.

For my daughter's second birthday, we spent the day at the San Diego Zoo. My kids loved the traditional animals—the zebras, monkeys, flamingoes, and whatnot. There were also penguins waddling around, polar bears playing with barrels in the water, and pandas eating bamboo. Ella enjoyed what she saw for the ten minutes spent awake. She loved the birds, including the sparrows flying around the grounds. Brooklyn selected a stuffed bear to proudly join the dozens of stuffed animals that sit on the shelf, never to be touched again.

Since we were on the West Coast, we caught up with one of my high school friends who I hadn't seen in years. The kids ran around the picture-perfect postcard backyard that looked like the set of a television show amid the desert foliage under the late-afternoon California sun before helping Brooklyn blow out candles on her birthday cake. The best part? Even though it was late, Screech Owl stared wide-eyed into the night sky on our way home. Peaceful at last.

After putting my kids to bed, I snuck over to the bar to see the future bride for a few minutes. Christine and I had bonded after meeting at an orientation in Washington D.C. but lost touch as I organized couples' dinners while she partied with the fun singles. I focused on marketing and strategy, and she excelled at the money-making and network-heavy trading. When I had shared the news of my pregnancy, she became a friend to count on. She dragged me out for good meals once my appetite returned, always an ear for me to talk to.

The morning of the wedding, my little family lazed at the beach in front of Hotel del Coronado, a cool breeze washing over us. Brooklyn wore a sweatshirt over her swimsuit under the gray sky. From her daddy's lap, Ella watched her older sister play in the sand.

Thirty minutes into our visit, cadets came jogging by, slogging through the wet sand. Though it was challenging to the men, it fascinated my girls. San Diego is home to the second largest naval bases in the country with Coronado hosting the Basic Underwater Demolition/SEAL (BUD/S) training. As you would imagine, it's pretty tough—eight weeks of Basic Conditioning, including 'Hell Week.' Those who excel advance to Diving and Land Warfare. The men we saw housed a deep burning to continue even when their bodies wanted to quit. Ironically, we probably saw them at their easiest part of the day.

After the beach, Brooklyn tore off her clothes to jump into our small, warm pool, diving from the steps into my arms. No fear of water, that one. The pool did not induce an easy nap, but after an hour of cajoling, she slept for three hours. I ran out to get AJ a surprise In-N-Out Burger. Food for Ever-Hungry husband and strong naps would bode well for the wedding.

Finally, we could celebrate our reason for coming—the wedding at the Hotel Del Coronado. Decked out in our beach formal wear bought for the occasion, we morphed into celebrities as we crossed into another world of money and opulence. This was where Rudolph Valentino starred in movies and the 1930s celebrities partied—Greta Garbo, Mae West, Rita Hayworth, Will Rogers, James Stewart, Clark Gable.... Considered the best comedy of all time, *Some Like it Hot*, filmed there with Marilyn Monroe, Tony Curtis, and Jack Lemmon. Spending a few hours at the 'Del' was a vacation in and of itself.

My baby was mesmerized during the ceremony on the outdoor grounds. Although we didn't really know anyone, I bonded with the bride's other friends and her family. Once we moved inside for the reception, I roamed around the floors of the hotel looking for a quiet place to nurse. Eventually I discovered a large armchair near the third-floor rooms, overlooking the ocean and away from the crowd. The thick maroon carpet cushioned my feet and the wide, ornately decorated hallways muted my baby's gurgles. After her feast, I put her in the carrier for a nap that stretched throughout the night. I rejoined the party, fine dining and dancing with a baby on my chest. Nothing bothered my sleeping baby, and she didn't trouble me. She climbed back into the womb that night.

The next day, I kissed Brooklyn's head as she looked out the airplane window with her sleepy eyes. All of the excitement was finally catching up to my sleep-resistant kid. Ella nuzzled against me for another four-hour nap. A trip to attend a wedding for a random friend, visiting two of our oldest friends, a college reunion, and days at the San Diego Zoo and Disneyland.

AJ and I shared a sly smile as we realized, it wasn't so bad with two.

Chapter Six

JUNGLE GYMS OF BELIZE

"WHAT IS THAT line on your face?" Brooklyn asked one night at dinner.

"What line?" I responded.

"That one in the middle of your head." I patted self-consciously at the deep line, a wrinkle I had inherited from my mom that, as kids, we referred to as her 'mad face.' Oh geez. I frequently catch my tight face when I'm focused a little too intently or squinting at the sun. It's my 'squint face.' Like inverse Kegel exercises, I relax my forehead for ten seconds when it crosses my mind.

That, along with buying overpriced cream from a friend with beautiful skin. With three kids the same ages, I figure it's worth any price to maintain our friendship—and hopefully also delay some of those wrinkles.

Like my own daughter, I could never imagine becoming my mom. Although I appeared her spitting image with my broad shoulders, strong legs, and blonde hair, I had always felt more like my dad. My mom is outgoing and will talk to anyone. And, as a mom, from my perspective she had it all together.

As I got older, I thought the transition would be like a composite, a slow morph until I had become a quieter version of my mother. After having my own children, I've found it more like one of those tilt cards given as a prize in a crackerjacks box. Look at me from one angle and I'm me, young and carefree, playing catch with my kids. Flip the angle and I transform in a flash, telling my daughter to wear an undershirt, yelling, "Hey!" to my kids, or pulling my son's pants up to his ears. As the years pass, the image of my mom appears more frequently.

My mom prides herself on her 'woo.' That involves talking to strangers, sharing stories about herself, and bragging about her grandchildren. She has rarely found an airplane seatmate she didn't like. Since I've had lap-babies for the past eight years, I am forced to acknowledge the baby in the room and hope my child will behave. Before kids, I opened my book upon boarding or, more likely, closed my eyes for a nap. When my mom traveled with my sister's family before this trip, she played travel one-up with the guy sitting next to her. Their conversation went something like this.

"I really enjoyed Germany," the man said to her. "Especially the castles. Have you ever been to Neuschwanstein Castle?"

"I have!" my mom exclaimed. "We couldn't find our way in. It was really confusing, and I felt a lot of pressure to hurry. It was crazy, wandering around looking for the entrance." My mom chuckled at her ridiculousness. Suddenly, she turned away from the man and looked straight at my sister.

"What?" my sister asked.

"I've never been to that castle!" my mom shot out. "That was on the Amazing Race." She roared with laughter. That's my mom—always looking to top others' stories to the point of thinking she had starred in a television show.

When I heard this story, I thought I would never be so outlandish. But I am. All the time. When I heard my jaw loudly popping as my mom's does every time she eats, I realized the transition is nearly complete. I am an introverted version of my mom, with books instead of woo.

I remembered this story on our flight to Belize City with a three- and one-year-old, thrilled that my parents would be meeting us at our layover. Until then, the flight would be challenging, with double the trouble.

On the way to the hotel in San Ignacio, the cab stopped at the Belize Zoo, a rehabilitation facility for 175 animals of over forty-five native species. In a pretty natural atmosphere, we saw tapirs lounging, jaguars prowling the animals in the cage next door (how would you like living next-door to that?), monkeys, peccaries, toucans, and many huge birds of prey. I got pretty close to many of the animals—a little too near for my worrying mom. It may not have been the world's safest zoo.

When we returned to the road, we saw trees loaded with a bell-shaped, apple-looking fruit with a greenish-gray kidney bean growing from the bottom. A sweet smell permeated the air. "What is that?" I asked our driver.

"Those are cashews," he responded.

"And how is that a cashew?" I asked.

"The nut is inside. It's actually the seed."

"Wow," I responded. "How do you get to the nut?"

"You need to roast the seed before eating it. The shell is actually toxic—like poison ivy."

"Really?" I had no idea.

"It's a big process. First, you pull the nut off and dry and steam it by hand. Then you have to remove the shell by roasting it. We can't do it indoors since it releases those toxins in the smoke." Our driver loved impressing us with his knowledge.

"What about the fruit?" popped in my dad. "Do you eat the fruit?"

The driver laughed as he pulled the car over. He ran up a little hill, pulled a fruit off the tree, and brought it back to the car. "Here, you can try it." My dad had fallen into his trap.

LESSON LEARNED

Flying with kids can be enjoyable or at least not painful. I have a few general things I try to do to make it just a little easier, including:

1. Not being afraid to book. The adventures in this book happened pre-COVID-19, so I benefitted from previous FAA guidelines about having a twenty-four-hour window to cancel a flight for a full refund. Personally, I like sleeping on decisions so I can be absolutely confident in my decision. It's a little obsessive, but it gives me a constrained time for second guessing myself. If I didn't have that slight flexibility, I would have paralyzing fear before booking anything. Fear like I had when I was forced to watch the school play of Wizard of Oz as a five-year-old.

And now, with COVID-19, airlines have modified their own cancellation and change policies. That may or may not change for some, but Southwest offers no change fees.

2. Traveling early (but not too early) so the kids can nap on the plane but, if they don't, they can upon arrival. Between nine and eleven in the morning is my sweet spot. I don't typically bring car seats onboard but have brought the infant seat so the baby could sleep in her own space. That depended on the child and only happened with my easy sleepers and when we scored a 'free' seat for said infant. Otherwise, I'd rather just have the extra space.

3. Figuring out, in advance, how to get to the hotel from the airport to minimize stress, especially after a red-eye. I may not actually purchase the tickets, but even knowing options helps.

4. Finding rewards and activities to pass time on the flight. My kids don't have too much electronic usage at home, so when they have access on the plane, it serves as a huge reward. In case the plane's entertainment system is down, we download games to the laptop.

Other, more thoughtful and creative parents arrange for a wrapped gift each hour, a toy, game, or treat. Those parents get a gold star for creativity. I simply bring along small snacks, like M&Ms or gummy bears, which can be divvyed and spaced out.

5. Reserving a seat that works best for the situation. With a lap-baby, try to get the bulkhead since it includes a small bassinette. Beware, the armrests do not go up between the seats in this row and you'll need to store your items above for take-off and landing. On domestic flights, we book a window and an aisle for AJ and me and cross our fingers that no one sits in the middle. Infants fly free (or cheap internationally) so we rarely spent money on a seat for them.

"What?" my dad asked incredulously in his Midwest ah-shucks manner. "Can I really eat it?" The driver took out his pocketknife, sliced off a piece, and handed it over. Brooklyn turned her head in her seat to watch as my dad extracted the cashew apple carefully from his hand. He popped it in his mouth. "Pretty good," he commented. "It tastes kind of like a mango and grapefruit." Then he pointed to Ever-Hungry. "His turn." The kids watched with big eyes, witnessing us trying something new.

A wide, beautiful lawn with large, colorful, tropical flowers greeted us as we arrived at Chaa Creek Resort. The pungent aroma of the plumeria and hibiscus overwhelmed us in the damp air. I had found a deal for the bungalow with two large connecting suites. That gave the kids plenty of space to play and a spacious, wooden outdoor shower. We started the adventure with the adults alternating daytrips to Actun Tunichil Muknal, or ATM, since kids were too small. The cave had been open to the public for less than twenty years and was relatively untouched.

After an hour or so bus ride, AJ and I easily hiked forty-five minutes through jungle to the cave opening concealed by mystical jungle vines. We swam through the entrance and along a shallow underground river before climbing to the dry chamber.

The deep inner chamber makes it one of the most sacred Belizean caves. To appease their gods, ancient Mayans held elaborate sacrificial ceremonies. Inside the chamber are contrasting natural stalactites and stalagmites and what humans brought in—pottery, the blood-letting devices, and the poor chosen humans. The Crystal Maiden, a young victim now coated with glistening crystal carbonate, ends the tour. The cave expands for miles beyond. I had never seen anything like it.

We couldn't take cameras since a tourist had broken a skull a couple of years earlier. It was a relief, actually, to just go and enjoy the experience. I was a little surprised my mom wanted to see ATM on their day off. If there was no photographic proof, what was the point?

We enjoyed a low-key picnic dinner that night—pizza and French fries, the local Belikin beer, and root beer floats for the kids. Okay, the last part was for me. Ella fed me French fries she had dipped in ketchup to show how much she had missed me before sharing her favorite part of the room—the three steps in my parents' room. Up and down. Up and down.

I'm blessed with young(ish) parents, but they were wiped out from their day with the kids, incredulous that we do it every day.

While my parents had their own "Indiana Jones" adventure, my quartet set out with a hotel guide on the 400-acre reserve. Instead of finding monkeys, Brooklyn spotted horseback riders. Ella promptly fell asleep on her dad. It wasn't all bad, of course. Colorful toucans and parrots soared overhead, and iguanas lazed in the sun. We ascended to an old Mayan site overlooking the valley below. We freed the baby, and she ran around the top like a puppy released from a kennel. The massive roots on the ground tested her running ability and my skills at catching her before she fell.

In exchange for napping, I had promised Brooklyn a night hike with my dad and me. With the equatorial early sunset, that meant we could head out before eight o'clock. The full moon tried to peek down between the heavy clouds but mostly failed, except for occasional moments it came through like a spotlight.

Our guide started the night with his favorite schtick. He shone his flashlight across the wide expanse of grass in front of the main lodge of the hotel.

"What do you think that is?" he said in broken English.

"Dew?" I guessed.

"The dots are the eyes of spiders." The grass glistened like the Milky Way, with hundreds of dots spanning the expanse of lawn. Since I scarcely believed him, he took us closer.

"There's one and there's one and that's another," he said pointing his thick finger at arachnid after arachnid. He shared the species names of each spider. I stepped back toward the path.

Our hike moved away from the bungalows and main hotel toward the woods and the namesake creek. "That's a wolf spider," he shared, pointing at one near the rocks. "It lives alone and doesn't make a web, instead hunting down prey and pouncing on it. He is fast and has great eyesight." I shuddered at the description. I didn't know that years later, living in the mid-Atlantic, I would see many, much larger wolf spiders in my own basement. Never one to kill spiders anyway, I leave them alone, hoping they control the populations of countless other creatures including the intrusive ants.

As we walked along the dirt trail lined with large rocks, our guide stopped at a small hole. We waited, and he called out in excitement. Our guide pointed to a spot near my feet.

"Here is a tarantula. She is waiting for something to come by so she can grab it." Like me or my child? I picked up Brooklyn to carry her. The spider was huge, hairy, and of course, quite daunting. The guide continued, "They may look scary but are fairly harmless. They only attack insects and small animals." And what, pray tell is a small animal?

"Does anyone eat them?" I asked the guide.

"Monkeys are their main predators," she responded. I guess that meant there would be no monkeys that night. She continued, "We can assume it is a female since the males are out hunting." I peered nervously into the vast dark night. Perhaps I should have listened to my nervous husband; a night hike with a two-year-old may not have been the best idea with the thousands of spiders on the prowl.

We moved beyond the spiders to the other animals in the jungle. The guide showed us tree frogs and sleeping emerald toucanets (basically a miniature toucan). We saw perched owls and bats fluttering around our heads and mating millipedes at our feet. The symphony of life came out when we would go to sleep. Brooklyn, ever appreciative of doing something cool and exciting, fell fast asleep as soon as her head hit the pillow. If only she could always be that easy.

AJ and I still have innate differences in our travel styles. In Dominican Republic, it had started with the taxi ride to the resort. Haiti sits 157 miles away from the airport, commonly regarded as the western hemisphere's poorest country. To me, I saw an exotic country not too far away. My guidebook said you could get there in just over two hours.

I had asked AJ, "What do you think the border is like? Could we go there for a couple of hours, just to say we've been?"

He looked at me like I was crazy. "Why would you want to do that?"

"Why not?" I responded. He likely sighed. Still trying to impress me but silently cursing his luck of discovering this character trait of mine.

A truckload of muscular machete-clad men drove by in the opposite direction. Our driver shared that they were migrant farmers who had crossed the border on the small island of Hispaniola to earn money. The Dominican Republic and Haiti are vastly different—different languages, standards of living, currency, and histories. Apparently, the Haitian migrants cross over during the day to work the fields just like our neighbors to the south.

Eventually, we arrived at our hotel, a small part of a breathtaking resort featuring every imaginable amenity. It was also behind an eight-foot-high barbed wire fence, patrolled by armed guards.

With Haiti in mind, I accomplished my greatest convincing coup with arranging a daytrip to Tikal, Guatemala. I had chosen Chaa Creek partly due to its proximity to the border and the potential for seeing another country. AJ expressed concern at crossing a border with small children, but after consulting with our resort staff, he agreed it was safe. The border was less than thirty minutes away, then we had only a hundred kilometers in Guatemala, less than two hours, along a tourist thoroughfare.

We set off on a private tour, arranged directly through the resort, for Ella's third country and Brooklyn's fourth. The roads to Guatemala were as smooth as a baby's bum, well-traveled and paved with the money of tourists. At the border, we transferred to a clean, fancy SUV for the trip to Tikal. Screech Owl came back to life in her third country. For the next hour and a half, she shared her unhappiness.

"I am so sorry," I apologized profusely to the driver. Her lungs shocked him. "She's only like this in the car," I added. "She'll fall asleep soon." She did not.

We passed through rural farmlands and by a large, clear lake in the mountains. The landscape gave way to trees, growing denser as we approached our destination. The last fifteen minutes of the trip was in dense jungle. Suddenly Tikal National Park, the largest excavated Mayan site in North America, rose out of the thick, lush jungle. The park, once a massive capital, contains thousands of structures and covers about sixteen square kilometers. It is estimated that the area was settled in about 900 B.C. and flourished from 200 to 900 AD reaching a population of close to 100,000 people. The amazing architecture and scale of the buildings within the jungle setting overwhelmed us. Astonishingly, the buildings were made with no animals, metal tools, or wheels. Just raw human strength.

As we climbed the first tower, Temple II, I let Brooklyn climb the stairs at the back, holding my hand. Once we had gone up fifteen feet or so, a wave of anxiety washed over me. As a child, I had a near-death experience when I ran up to a cliff's edge at Bryce Canyon in Utah trying to find a short cut across the canyon. (There is none—that's why it's important to stay on the path.) Staring into the abyss hundreds of feet below, I felt my life flash past me, pulled toward the hole by inertia and back by something else.

I maintain what I consider a healthy fear of heights; I like views but don't put myself near a dangerous situation. More specifically, I keep a five-foot perimeter from the edge. As a mother, however, I hyperventilate and get weak-kneed if my child so much as looks toward an edge. For Temple II, I found the nearest landing and loaded Brooklyn onto my back. The next time, I put her in the carrier before leaving solid ground. We climbed the ruins of Temple IV, at 230 feet high, with our babies so we could see the breathtaking views.

Cool animals attracted us—rival bands of coatimundis like the Jets and Sharks begging for snacks near the food stands, a troop of monkey spiders swinging through the trees like a Belizean jungle gym, giant guinea pig-looking agoutis running in the brush, and large bright toucans soaring through the sky.

"Mommy, look!" the girls shouted at every encounter. The juxtaposition of ancient city with wide paths, vast wild jungle, and dynamic views surpassed any expectations I could have held.

Toward the end of our tour, on an isolated tract, Brooklyn pointed excitedly. "Jaguar!" she announced. After a day of searching, she insisted so vehemently that we'll never know for certain. In addition to the jaguar, seen most days around dusk, the park is also home to much more rarely seen tapirs, crocodile, and cougars.

We grabbed a late lunch at Comidor Tikal, a cafeteria style restaurant near the parking lot. There were minimal food options in the park, but this was good for the price and laid back. A group of schoolgirls, about twelve years old or so, had come on a field trip. They adored our baby.

"Oooh!" they'd coo as Ella would turn her head in the highchair.

Ella would smack her hands on the table for attention. Big smiles from the girls. She would throw her cup on the floor. Three girls instantly jumped up to get it. I had conflicting thoughts—these girls were going to grow up to be like the Italian women, and wow, I hope they learn about birth control. They were way too young to be mothers. I still nearly let them change a diaper.

Brooklyn fell asleep on the drive home, so the driver carried her across the border in her car seat. It was really cute, since it's quite rare for her, and like most kids, she's adorable while sleeping. Looking back, however, it seems a bit sketchy that border patrol would let us bring a sleeping child. I cannot imagine that back home.

We were bummed to leave our paradise jungle vacation and go to our paradise beach vacation. For one last activity, we decided to take advantage of the resort's inclusive canoes. Negotiations were tough while formulating a plan. It was like the riddle, 'How do you get the goat-eating lion across the river?' A person wants to cross a river with a lion, a lamb, and a bundle of grass. He only has one boat, and it can't hold more than two things at a time. How do you get to the other side with all intact?

Challenge: Paddle six miles down the Mikal River to San Ignacio
Participants:
- A strong rower who does not want to accidentally view a woman's breast.
- A dead weight child, who may or not become a monkey in the canoe.
- A man who can't steer a canoe.
- An out-of-shape nursing mom who may or may not help. Has trust issues with her husband in water.
- A baby who will want to eat if she's near her mom and who will cry if not near said mom.
- The wildcard? The woman who says she can do anything but is almost sixty years old and may flake out.

Answer: Chauffeur the mom and baby in the front like a Queen of the Nile by her father and have the young buck steer the canoe with his mother-in-law and two-year old. My mother wouldn't be afraid to correct her son-in-law when he errored.

As suspected, I offered little help. I played 'reach for the paddle' with Ella, the best game since peek-a-boo. Getting her to sleep should help, I thought. Unfortunately, I had only brought the back-up pacifier since I feared it dropping in the water. To her, the emergency pacifier was only for dire situations, not for use when there was a perfectly good nipple within reach. I gave in to fate and lounged with a nursing and napping baby in my arms, happy I had convinced everyone to come.

The painfully slow river took three hours to navigate, twice the stated hour and a half, due to the little rain over the past few weeks (the downpour while at ATM the rare exception). We saw more iguanas, turtles, and tropical birds like the kingfisher. When my dad and I steered ahead, we heard a shout.

"Jaguar!" my mom and husband shouted.

"Really?" my dad said. "You think you saw a jaguar?" We looked up in the open hills overlooking the river.

"Well, maybe it was a bobcat," my mom conceded.

"I bet it was a dog," my dad murmured to me. "I heard it bark." Whatever it was, it provided excitement until my dad ran us into a rock.

"Aah!" I yelled as we careened into the boulders under the trickling water. As we tried to free ourselves, we tipped, and my foot fell out to catch us. "Ella is still sleeping," I called out in relief.

After dropping off our canoes, we walked up the hill to the San Ignacio Resort Hotel, a sanctuary for the endangered Green Iguana species. Our curiosity rewarded us with a surprisingly fun and unexpectedly random experience.

The Iguana Project looks to conserve and create awareness on the species through its hatchery and educational experience. They aim to raise the iguanas and release them into the wild to accommodate for the overhunting and introduction of domesticated animals.

Our guide shared the life cycle, gave a tour, and let us hold some large females. At the sanctuary, there is only one mature male to reduce fighting and inbreeding. In the wild, they can get up to five to six feet long. The dominant male-in-training had only reached three feet or so. The guide shared that iguanas are drawn to bright colors, especially fluorescents. These could trigger an attack response in the adults since they are colors they may see on another iguana that is mating. The babies would just be intrigued. He glanced at our outfits—my dad wearing a faded orange linen shirt, the baby and I both sporting bright pink shirts, and my mom's purse boring a neon yellow reflective strip—and shook his head. We could not have dressed more ridiculously if we tried.

The iguana-filled room horrified AJ. During the experience, he used Ella as a shield between himself and the iguanas since he figured we wouldn't allow her near any of them or put her in danger. He tried using her as an excuse to skip the nursery.

"She seems hungry," he said. "I think she wants me to take her outside."

Yet, we still moved to the nursery. In that greenhouse room, dozens of the baby lizards scrounged around, ten centimeters or so long. I held the father-of-all-iguanas, literally, as Brooklyn fed him a big green leaf. When he had finished, he crawled over and stuck a talon on her. Incredibly, she maintained her Poker Face.

AJ had a much more pampered upbringing than me, so he was not used to being outside his comfort zone. I tease him that he was born with a bronze or platinum spoon in his mouth, not quite silver. When we traveled in Costa Rica, I killed the scorpions in our room and captured the cicadas to release outside. His herpetophobia, fear of reptiles, was not shocking when it paralyzed him with fright. What did my parents and I do in response? Comfort him and tell him it was okay? Not in my family.

"He really does want you to put one on his back," I told the guide after I had taken Ella to let her gently pet one. (We have dogs at home; she was game.) AJ cringed and jumped as the iguana scratched up his shirt and onto his neck. He was, as always, a great sport.

Then the guide piled baby iguanas on my mother, one after another pinching her shirt, probably close to a dozen, like the finale of a fireworks show on the Fourth of July, as she cowered good-naturedly under their weight. Perhaps it was all an act; she expertly passed the camera for a photo.

I can say I'm my mother's daughter. If it hadn't been her, it would have been me in that shot, smiling with a dozen raptors for the family photo album. Somebody has to take the risk and try something new. I love that she tries to keep a positive attitude and am happy to inherit that from her. I wonder which of my three girls will be the next in that family chain, the poor woman who will say, "How on earth did I turn in my mother? Why do I have Mom's squint face?"

In the future, I hope to travel with my kids the way that my mother does with us. I hope I'll be as helpful as her and can watch the grandkids while my children hike or dive with their spouse. As my own mom likes to say, that's the circle of life.

Chapter Seven

SHARKS AND SWIMMIES IN THE BELIZE BARRIER REEF

*E*VER SINCE A trip to North Carolina's Outer Banks in our early years together where I convinced him to river kayak through the estuaries near Kitty Hawk, AJ has been repulsed by shrimp. Pre-kids, we had taken our dog, Artie, wearing his life vest in case he fell overboard, and we had to pull him back on. We rowed slowly among the mangroves, butting into the shallow trees due to poor steering but enjoying the experience in the safe wild.

All of a sudden, we wandered into a troupe of shrimp. At first, a few splashed in the water, appearing like raindrops as they reentered. Suddenly, they were everywhere, jumping up and down in the water, popping up like corn in a hot griddle. Sitting at the front of the kayak with a dog near my feet, I instinctively covered my face and probably "ah, oohed," a few times. In the back, AJ didn't immediately notice. The shrimp jumped a meter in the air, over the boat, and whizzed by our heads. Artie started snapping his mouth toward the sky, hoping to catch one midair. The small crustaceans pelted my arms and face like snowballs in fights I had as a kid.

"What is going on?" AJ shouted, impatient at another thing to distract from his steering efforts. He quickly ducked as a shrimp flew by.

"Shrimp!" I shouted with my head facing forward. I didn't dare turn my head to face him. Artie peered his head over the side of the kayak as if contemplating how best to dive in.

"Keep paddling," AJ ordered, attempting to free us from the barrage.

But I couldn't. I was laughing hysterically at the absurdity and trying desperately to keep my dog onboard. My laugh started in my belly and worked itself up. My shoulders were shaking, and my face hurt from a smile that stretched from ear to ear. A shrimp smacked into my head and landed in the boat. Artie dog sniffed it and reached down to eat it.

"No!" AJ shouted at Artie. "No!" he added desperately. "No!" he continued to repeat. "Let's get out of here." But the more he panicked, the more I laughed. Our eyes locked and smile caught on this face, a smile deep within his pale hazel eyes that melts my heart. "Can you please help get us out of here?" he asked more calmly, resetting the mood.

"Sure," I said as I drove my paddle back into the water. Artie, realizing he was free, promptly hopped into the water.

After our time in the jungle, we were ready for the beach. Unfortunately, our plane was overbooked, and we got bumped. It didn't matter since the air strip was, in and of itself, another experience. I'd call Maya Flats an airport but then I'd have to call my son's kick-each-other-in-the-shin team part of a soccer league. A glorified cow pasture held a long-enough dirt runway down the middle. It was quite picturesque, backing to the forest of Chaa Creek in the Cayo District.

Our two curious toddlers howled with excitement as they watched the first plane land, people get off, others get on, the plane go into the sky, and another one appear. Ella slapped the floor-to-ceiling windows, mirroring her sister's enthusiasm. The adults indulged in free coffee.

It was a speedy flight on our ten-seater to Belize City, no more than thirty minutes, to exchange a couple of passengers, then to San Pedro on Ambergris Caye. I missed most of the scenery with my head between my knees, but it sounded phenomenal. Brooklyn enjoyed looking out the window as we flew low over the mountainous forests and dipped over the expansive farmland, and Ella slept on her daddy.

The second leg was even more spectacular. Belize has the second largest reef in the world, covering 370 square miles. This includes over 450 islands, three atolls, and over 500 species of fish. We could see the massive reefs from above, beneath the shallow, crystal-clear Caribbean Sea. I felt like I had paid the big bucks for a scenic air tour—which I would be hard-pressed to do without taking some motion sickness medicine beforehand.

The Pelican Reef hotel welcomed us with open arms, a caring staff, and a greeting sign that misspelled my name. The hotel sat on the beach, just down the street from the city center. The front desk clerk described the two-bedroom apartment with full kitchen and laundry to my mom and me at check-in. Then he added, "You overlook the pool." I looked wistfully at the gorgeous expanse of glistening Caribbean Sea.

"How much more for the beach view?" my mom inquired. "I'll pay the upgrade," she stated for the first time ever. Usually she would say, "We can go to the pool for a view" or "We can use the money for a nicer dinner every night."

I must have looked desperate, a young mom who would be trapped in the room with the balcony as my only outlet. "Just don't tell your dad," she added. I thanked her by encouraging her to play her Sudoku on the balcony with her complimentary glass of wine while the kids ran around like banshees.

We were in paradise. With the other guests out at sea, we seemed to have our own private beach and pool. AJ immediately set to work, washing the cloth diapers for two kids I had insisted on bringing. Perhaps it wasn't quite as incredible for him. I hung multiple sheets on our east-facing bedroom window in an attempt to darken the room and allow us sleep past the bright sun rising on the water.

My efforts failed. Ella awoke around five the next morning, at the first sign of light. My mom, the early bird, blessedly took her as part of our unsaid vacation agreement. They grabbed the beach toys and walked down the flight of stairs to our slice of paradise. I felt slightly bad as I rolled out of bed after a long rest, but that trivial feeling disappeared upon seeing the others. Nana got her baby time and adorable photos for her album, my kids loved the attention and the sand, and of course, Mommy got some sleep.

AJ and I departed directly from our dock to the dive shop for a tour we had booked the night before. Ambergris Caye has fantastic reefs and diving locations spanning twenty-five miles of barrier reef less than a mile off the coast. There are options to see canyons, tunnels, and grottos, along with traditional coral. There is also incredible, seemingly unlimited visibility there, up to 150 feet in places. It is also home to the spectacular Great Blue Hole.

None of those options were for us, though, as we took scuba-diving lessons in Jamaica three years earlier, a few months before learning we were expecting. Once we got the scuba certification, we hadn't gone again due to constant pregnancies. Or rather, it seemed like constant pregnancies, but I wouldn't truly know that feeling until I had two more babies.

Based on our sub-par skills, we joined an intro dive at two of the best preserved and popular locations. AJ seemed relieved; neither of could really remember much of the former guidance. He still had panic attacks thinking of the training exercise where he had to remove and then replace his mask at thirty feet underwater. That had coincided with spotting my first wild lobster and just two minutes before we saw two enormous nurse sharks. Though harmless, to a flustered man with water in his goggles, they probably seemed like Jaws.

After relearning five lessons in fifteen minutes, we took off, passing a man in a ragged fishing boat handfeeding an enormous loggerhead sea turtle. Our guide shared that the turtle was quite old, and the man had been feeding it conch daily for years near Shark-Ray-Alley.

We paid our entrance fee at the southern tip of the Hol Cha, 'little channel' in Mayan, to join the dozens of people already in the water. After years of overfishing, the diminishing populations had been rebuilt by the time we visited twenty-five plus years after it was officially established in 1987. Although we only covered a small portion of the narrow channel of twenty-five yards by thirty feet deep, it covers three square miles, housing a plethora of bright, diverse sea life and coral—morays, barracuda, and parrotfish greeted us as our training came back to us underwater.

Back at the apartment, Brooklyn found the toys left behind by the condo owners and bossed her sister around. Ella was happy to be included, allowing her sister to dress her up and listening as she was ordered to create a fort or play dolls. Basically, doing the same things as back home, except that we were over 2,000 miles away.

Our day ended with dinner at a nearby delicious restaurant, the Black Orchid, where my pasta dish came covered in large, fresh shrimp. My children had become perfect angels, using their napkins and saying please and thank you. Well, the baby didn't throw her plate of food on the floor at least. We put on a rare façade. Then, we walked home under a large moon with the sound of waves lapping the shore, the bats flittering above our heads, eating their fill of mosquitos. They could have done a bit better; the mosquitos enjoyed us as much as I had that shrimp.

At the beach, Ella scarfed her Nana's eggs. Brooklyn loved the banana pancakes and orange juice. Either that or I had been starving my kids at night, and when they woke up, they would eat anything in sight. We had also been spoiled at Chaa Creek with inclusive made-to-order breakfasts.

After the gluttonous gorge, we rolled our babies into their life vests for the morning's boat tour. With the size of our family, renting a boat and guide made more sense than joining a tour. That also supports my super-introverted nature, but that's not as easy to say to my husband as, "It's the same price, and we can follow the kids' schedule." This guide also promised to fulfill my goal of seeing manatees. Upon boarding, we made ourselves comfortable, my baby so much that she promptly passed out as soon as we left the dock, within site of the hotel.

LESSON LEARNED

Finding a good, inclusive breakfast drives our hotel selection. With children especially, there are a few reasons for that: savings, convenience, and the ability to easily indulge in local fare. In Costa Rica, we ate massive servings of fresh tropical fruit and homemade breads along with milk-brewed coffee. Not much beats hot food served with refreshing carafes of fresh fruit juices. In Scandinavia, our kids got mini pancake puffs on the cruise ship, crepes in Stockholm, and croissants (plain and chocolate) in Denmark. Since the kids stayed free, the kids ate free. Stateside hotels provide full American breakfasts with eggs, waffles, and cereals for the kids. Even at Disneyland, I was so ecstatic about an inclusive breakfast that I didn't mind eating Mickey Mouse-shaped pieces of cardboard in a cattle-car atmosphere. There, it tasted like savings.

Last, is convenience. At home, I make scrumptious French toast, pancakes, and eggs, but on vacation, I avoid most cooking. If we're responsible for breakfast, it's usually a box of some foreign Coco or Rice Puff-esque cereal. Waiting for breakfast when small (or Ever-Hungry) bellies are empty can cause a rough start to the day.

Though we tried a few spots, we did not find any manatees. Unfortunately, they were not frequenting their usual hangouts—the McManatee or Star(fish) bucks that day. Undeterred, we went to Coral Gardens instead, another fascinating location known for its beautiful coral formations (duh) and shallow depths of only a couple of meters. Although we had gone diving the day before, it was powerful seeing it through our daughter's eyes. While Ella softly snored, her sister bravely jumped in and witnessed the entertainment on the other side of her mask while AJ gripped her and her life vest. We pointed out the purple, pink, and orange coral formations, and she gasped at the fish swimming by in the crystal-clear water.

As we headed back toward Caye Caulker, we saw a familiar figure: the fisherman feeding the old turtle. For years, fishermen would park in these shallow waters to clean their catch, only about eight feet deep. Just inside the reef, it served as a safe harbor. The fishermen reported the abundance of nurse sharks and Southern Sting Rays to dive operators in San Pedro who quickly sent out guides. The sharks seemed harmless and ideal for tourists hoping for animal encounters. It quickly became a popular dive site and the name, "Shark-Ray-Alley" was formed. Our guide had brought our family with curious kids.

I knew where we were and why the guide brought us. However, we didn't share that with my mom until the dark shadows moved toward us and sharks surrounded our boat. If these had been man-eaters and our ship went down, we would have been goners. Thankfully, our boat stayed afloat, and the sharks just wanted a little fish chum, not a baby.

It's really amazing to be with a child when they see something new. I mean, that's a huge driver in continually having children! That, and spending multiple maternity leaves from work with my older children. I would sign the second youngest up for a tumbling class, strap the newborn to my chest, and off we would go for the next few months.

Seeing something through a child's eyes humbles and inspires me. Blank expressions morph with an initial look of confusion like, have I seen this before? The baby approaches slowly, staring at the object or creature, trying to figure out whether it is new or just something she can't remember. Then, she looks up toward Mom or Dad to see whether it's dangerous or exciting. When Mom smiles or nods encouragingly, the baby starts working up the courage to approach or just watch more closely with an open mind.

Ella pulled us all in when she saw something new, on the trip and in life. My mom shared watching her encounter her first downpour one day at Chaa Creek. The rain started with just a couple of drops, and Ella smiled at the water hitting her head. The kids were on the patio, just outside the large glass doors, my mom sitting inside with the door open. The drops fell larger and faster as the sky cracked open. My baby confusedly looked at her now wet clothes. She took a couple of steps toward the thick, thatched roof, away from the rain. Then she'd step back out and the fat drops would roll down her face. In and out of the rain she went, watching my mom's reaction. Eventually, she started to laugh.

Ella laughed the way only a baby can, with loose abandonment and a shaking throughout her whole body. She laughed like she never had before, as if she and the rain had their own private secret. She laughed as she discovered the meaning of true joy and the pleasure one can get from a simple action.

Ella looked up at my mom with her big, oversized doe eyes and beautiful long lashes, soaked from the rain. My mom claimed that she could see her soul. Rain had made her the happiest my mother had ever seen. Simple water, two of the most common elements on earth.

On the boat, Ella woke as the boat pitched when AJ and I jumped in. She looked curiously over the side at us. Were the sharks going to eat Mommy and Daddy? Or was something fun going on? A few minutes later, Mommy was still there, so she determined it must be the latter.

As the sharks and rays thrashed toward the food from our guide, Ella started quaking excitedly. She didn't have much of a vocabulary, so her words were just loud, high-pitched chatters and squeals. I was living with a cross between a piglet and a squirrel.

I hopped out of the water to be with her as she watched the sharks and stingrays. I held the baby near but not over the edge of the boat, Michael Jackson-style. Our guide offered a ray at the surface of the water so she could pet it. I rubbed the soft, silky skin to show that it was safe. In response, she reached out her chubby little fingers and patted it gently. She smiled up at me, that all-encompassing baby grin which expressed so much wonder. Then he repeated it with a shark. Really.

My mom worried that we had brought our kids to this spot and were letting them pet the sharks. We calmed her by explaining that although these were sharks, they were nurse sharks, not aggressive or mean. To hit on that point, our guide jumped in the water, rubbed one's belly, and held it. I wasn't willing to go that far, but I did feel pretty safe on the boat. After all that excitement, Ella was ready for her second nap. So was I.

I wanted to do something nice for my mom so, for Mother's Day, I rented her a golf cart. Driving the cart down to San Pedro made her day. She behaved like those adults at Disneyworld who wait in line for an hour to drive the mini cars. I want to shout, "You have a license. You can drive whenever you like. Please don't make the line for my children any longer." But I don't say anything and just waste my FastPass for my daughter to get that joy she will be getting when she turns sixteen. I shouldn't criticize; I loved it as a kid. There's just something about tiny vehicles.

My mom and I sped toward the town of San Pedro, acting like we were fifteen-year-old kids borrowing our parents' car. (Not that I ever did that with my older sister.) San Pedro used to be a small, sleepy fishing village but was now a full-fledged tourist destination. Perhaps it was because it served as the inspiration for Madonna's song, La Isla Bonita, "Last night I dreamed of San Pedro."

My college used to have a Madonna-Rama party where we'd dress up as the Queen of Pop through the ages. Girls would deck their hair out in crimp and wear tons of hair spray. Almost everyone wore some type of 80's outfit with lace, layered necklaces, or shoulder pads or mini-skirt. One crazy girl even brought out the cone-shaped bustier.

My sister loved Madonna. She went to her concerts, watched her movies, and knew everything about her. My sister embraced women's empowerment, and Madonna knew how to command that. Not only that, she came from my home state.

I understand the Madonna fascination, but I'd have to say that the diving is what attracts the multitudes to the town. This is one of the few native English-speaking world-class diving facilities outside of the Great Barrier Reef in Australia. The town still has the sleepy-town feel with low buildings, only ten streets, and dirt or gravel roads. It is truly paradise—if paradise comes with mosquitos.

We drove to the open-air markets and bought handmade bowls, carved out of driftwood. Then we picked up the guys and babies for a filling dinner on the beach.

"You have to see the Great Blue Hole," an experienced, middle-aged, weekend diver had shared as we were learning to dive in Jamaica. "Though…it can be really dangerous if you don't know what you're doing. Some people in my group went further than the 300 feet that you're allowed. So risky." I knew AJ and I wouldn't attempt that—we were only certified to forty feet—but it's good to go in with a healthy fear of the atoll. It's like that feeling when you're a week late, you're really tired, and you already have multiple kids. It's not real worry, since you've done it before, but rather than relaxed exhilaration, you feel a stressed calm.

People come to Belize simply for this excursion, testing yourself at one of the world's best dives. I had read about it, seen the aerial photos of the sapphire blue water surrounded by the aqua Caribbean blues. The sinkhole forms a near-perfect circle, 980 feet across and 410 feet deep.

Unfortunately, we could not find a boat to take us. Though it looked fine to us, the sea frothed angrily. We were trapped on land in a water wonderland. To say I was bummed is a huge understatement. I couldn't believe that we'd come all the way to Belize and couldn't see the most famous landmark. It's like seeing New York City and missing the Statue of Liberty or visiting D.C. during the government shutdown and missing the free Smithsonian. I dwelled and complained for a healthy period of time to get it out of my system, then tried to sort out a Plan B. My stomach silently thanked me for avoiding that three-hour boat trip. At the Great Barrier Reef years before, I got so sick I couldn't even get off the boat at a planned stop. It is what it is.

My kids were my everyday Blue Hole—unique, challenging, beautiful, and deep beyond comparison. I felt I could only manage them with lots of preparation and gear. Missing out on the exhilaration, I instead focused on the relaxation. We went to the pool, walked on the pier, and played on the sandy beach. I popped the girls into their life vests, Ella gazing up at the cloudy sky as she drifted on her back like a floating flower petal, and caught Brooklyn as she jumped in. The hours at that pool and in the Chaa Creek pool were the kids' favorites of the trip.

In the afternoon, I chatted with tourists who had arrived a day earlier. They hadn't left the resort. I counted my blessings. We had gone on the water twice and the clouds had lulled the mosquitos to sleep. Those were my wins.

LESSON LEARNED

'But aren't you scared of the danger?' I hear from well-meaning friends. 'Aren't you worried about safety?' I can honestly say, not any more than anywhere else.

I have not personally encountered a lot of trauma in my life, but with random mass shootings, kidnappings, and other bad news in my broader area, I know that danger can be anywhere. I've lost extended family and friends too young, too soon. Within our own small community, we had three shocking deaths of middle-aged adults in one month. Two little boys and three girls lost their seemingly healthy fathers, a friend lost a sister. You never know what tomorrow will bring, so I try to do what I can today. My approach is to be aware of our surroundings, visit the U.S. Department of State site for travel advisories, and go in with a healthy dose of caution. (And that's before COVID-19!)

For me, caution involves three things: prepare beforehand, be aware while traveling, and remain vigilant. I ensure my kids know the ground rules before we leave. Since they are still young, that's basically listen to me and Dad and a reminder to act as they do at home. But as they get older, it will involve more of don't wander off, don't talk to strangers, etc. Additionally, with four children, my husband and I try to always divvy up the kids to lessen the stress. Last, if something does happen, we have taught them how to ask for help. Find the person in uniform, know our names, go to a parent with a young child for help. And don't move too much! But, while in crowded places, we always maintain physical contact with them as we do while crossing a street back home.

After a last dinner together, we walked along the sandy beach to a fancy chocolate shop. It clearly wasn't that posh since it lined a dirt road and had dogs sleeping outside, but it did feature glass shelves and individually sold chocolates.

During our shopping, my dad had stood near the door, holding it open, hoping to keep his tall frame and size fourteen feet out of everyone's path. All of a sudden, we heard a piercing, high-pitched shriek, wailing like a siren. It just went and went, seemingly forever. I immediately sought my baby, my little Screech Owl, to see what had happened. My mom was holding her, and she was fine, if not surprised by the commotion.

Where was that stabbing sound coming from? It was the most horrible sound I had ever heard. In an instant, I saw. My sweet two-year old Brooklyn, always quiet and behaved, was wailing at the top of her voice. Her scream was only topped by one thing: the growling of a mother bear as she sees what is hurting her baby.

"DO NOT MOVE!" I barked at my dad in the most primal voice that had ever left my mouth. He was releasing the door and didn't realize that my poor daughter had put her hand in the small crack. He was slowly crushing her fingers with the weight of the door. In one second, I had pushed the door open and scooped her up. Brooklyn's purple fingers had condensed to about a third of their normal width. I was certain, absolutely certain, that at least one had broken. I was nervously calculating if she could wait a day to go to the doctor when we got home.

We went out into the cool breeze, and I rocked her as she cried. I kissed her face and her fingers. I held her as only a mom can. After a couple of minutes, I convinced her to let me touch, then bend them. It's amazing that as hard as she screamed and as terrible as she looked, within five minutes she was back to normal. Kids are resilient. Brooklyn earned her own ice cream cone that night.

We joined my parents on the flight to the mainland, checking our luggage before exchanging sad goodbyes ahead of their early flight.

AJ turned to me and asked, "Is that our driver?" Sure enough, the man who had driven us all the way to Chaa Creek was at the airport, shooting the breeze with friends.

"Maybe he can take us somewhere fun?" I offered. We needed to entertain two small kids for six hours.

In small countries, everyone seems to know everyone else. Our driver shook my hand and slapped AJ on the back like old friends. AJ connected with him like he tends to do, avoiding the awkward conversation I would have mustered. The man showed true disappointment that he already had a fare. Instead, he introduced us to his "brother" to take us to the Community Baboon Sanctuary. I doubted this guy was actually his brother, but why not? I asked someone to be a bridesmaid in my wedding because she had referred to AJ as her brother. Then we didn't see her for the next year.

The sanctuary embraced a simple but cool mission. The goal was to "sustain the Black Howler Monkey habitat while promoting the economic development of the participating communities." Over 200 private landowners participate, and over 2,000 monkeys live in the twenty square mile sanctuary. It combines grassroots conservation and old-fashioned tourism.

"Do you have any bug spray?" I asked our guide upon arrival. Brooklyn and I wore shorts and t-shirts and our liquids were trapped in the checked suitcase. Thankfully, Ella was garbed in her standard long-sleeves and pants, worn to prevent chunky baby thigh and arm chafing while in the carrier.

"Here," the guide replied. She, I kid you not, handed me an old fly swatter. I severely doubted it had ever been washed. I do not use fly swatters because they are disgusting and have fly guts on them. And what was I supposed to do with it? Hit flies against trees?

Add to that, the monkeys were nowhere to be found. We wandered around the edges of a jungle in a grassy savannah, getting eaten alive. Thankfully we happened upon another tour group who fell in love with my girls and were willing to share anything for their comfort.

"I have sunscreen," one volunteered.

"Here's some bug spray," offered another.

"Do your girls like lollipops?" a grandmotherly type asked.

Their guide simply pointed and said, "The monkeys are that way." Heeding his directions, we found a troop of howler monkeys! The family swung from the trees and climbed down to investigate us. My kids were captivated. The guide handed AJ and Brooklyn a tree branch full of green, delicious shoots. One of the monkeys cautiously came closer and pulled the leaves off, throwing them into his mouth and chewing thoughtfully. A small baby monkey peered down at us from his mother's back. I made eye contact with his mom, two moms doing the best we could for our clingy babies. After all of that searching, I was disappointed to leave, but we had a flight to catch.

The flight home landed early but with no gate for our layover, we held on the tarmac. Small kids love being trapped on a plane after a long flight even more than adults. Upon deplaning, we heard that the baggage door had jammed. We could not clear customs without our luggage. It took over two hours for the airport officials to open the door. Two hours with two over-tired children. Brooklyn was thrilled she got to experience fifteen straight hours of living.

I'm happy we only had two children at the time, and they were able to make the best of it, loping around like the monkeys we saw earlier. Ella devised a game of 'run to the other side of the large chamber without Mommy seeing.' Brooklyn countered with 'unstrap all of the temporary guard rails.' Needless to say, we missed our flight home but thankfully found a loud, cheap motel near the airport. We were extremely fortunate to get a flight out the next morning. Not everyone did.

We arrived home a day later than planned, exhausted but fulfilled, covered in dozens of mosquito bites. AJ drove straight to work while a friend gave a ride to the girls and me. On the way, I called my parents to thank them. Without them we couldn't have gone diving or seen ATM. We couldn't have kayaked with two small kids and a man who can't steer.

But we gave them something, too. My parents will always have those memories of a trip to Belize and Guatemala with two precious grandkids, beautiful sunrises, and belly laughing in the rain. Losing that day was crazy but, in the end, it was fine. Things have a way of balancing out. The stressors of today are the memories of tomorrow.

Chapter Eight

CONVENIENT SLEEPERS IN BAHAMAS

"I'VE BEEN TO thousands of slaughterhouses," my Indian future father-in-law shared with me one afternoon, a few months before my wedding. He loves his gross exaggerations. This one came up during our discussion on my near-vegetarianism and his family's Jain tradition. Jainism is an ancient religion that promotes ahimsa, or noninjury to all living creatures, even bugs. Like Hindus, Jains clearly do not eat cows. However, Ever-Hungry wanted us to serve a juicy prime rib at our wedding.

A place where animals are killed, many times inhumanely, is a place that most reasonable people would avoid. Yet somehow, my father-in-law (who, we'll say, "doesn't eat meat") has visited thousands. This is why I struggle to believe him.

AJ had warned me of his father's idiosyncrasies. Before our breakfast introduction at the local diner, he implored me, "Do not talk politics. You will just argue." Only one month in, I agreed to do whatever he said regarding his parents. Twenty minutes later, his father and I were debating the merits of a former president. I showed that I was different from girlfriends past; I certainly had an assertive streak that contrasted with a docile woman his dad may have expected.

I traveled with my father-in-law once when a furlough at work coincided with one of his trips to India. I had an amazing experience in India, seeing a part of the world I hadn't dreamt I would be able to visit so soon, being welcomed into my husband's family, and watching the thousands of people walking the streets or farming in the fields, colorful saris brushing against the brown dirt below.

However, traveling solo with my father-in-law was tough. He would burst into my bedroom without knocking on the door. Then he was curious why I locked it. "Katie, the door is locked," he'd call through the door. No kidding! I thought.

He criticized my naturally curly hair, volumized by the humidity of monsoon season to look like a ferocious lion. "Here, borrow my comb," he commanded. 'Never criticize a woman's appearance,' I should have said. Instead I choked back tears and complained to my husband by phone. I had to remind myself that he had no experience with daughters or even granddaughters and he was just trying to help.

That experience caused me some trepidation about traveling with my father-in-law. However, at the time, we lived six hours away and wanted our kids to have richer experiences than just seeing their grandparents every other major holiday. My in-laws balked at previous proposals, based on our comparatively frenetic pace and inclination to exercise, but somehow, we convinced them to join us. Perhaps they thought my being six months pregnant with our third child may actually slow us down.

Personally, I looked forward to one last hurrah trip for our small, still-manageable family. I had heard that transitioning from two to three kids could be brutal, moving from the cliched man-to-man defense to a full-on zone defense. Moving to three kids means accepting that freedom is the rare night you overpay a high schooler to sit in your home with already sleeping kids, then waking up exhausted wondering why you stayed up past ten.

We settled on Paradise Island in The Bahamas. At fifty miles southeast of Florida, it was less than an hour flight to Miami and first-class hospitals in the event that my thirdborn decided to make an early appearance.

I would have preferred to dive into a more adventurous voyage, like their coral reefs teeming with life. Perhaps we could have rented a catamaran and sailed through the 700 islands and islets, snorkeling through 2,000 cays. We would eat fresh tropical fruit we had purchased from Bahamian locals as we picnicked on an uninhabited oasis. As it was, we were already at the mercy of my unborn son, so I happily got my new passport stamp and tried to embrace my aversion of crowds. Late February helped us settle into a niche between the busier seasons.

We booked two rooms at the Comfort Suites, across the street but still part of the famous, glitzy Atlantis Resort. Though our rooms were smaller, less fancy, and an entire crosswalk away, we still garnered free admission to the site and waterpark. We requested connecting rooms with the hopes that my in-laws could stay with the kids during naps so AJ and I could get out alone. And for quality time with them, of course!

Our first morning, my father-in-law bailed on our first expedition, citing a desire to rest. We dragged my mother-in-law out after much negotiating. My kids held her hands to walk the short distance to the marina that would take us away.

"Yippy doo!" I exclaimed on our short boat ride across an inlet of crystal blue Caribbean Sea on our way to Blue Lagoon Island. My girls sat on opposite sides of their grandma, pointing out the boats and seagulls for her. I had arranged for a dolphin encounter. I had read that the mammals adore pregnant women and that they may even be able to see the fetus via echolocation. Some people even give birth with those carnivores. That boggled my mind, and I had to try it. Seeing one that is, not giving birth with one.

I booked an encounter that not only allowed small children to pet the dolphins but also gave them free entry. Yet another reason to space your kids as close together as Mentos in a pack. Although I wasn't about to go all Free Willy or anything, I was somewhat concerned about the poor treatment of such smart animals in captivity. Reading that none were captively bred and many had been relocated from New Orleans after Hurricane Katrina in 2005 eased my concerns. The Blue Lagoon has also earned the Humane Certified seal of approval from the global American Humane Conservation program.

Our guide greeted us at the dock upon arrival and shepherded us to our dolphin. Since I was quite large and awkward, I lumbered in first, splashing with a thud into the knee-deep water. AJ handed newly minted two-year-old Ella to me to hold on my hip while he and three-year-old Brooklyn easily skipped down the ladder. Brooklyn clasped her daddy's hand tight in the water, and my mother-in-law watched from the platform above.

The dolphin sliced through the water toward us like a torpedo and popped up to join us on the ledge. After feeding her some live sushi, her trainer encouraged us to pet her. I felt the soft, rubbery skin that gave slightly under light pressure from my fingertips. She nuzzled close (but not too close) to my belly. Ella was quite apprehensive at the whole situation and glared at the dolphin. I took her tiny hand, cold and starting to wrinkle from the water, and touched the top of the dolphin's head. She snatched it back like a spring upon contact. Her eyes opened wide in curiosity and amusement on a second attempt.

"Aah! Aah!" Ella shouted. Or the dolphin. Based on pitch alone, it was hard to decipher the source. Though my baby had little desire to be part of the action, she loved seeing an actual dolphin up close.

Then, as soon as she relaxed and started enjoying herself, it seemed that it was over. I watched the dolphin swim back to her pod and hoped the staff in the tropical surroundings treated her well.

"Mom, are you coming?" AJ asked his petite Irish mother as we left the dolphin pool. Before leaving the island, we had an hour or so for the beach.

"No, I'll just stay here and read," she announced in her brogue accent with a wave of her hand. She was as composed as if she was sitting down to a cup of tea rather than abandoning us while the girls excitedly bounded down the sand. I admired my mother-in-law's calm demeanor as I waddled quickly behind the kids before they hit the surf.

On the boat ride back to the hotel, I discovered that although the girls loved the beach, nothing could compare to a ride across the scenic harbor. "Bird!" Ella called after a common seagull.

The wind whipped through their hair and blew into their faces as we sped across the water. From their perch on the boat's second level, they could see the world from a new perspective. They squinted out at the water against the piercing blue sky. They each sat under the crook of my arms and giggled about life, the smell of salt water deep within their sandy hair. For my part, I exceeded an admittedly low bar by avoiding anyone vomiting on the boat.

Back at the hotel, wholly exhausted, I fell asleep patting Brooklyn to sleep. The phone jolted me awake. Our originally request adjoining room was available. After a loud but muted, "Are you kidding me?" AJ lovingly moved our sleeping child to the opposite wing of the hotel, going up and down two separate elevators, past the crowded lobby. And blessedly, for once, she slept the entire time. I wished he could carry me too.

Atlantis Resort boasts everything you could possibly want in one location. That worked out well since my in-laws don't care for walking, and my mother-in-law is all about convenience. We learned this a few years earlier when we moved to our small town. The dogs' vet was next door to the high school.

"Well, that's convenient," my mother-in-law announced as we passed.

"What is? Why is that convenient?" AJ responded. "In case we have a dog emergency in fifteen years and our daughter needs to be retrieved from soccer practice?"

Atlantis exuded convenience. Casinos and clubs splayed around dozens of stores from the rich and glitzy to the touristy and kitschy fare. Over twenty restaurants and nineteen bars and lounges of every different cuisine—Chinese, American, Italian, local seafood—fed the masses.

In addition, the island boasts the largest open-air marine habitat in the world with eight million gallons of ocean water. Before dinner, we wandered through the aquarium tunnels with over a thousand fish, jellyfish, and massive Moray eels. Ella's face lit up watching the sharks patrolling the tank, her big green eyes glistening like the sun off the scales of the fish. The stingrays glided across the floor with their gentle flapping, and the expressionless orange and blue fish swam in large schools around the perimeter. I felt the damp humidity penetrating my hair.

We decided to try Asian fusion for dinner since a) the restaurant had cloth napkins and appealed to my in-laws, and b) there were no age restrictions. Brooklyn and Ella happily slurped rice before convincing their Grandpa to buy them ice cream.

"Mommy, can I get something?" Brooklyn asked when we passed the gift shop. A small shake of the head was all it took for her to change tack.

"Grandpa…" Before she could finish her sentence, he was at the register buying two stuffed animals. Grandparents are the best.

With few other options at the artificial playground, we devoted the next two days to Atlantis Aquaventure, the 141-acre water park. Brooklyn was up early, raring to arrive at opening.

"Are you ready?" AJ asked his parents at breakfast.

"No, no," my mother-in-law said with another wave of the hand. "You go ahead."

"But we're here," AJ said incredulously. "You have to see the park."

"It's too much walking," my father-in-law responded. "We did so much yesterday." I stayed above the fray before suggesting we meet in a few hours. Neither was happy with the compromise, but it was the best solution.

Growing up, I loved amusement parks. Every summer, my family would visit Cedar Point in Sandusky, Ohio with our cousins. Before a porch swing became too much movement for me, I loved spinning rides, especially the Witch's Wheel. The name describes it pretty well, the ride spinning round and round as if a witch was at the helm. I didn't realize my problems went beyond spinning until AJ's introductory visit to Cedar Point when we were still dating. I dragged him into line for Millennium Force, at one point the world's highest roller coaster at 310 feet. He was terrified of the height as the coaster climbed higher and higher.

"Where is the top?" he asked incredulously, still fifty feet from the peak. I laughed. Amateur.

I screamed with exhilaration as we descended quickly, my stomach dropping, and my hearing and vision fading out. Uh oh… something was wrong. I was losing consciousness. I had no idea why it happened, so I shook it off and assumed I imagined it.

A couple hours later, AJ wanted to go again. "That was the best ride," he said. Earlier must have been a fluke, I thought.

Up we went, overlooking sparkling Lake Erie. Again, my stomach dropped, a veil of black covered my vision, and I groggily came to a bit later. I had definitely passed out. I wobbled weak-kneed off the ride.

"I need some sugar," I told AJ. "A cotton candy or ice cream or something." He looked at me like I was crazy. "I just need something right now," I practically shouted.

"How about a sandwich?" he countered. "We haven't gotten lunch yet. I'm hungry, now that I think about it." I was not in the mood for Ever-Hungry.

"I need some sugar right now!" I demanded. "Please get me some." The argument continued for far longer than it should have, but I eventually got my sugar and he got his sandwich. I also had to admit that I had already fainted earlier in the day.

I later looked it up, and what happened to me seems to be relatively common and seemingly harmless. It did have the longest drop, hit 4.5 Gs, and top out at 93 mph after all. I am curious what I'll decide to do when I take my kids in a couple of years. Do I ride again and most likely blackout a third time or tell my kids why I won't ride?

The memory flashed in front of me upon arriving at Aquaventure. Some trips, like Italy, we do for ourselves and drag the kids along with us. Aquaventure was almost entirely for the kids. It really wasn't all that surprising they loved their first waterpark, but watching unfiltered, complete glee warmed my heart more than pregnancy heartburn.

The girls splashed and played in the pools and on the slides. Most of Brooklyn's initial apprehension disappeared once she saw her fearless baby sister. They splashed together and dropped six feet on parallel slides, their eyes locked in contented excitement.

I found a hidden twelve-foot twisty slide within the rocks of an adult ride. AJ carried my cautious three-year-old to the top. "Look." He pointed toward me at the bottom. "There's Mommy." After placing her down gently on her bottom, feet first, he pushed her down like Ralphie in the 'Christmas Story.' It wasn't quite that rough; he wasn't wearing Santa's big black boots after all. After a clean landing, her baby sister careened toward me, speeding face-first as if entering the world. When I caught Ella, a look of stunned silence spread across her features. Then a big smile as she pounded her feet on the concrete to run toward the stairs. I held her soft, warm hand and traded places with AJ so he could witness the landing. That time, she flipped from her back to her belly but stayed feet-first. It still makes me smile to think about it.

I was bummed to miss out on the adult slides but secretly relieved. Nearly twenty years earlier, I feared for my life at a water park. As the youngest tagging along, I rode an inner tube far too big for me down a hill far too fast. Inevitably, I slipped through as the tube crashed into the plunge pools. Other tubes landed on mine, crushing mine and pushing me beneath the surface. There were no lifeguards there in the '80s. My big brother, my hero, tossed the older kids out of their tubes.

"Out of the way!" he shouted as he dumped the teenagers. "My sister is under there," he barked. "Pardon me," he said to the cute ones as he helped them back in.

At Aquaventure, I insisted that AJ enjoy it in my place. First, like he did when he married me, he took the Leap of Faith. This sixty-foot slide dropped through a Mayan Temple replica into a tunnel through a shark and ray-filled lagoon. The girls and I watched him zip by from our lagoon viewpoint. He looked like a child himself at the bottom, the excitement removing years of his life.

"That was fun," he said, starting to towel off, seemingly done for the day.

"Try another," I urged him, pointing to the Serpent slide. He smiled broadly when he returned, the adrenaline rushing blood to his fingertips and toes.

We walked through the lush environment, the breeze forever at our backs as we crossed bridges and walked along a beach to meet my in-laws at the opposite side of the park. Brooklyn trudged along for the reward of a ride down the lazy river with her dad.

AJ, the girls, and I repeated the cycle the next morning—water, slides, and fresh mango milkshakes. I took my inspiration from a shampoo bottle I read when escaping in the shower: "Rinse. Recycle. Reimagine."

In the afternoon, AJ and I took our daughters to a quiet beach as a break from the artificiality of the resort. That peaceful walk along the sandy path and Caribbean cool streets, seeing turtles, duck, and cranes, calmed my spirit immensely.

My in-laws had a more eventful day than ours. They spent twenty minutes trapped inside an elevator after breakfast, probably cursing their daughter-in-law for finding a bargain hotel. When they finally escaped, they barricaded themselves in their room for the rest of the day to comfort their nerves. They apparently missed the irony.

After our foibles in India, I had anticipated more stress with my father-in-law. It turns out, my only complaint was how he spoiled my kids. What grandparent doesn't? AJ was frustrated by his parents' lack of interest in joining us for activities, but I wasn't surprised. The two of them were in their seventh and eighth decades of life. And though my family was slowed by my pregnancy, we were still chasing two lively girls. That's a lot for people accustomed to a daily routine that revolved around television, food, and tea.

Mealtimes served as our opportunity to come together. For our last night, we dragged them back into the elevator (they refused to use the stairs) and out to dinner on the harbor. We ambled down to the Atlantis Marina on a warm, steamy night. We were still 'on property,' I suppose, but with the cruise ships gone and the out-of-season February sun setting, it felt more like a Caribbean outpost than an island resort.

"Grandma, look!" Brooklyn screeched as she hopped on one foot.

"Me! Me!" cried Ella. As my kids led their grandparents to buy them even more stuff, Ever-Hungry intervened.

"How about here?" AJ said as he led us into Carmine's, a lively, family-style restaurant with sumptuous pasta. Though it is a chain restaurant featured in Times Square, when paired with yachts and docks, the atmosphere felt subdued.

My father-in-law treated us to our fancy meal and amused us with an animated version of the elevator adventure. I dug into shrimp the size of my baby's fist. Time, even a few hours, certainly changes perspectives.

"Would you consider moving back to Maryland?" AJ asked a few weeks after our plane landed in Connecticut. Seeing his aging parents had initiated something deep within him that expounded the expanse of our distance on him.

I loved the peace and solitude of the ranch home we had bought only two years prior. Even though we were only two miles from the conveniences within a trendy suburb of Hartford, some combination of deer, raccoons, and boisterous flocks of turkey visited our wooded acre lot daily. AJ had even seen a bear while running near the enormous reservoir down the street.

"Sure," I agreed. He did so much for me in encouraging me to attend business school, acting as bedtime leader extraordinaire, and just being my biggest cheerleader and supporter. He moved to Connecticut for me. Connecticut! "Of course! But I am not doing anything until the baby is born. I am way too tired to show the house." The next week, while working from home, I spotted a strange car in the driveway.

A petite woman in her early forties was standing on my doorstep. "Hello," she said. "My family lives nearby, and we're looking to move within the neighborhood. I'm leaving this info at the ranches. In case you were thinking about selling," she added. She pointed to the envelope in her hand as proof.

Ever trusting, I waved her in. "Come in. Let me show you around." I shuffled ahead.

When my son, Lucas, turned six weeks and was big enough to leave his birth home, that owner of a boutique pizza joint closed on our house. Since I couldn't travel or walk more than a couple of steps without needing to pee, AJ drove down to Maryland on weekends and found a home I loved in an amazing community. The kids see their grandparents nearly every week and Brooklyn's grandma taught her to knit. Plus, we got free pizza and eggplant fries until the day we moved.

LESSON LEARNED

Consider mixing up who you bring as your travel companions. Kids, dogs, or grandparents can change the trip trajectory. You will see things another way, noticing the worms on the ground, the squirrels in the trees, or the eagles in the sky. I learned this, of course, while traveling to India with my father-in-law. He shared a new destination with me as a local who had taken a chance on leaving. I helped him see his country's beauty (and his first wild tiger).

My parents offer a different experience. Along with enjoying our time together, they babysit so AJ and I can engage in kid-free excursions or simply sleep in. It can also be as simple as visiting an all-inclusive resort with a large family (especially organized by someone else). There's always someone to hang with or help with the kids. A close friend recently returned from an island trip for her grandmother's birthday. That sounds ball pits of fun better than the party we would have at an all-you-can-eat Ponderosa Steakhouse with my own grandpa.

Before our trip to the Bahamas, I fretted about my in-laws' contrasting travel style. I needn't have worried. My massive pregnant body greatly benefitted from their pace—I slowed down, got more sleep, and walked less than I would have otherwise. They also share a similar schedule with the little ones with naps, early dinners, and bed before eight. Looking back, we appreciate the memories and time spent with them. We could all be happy, even if our group spanned nearly eighty years. Sometimes it's worth trying something you're not sure you'll enjoy. Like my second-grade daughter's science experiment on melting ice, new variables yield new outcomes.

Chapter Nine

CELTIC CRADLES OF IRELAND

SHORTLY AFTER WE moved to be closer to them (and presumably for their help), my in-laws graciously agreed to watch all three kids. I peeled off my sweatpants and actually brushed my hair for the romantic dinner AJ planned for us. Then, just after we ordered and I could practically taste my arriving veggie lasagna, his father called.

"Come home now," he ordered abruptly.

"We just ordered," replied AJ. "What happened?"

"You need to come home immediately," was the response. Then he hung up. We jumped up from the table, AJ apologized to the staff and left a tip, and we hopped in the car.

"Oh my God, what happened to the kids? Which one is hurt?" I cried. Full of hormones, my tears were kicking in.

"The kids are fine," he lied. I mean, what else do you say to a hysterical wife?

"Then it's Artie. I bet the kids let him outside and Cujo killed him." That's not her real name, of course, but the description fit. The neighbor's dog made a game of breaching her electric fence.

"What?" He didn't know how to respond to my wild conspiracy theories, so we continued home in silence. When we arrived, nothing seemed amiss with the kids or the dogs. I breathed a sigh of relief, and then saw my mother-in-law cradling her arm. She had broken her wrist chasing the kids in my hilly backyard while my father-in-law walked the dog. My theory was so close yet so far away. I still wasn't quite sure why they had gone outside in the first place.

My mother-in-law's injury disrupted her upcoming travel. She had planned to go to Ireland for her brother's funeral but worried about traveling alone with a broken wrist. AJ offered to accompany her. And where he goes, we all do. The next day, we snapped some adorable baby photos and sent them off for expedited passport services. Who needs the photo studio when you have the post office?

We left with a sense of foreboding from my little Screech Owl at the completely unpredictable age of two-and-a-half. Even though she had napped, she was a bit high strung and melted down at the airport. It could have been anything that happened. She wanted the big yogurt, to hold that thing, or some other random desire. Then in the restroom, she dropped her pacifier as I tried to put her on the toilet. We are not the type with dozens of pacifiers. We brought one. Maybe two.

I had to think quick since it was auto flush. The water was clean. Would I use the usual method of putting it in my mouth? Multiple studies have shown that babies whose parents clean their pacifier in their own mouth have a reduced risk of developing allergies, asthma, and eczema. Would I leave it? Quick. Decide. Auto flush. I plucked it out, scrubbed with soap and hot water, and handed it to AJ with the story. "You make the call," I said. Passports and pacifiers—the two most important things to bring on a trip for our family.

It was a long flight to Dublin for AJ as he juggled the girls and tried to soothe them to sleep. My mother-in-law could not help. The baby nursed and passed out on me for almost the entire flight. The others slowly inched their way over to me until all three were cuddled asleep against me.

Since we had a two-hour drive to my mother-in-law's hometown of Mallow, we arranged a short break in Dublin at the home of a family friend. While Brooklyn and Ella watched old American cartoons, I slept with my baby. I awoke in a dizzy fog, confused as to my whereabouts, willing to sleep some more, but strangely satisfied. We were in Ireland.

I missed efficient American customer service as I waited in an excruciating car rental line after our long red-eye flight. Then, I proceeded to argue with the Irish representative about needing insurance for the car. This experience was not mine alone; reviews of renting a car in Ireland are miserable compared to most other Western countries. I'd love to regale how the kids were behaving at that point, but I was too tired to care. All I know is that they were safe and didn't cause a massive scene. Sometimes the bar is set lower than a limbo contest. Or maybe, I was just lucky to have a spouse who kept them entertained when Mommy was a tired zombie.

After finally getting the car keys, I discovered that our minivan was literally a van squeezed into the size of a car. There was no leg room for the toddlers or space for our American car seats. Short of cutting off their legs, we tried every configuration to squeeze them in. Eventually, we all had to troop upstairs to pay for an upgrade. I gave them whatever they requested and we took their only large car. Since AJ only drove automatic, I would be driving a stick shift on the opposite side of the road the entire trip. I had driven friends' cars in Australia, but it's disconcerting when you set off. I forget how hard it is until at the wheel again. So much for all of that planning.

Passing through the green fields that reflected how I have always envisioned Ireland, I saw a tourist sign. The Rock of Cashel. With no Euros, we pulled in five minutes after last entry. They took pity on us with our gaggle of kids and let us in for free. The grounds didn't actually close for another thirty minutes, so the kids ran around the rocky, limestone hill, and explored the open grounds. In all directions, grassy plains with grazing cows surrounded us. Over six hundred years old and impressive, it was one of the first castles I visited and definitely my kids'.

"Elsa lives here," Brooklyn declared.

After our excursion, we continued to the Springfort Hotel. Other than a couple of aunts who had come to our wedding, I hadn't met any family members. After long hellos and a solid sleep, we were ready to say our goodbyes.

When I was a child, I went to two funerals within two years—my mother's grandmother and my father's grandfather. I always remember Granny's as my first, but as I was older, my memories are much stronger from the second. Since their deaths were fairly expected, my parents let me see the open caskets at their funerals. It is strange for a child to see a dead body. You don't have a real concept of life and death at that point or any sense of finality.

When my own grandfather passed, my sister struggled to explain it to my three-year-old niece. My niece didn't believe her at first but after a pause, asked, "Is Grandpa an angel?"

Not deterred by my past speaking challenges, I spoke at his funeral, starting off with a quote from a noted author, "To the adventurer, death is but the next great adventure." I followed up, "Grandpa led a full and long life, full of adventure and love. After meeting my grandma, he raised five children. He was strong—my mom thought he was as strong as Popeye and as handsome as President Kennedy." And I wonder where I got my corniness. "Near the end, my husband and I spent one long evening with him, laughing over Arby's Jamocha shakes. When I gave my last hug and said my last goodbye, he said, 'I'm proud of you, and I really like your husband.' That stuck with me."

I don't know how AJ reflects on Uncle Sam or if he feels he got his goodbye, but he probably wasn't ready. People are gone too soon, and things happen, often in the blink of an eye. It could have been my kids when my mother-in-law got injured, not just a broken bone. With the struggles we face, it's challenging to appreciate the little things in life.

I try to remind myself of this with my kids. I inherited so much from my grandpa—the broad shoulders and extra-large head, his love of Boston Terriers, and his thirst for reading, travel, and learning. I hope his lesson on appreciating life sticks the most.

With my limited knowledge of Uncle Sam, I wonder if these final words apply, "If he were with us now, he would not want us to focus on the sadness of his death but to look at the happiness we still have in our lives. He led a good, long life." I hope so.

We introduced our kids to those emotions on our first full day in Ireland. It was outstandingly beautiful with a brilliant blue sky and verdant green grassy hills leading to an old stone church. There were so many relatives, all with varying memories of AJ or accounts of me. We saw AJ's many aunts and uncles with their conventional, one-syllable Irish names—John and Jean and George and May. Then the cousins, so many cousins! It was a heap of people—a mass of warm, loving relatives. After years of wondering why my blue-eyed kids looked so little like my (not quite) tall, dark, and handsome husband and how I could produce a precious baby boy clone of my fair grandpa, his kin gave the answer.

At the church, Brooklyn and Ella sat upfront with their dad. Even Screech Owl sat silently, paying her respects. AJ bid farewell, his uncle's ashes to be buried in an urn made with his own hands.

In a time of mourning, when the sad want simplicity and stoicism, life rarely allows it. Funerals rarely go off without a hitch. The dead always seem to have one last gotcha to make you question the absurdity of life and the death that inevitably follows.

At the burial site, the priest had finished when we arrived, leaving little time for people to exit their cars. Especially those who had to buckle and unbuckle three car seats. Or account for the out-of-towners getting lost. Even though we attempted to follow the funeral procession, the one-way circle of Mallow pulled us away. My mother-in-law blasted at the priest, her Irish temper erupting in her homeland as a vent for her grief. She forced the priest to redo it fully. Not the burying part, of course, just the blessing and the prayers. Good on her, I thought, as my girls watched curiously.

After the reception at our hotel, my mother-in-law needed a rest, so she took Ella for a nap. The rest of us went to Cousin Rob's house to see the old family farm. We drove a few miles through the open pastureland, up into the hills. The family greeted us outside, including a large nursing female boxer and her mutt puppies. I felt a kinship. We walked into the ramshackle farmhouse, and to the delight of my son, discovered even more puppies. We learned that my mother-in-law had grown up in the house.

Cousin Rob gave us a tour, sharing the details of who slept where and which rooms had been renovated in the past sixty years. Answer: Not enough.

After a few minutes, we realized that we had left Lucas's pacifier in the car. "Out! Naughty!" I heard AJ shout as he went out to retrieve it. The Boxer was in the trunk and the Cheez-its and graham crackers, brought from home, were gone. He couldn't figure out how to open the granola bars and left the oranges. I hoped the dog would get scurvy.

My mother-in-law had encouraged us to take a day or so to explore the countryside while she visited her sister. I planned wisely. Killarney National Park, green and mountainous, spanning over 25,000 acres, includes a large lake and native woodlands about an hour or so away via the Ring of Kerry. The beauty overwhelmed me and made me believe Uncle Sam was at peace.

After passing through the central town, we visited the grounds of Ross Castle where Brooklyn and Ella could run around and throw rocks in the water. Then they watched as AJ helped some locals transport a large boat out of the water. The boats visit the ruins of an Abbey in Innisfallen. The site goes back to the seventh century and was occupied for nearly a thousand years. I love the history.

In Killarney, we continued along the Ring of Kerry. "Gorgeous," I said as we encountered some absolutely amazing views.

"Gorgeous," I breathed, peering across the hills with craggy mountains hiding amidst the fog.

"Gorgeous," I proclaimed, amazed at the juxtaposition from driving just over a mountain or around a bend.

"That's enough," AJ declared. "Find another word."

Eventually we turned onto a narrow, precarious one-way street to traverse down the mountain for our shortcut. We weren't sure if we were going the right way, but we were descending fast through the windy path. At one point, I had to reverse nearly halfway when we hit a dead end with nowhere to pull off and a truck coming toward us.

"Sheep! Sheep!" Ella bleated joyfully out the window.

"Why does that one have blue on it?" asked Brooklyn. Small herds were grazing in the valley. We were just outside the perimeter of the official park and had veered onto a farm. We passed a large bog. At the other side of the valley, we began our ascent back up the mountain.

We were now at the highest point in the park and approaching Dunloe Gap. This seven-mile narrow mountain pass was formed thousands of years ago by melting glaciers. We approached the gap from the opposite direction of most, near Moll's Gap. Signs near the start stated that the road was poor for cars. It was our path home and technically legal, so we decided to give it a try. The road narrowed as it wound through the Black Valley. When we'd approach another car, one of us would find the nearest pull off and wait for the other to pass. There weren't a lot of options for that, so sometimes that meant going backwards. It became a game of musical cars—keep your eye on the nearest spot and hop to it before there was a collision. Luckily, traffic was sparse. We passed five beautiful lakes of differing colors and sizes connected by the Loe River, and then stopped at a pull-off. Brooklyn and Ella burst from the car to run near the base of the stone bridge and dip their fingers into the cool water.

We ended at Kate Kearney's Cottage, a large parking lot for those hiking, biking, or riding a horse-drawn carriage through the Gap. The horses pull jaunting cars with up to four people through the pass.

At the bottom, Brooklyn asked the inevitable, "Can we ride the horse?" With two adults and three children, we still qualified—though we did push the limits adding in the driver and his two-year-old son. Our guide, like generations before him and his son after, lived near the Gap. He received our family through their fair rotation system, termed The Turn. The man we had initially approached actually directed us to our driver.

No longer driving the hairpin turns, I could enjoy the majestic views with a warm bundle of baby in my lap. Close to the cottage was an old arch bridge known as the 'Wishing Bridge.' Here, many hikers turned around after making wishes that were destined to come true. It was simply breathtaking, gorgeous really, and the weather breezy but clear. Before kids, AJ and I would have hiked the whole Gap and shaken our fists at those driving the path. Thanks to my three, I went on horse-level and saw it from a whole new perspective, within the Celtic cradle of earth.

After our peaceful day, our little family drove to Aunt Nuala's house. Nuala's husband, AJ's uncle, had died years earlier. She had six children, a plethora of grandchildren, and her own bakery behind the house. We tried to give my mother-in-law the same experience back home, but she bakes from a box and we've topped out at four grandkids.

To get to her home, we took N22 to N23 to N21. Not the least bit confusing to my directionally challenged spouse and me driving a manual stick shift through hedges about one-and-a-half size my car on the wrong side of the road. At the Newcastle roundabout, we got on R520. We took N20 north one exit toward Limerick and got off in Croom. Once we exited there, it was basically, "Go right at the exit, drive a bit, go up a big hill, don't go right at the roundabout, and follow that road. At the pub, go left at the roundabout. If you've gone to the church, you've gone too far." The roads were all similar with road hugging hedges and miles and miles of pastures and farmland. Addresses were non-existent. We stopped at a funeral, of all places, for directions. We gave his aunt's name and got further insight. "Go back to the roundabout, take the first left, then there's the pub. Follow that..." And off we went.

When I had my first child, I joined a local parenting club in my Connecticut suburb. The (primarily) women hosted playdates, organized a Halloween stroll, and gave each other meals and support. Since I had moved to the area for work, it gave me an opportunity to meet others outside my corporate bubble. When we moved back to Maryland, I actively searched to no avail for a similar group. On Halloween night, I eventually met Be the Jenny, who shared the details of a group that fit my narrow specifications. Through that club, I made some amazing friends, not to mention carpool drivers.

A couple of years ago, we launched a book club, a cathartic release to my month. Seven or eight of us meet to drink wine, gossip, and, oh yes, discuss the chosen book. It's usually historical fiction because we tend to be introverted nerds, the extroverted librarian the oxymoronic exception. One evening, while we spent our half-hour picking out the next book, someone mentioned a book about a woman with early onset dementia. One of the first things to go was her ability to remember names. Though well-written, I found it painful to read.

I became convinced I was developing Early Onset Alzheimer's. In the past few years, things suddenly drop out of my mind as if they were water. A phone number? Too many digits. A name? I can't remember it five minutes from now. During a job interview, I could not commit the woman's name to memory and wrote it down on a post-it as a reminder. My recall of past events and memories remain. I can recall the order we rode the rides at Dutch Wonderland last month and will always remember the births of my children. But tell me your name, and I will forget it within two minutes.

One night, I could not remember the name of the high school sitter I had hired. "Please ask her to tell you her name," I implored Brooklyn, the most competent of the bunch at seven years old.

"Sure, Mommy." She did her part, giving a big wink with her whole face as she asked. "And don't forget to tell her about the ants."

Even as my ability to remember names has declined, I still have fantastic recall for events. I may not know the location of Aunt Nuala's home, but I remember nearly everything we did, how the warm baby felt in my arms, and the permeating aroma of baked goods that infused the air. The house sat on what seemed a large estate surrounded by farms. The family was sincere, friendly, and utterly familiar to AJ, though he had only met them once before. They welcomed my children and me with open arms. They were entirely everything I had imagined of them when he shared his Irish heritage on our first date. Lucas cuddled against these strangers, and the girls ran with their second cousins alongside the horses or cows or some other large livestock. After showing us her ovens, Aunt Nuala placed a fresh, delicious cake in my greedy hands. Those memories—sharp, vivid, alive—demonstrate why I love travel so much. The adventures roll through my mind like a never-ending movie. However, as soon as we left, I forgot nearly every name.

That night, we drove a quick twenty minutes to Charleville Park Hotel on the way back to see my mother-in-law the next day. Screech Owl flew in that night. She struggled to sleep, swapping with her sister between the bed and the crib. She just wanted me, but I couldn't help since I had her nursing brother. We tried nestling a little cot on the floor between the beds. Eventually, I let her join me. The lack of routine had finally caught up to her. It was the worst night she ever had.

The next morning, we veered back on course with a filling breakfast for our tired stomachs. But then the tantrum returned. The stress of the night fed back into our souls. We tagged out in helping, trying to maintain some semblance of balance. That, unfortunately, did rule out our desired trip to Adare, a cute little town his family had recommended. We were going to drive straight toward Mallow with just one final stop.

The previous year, my mother-in-law had adopted a donkey for my kids at a sanctuary in Knockardbane, County Cork. We thought it would be fun to visit their donkey, pet her, and snap some photos to share with Grandma. It turns out, the roads had become even more confusing. This time, we had to stop and ask directions in town and were directed to another man who could give them to us. The friendly gent told us to follow him as he hopped in his truck.

LESSON LEARNED

Like it is in general, discipline can be especially tricky when traveling. For those who use them, time-outs are nearly impossible when on-the-go and even harder in a Polly Pocket-sized hotel room with siblings bouncing around. The routine is off and traditional privileges can't be taken away. You can't cancel a play date with Harper. However, being flexible and creative with incentives while staying consistent with your home parenting style can pay dividends.

As a parent, I lean toward authoritative parenting, creating positive relationships and enforcing rules with our kids. Our most effective form of correction when traveling is addressing it before departure. We share what they will see and get them excited for the trip. (That helps before leaving too.) Travel, in and of itself, can be the reward. But first it's important to provide the resources and support they need to succeed—for us, that's enough sleep, exercise, and a healthy diet.

We may have high expectations, but that doesn't mean our kids never act up. Clearly, they do—at some point on every trip. Usually when one of the needs above isn't met. We try to remember that each tantrum will end, more quickly with a distraction. Luckily, a new place offers distractions in droves, like the endless cheese puffs in the giant plastic tub from Safeway. That list of like-to and must-do items also comes in handy with overtired kids. They don't all need to walk along the waterfront, but you want everyone to see the Taj Mahal. Let meltdowns serve as an opportunity to split up, taking some kids to the pool and others for a rest.

At the sanctuary, we learned that donkeys have remarkable memories. They can recognize donkeys from twenty-five years ago (at donkey school class reunions?). They also are herd animals that love a good crowd. Lastly, we discovered that our adoptee, Shelly, was not even ours. She was just a token donkey that belonged to the masses. It's a bit strange, multiple orphans and everyone adopting a select few donkeys. The donkeys didn't seem to mind. They seemed happy, the girls pet another one altogether, and the weather was serene. Only one word could describe it—gorgeous.

We met my mother-in-law at her eldest sister's farm near Mallow. For the zillionth time that trip, we crossed our fingers and hoped we were going in the right direction. We followed a massive tractor down the road and passed farm after farm. AJ surprisingly recognized the path from twenty-five years prior. The estate was exquisite, set atop a hill and overlooking green pastures below. The home, trim and tidy, looked like it belonged in a fairytale. It sat in the center of a neat square of a vast, colorful garden.

AJ's mom was thrilled to see us and listened to our adventures as we watched cows grazing in the field. Brooklyn and Ella ran along the fence while the cows watched with their monotone stare and mouthful of cud.

At the home were more relatives—his aunt and uncle, celebrating nearly sixty years of marriage, cousins, and grand-cousins. A lovely, giant Irish family. I'm sure there were dynamics and love that pulled my mother-in-law away, as there always are, but to me, it was paradise. Having Ella nap at the home to give me a breath of fresh air may have also contributed.

Alas, the ease had to diminish. Poor Lucas cried on the way back to Dublin for the night before the flight. They took turns, the rare symphony of kids alternating tears for the two-hour drive. That night, Ella insisted on sleeping with me, and we gave in to avoid the conflict of the night before. Three of us in a double bed exhausted me. Then an early morning flight lasting throughout the day. AJ relaxed on the plane with the dream baby asleep in his arms and Brooklyn napping against him. My poor middle child had the last throes of her epic tantrum with an utter meltdown on the plane. Neither AJ nor I could not calm her, and she punched me for the first time in her life. Hard. It was her worst tantrum, pulling in multiple flight attendants. I feared they would ask the pilot to turn the flight around. I felt completely helpless—there was nothing I could think to do. I just held her and tried to comfort her. She was so, so tired.

Just like every other parent on the planet, I worry about my kids and that I'm not being the best mother I can. When she couldn't speak at two or read in kindergarten, I worried for my oldest. I worried my middle daughter would never outgrow her pacifier. Since she lost it and was forced to, I worried she wouldn't ever surpass the seemingly unending temper tantrums that replaced it. In life, whenever I learn something new, like every new day as an adult and now as a parent, I worry about what else I've missed.

That's just part of being a parent, I know. You never know what your kids are going to be like when they're grown. You don't know what you could do better until it's too late. As they grow, it's just important to continue to nurture the seed you've been given and do the best you can. And try to enjoy it.

I try, and fail, to not pressure myself since fate and God, or whatever you believe, plays a large role as well. One of my children pushes me more than the others. It's hard to know what plays the biggest part—birth order, personality, age? I can say that energy, that passion, and that inclusiveness will drive her to greatness someday. She's certainly charming. But when we're in the thick of it, when a couple of kids are crying and I'm struggling to put dinner on the table, wash dishes, and help with homework, I lose that perspective.

Even an orange isn't that until it matures. As it grows, it needs to spend some time being green. Some days I see that beautiful, self-assured girl and appreciate the path that is guiding us. For now, I don't know what that little fruit will become.

Chapter Ten

BUBBLE BATHS IN THE AZORES

I IMAGINE I'M NOT alone in feeling great satisfaction when organizing a drawer or finding a place for the toys that seem to flow from the gills of our home. I'm not as put-together as those friends who host pumpkin Pinterest playdates or large crafting events, but I hold my own. I'd say that my house is about ninety-percent composed. It appears tidy, and I can whip it into shape if I have fifteen minutes' notice to pick up those couple of things I catch out of place. The fact that they have a place is a win. The floor in my home probably could use a sweep or a vacuum, at least, according to my mother-in-law. She bought me a wooden sign that says, "Good moms have dirty ovens, sticky floors, and happy kids."

However, one morning, as I waited for friends to arrive for a baby playdate, I congratulated myself for pulling off the farce of appearing organized. Then came my self-correcting device. Whenever I find myself perfectly content, feeling that I've mastered a skill, I seem to get a scolding from above: "Don't get too cocky." Things have a way of balancing, either in reality or through perception. My bubble burst. I noticed a new wrinkle on my face to accompany the line down the center, my mom's mad face. I pulled out the cream from my friend.

This balance happened quite noticeably at work, one day after securing a promotion at my first job to manage a couple of summer interns. Proud of my new status, I showed up to work wearing two different boots. Literally one black and one brown knee-high boot, shown off beneath the hem of my skirt. I hadn't noticed on the D.C. Metro or at my desk.

A coworker came over and asked, "Did you get dressed in the dark?" Apparently.

From my favorite weekly travel email, *TravelZoo Top 20*, I noticed intriguing, repetitive photos from a place called the Azores. A young, fit person appeared front and center, overlooking a cylindrical crater-formed lake. The hills are a brilliant green, and the sea beyond is a dark blue. It's like a 120-box of Crayola crayons, composed entirely of differing shades of blue and green.

Although I had never heard of them, I found the island chain in the middle of nowhere, saddling the borders of the North American, European, and African tectonic plates. These Portuguese islands are relatively young, the first island formed eight million years ago and the last expansion into the sea within my parents' lifetime.

Since the islands are scattered among the differing continental plates, our first stop, Faial, was considered to be the westernmost point of Europe. Since pictures can lie, I knew the hikes might not be as good as they seemed.

However, chances not taken are opportunities missed so we wouldn't know unless we explored. Like the lava bubbling from the depths of the earth that had formed this archipelago, I had to burst out of my comfort bubble and see what it was all about.

More importantly, there was a direct flight from Boston, less than five hours to get there—closer than the West Coast. I then discovered that one of our former neighbors, still friendly through holiday cards and email even though we're political opposites, had recently gone with his adult children. He had ingratiated us to the neighborhood gossip so I knew he could give great advice on hotels and must-dos—hopefully with minimal comments from his favorite cable news host. I convinced AJ we needed to go immediately and persuaded my parents to meet us in Boston.

There was one little minor, miraculous hitch in the plan. Two days before our flight, via an at-home test on Lucas's first birthday, I learned we were pregnant for the fourth time. During my first pregnancy, we had visited the famed Blue Lagoon in Iceland, a touristy but amazing natural hot spring spa near the airport. On advice from my medical provider, I kept my bulging belly near the surface and was careful not to overheat, avoiding water above body temperature—one-hundred degrees max. I would use that same advice in the hot springs of the Azores.

After our torturous journey, the one that Ella melted down at the security line and threw herself on the dirty floor, we finally reached Horta, Faial. Some overnight flights are horrible for AJ and me, some merely bad. Regardless, we try to acclimate our kids to the current time zones upon arrival. On flights across the Atlantic, that usually means they are up for the day on arrival, only getting the four to five hours of sleep they got on the plane. The younger kids nap later in the day, fingers crossed, but everyone goes to sleep after an early dinner. The initial day can be tough, so we generally walk around town near the hotel. The next morning, the kids sleep in an hour or two, but generally recover from jetlag quicker than the adults.

LESSON LEARNED

My parents instilled a slightly obsessive habit of setting goals and bursting them like the bubbles around us. Varsity as a freshman. Check. Done with kids by 35. Check. (I think.) Unfortunately, many of my goals revolve around mundane things—finish reading that book in three days, do twenty-five pushups a day, make one major home improvement a year. Never opening a box of cereal before we finish an old one must be my husband's favorite!

When I first embarked on traveling, I set a goal of visiting all fifty states, all seven continents, and one new country a year. I love reading and learning new things to see what's out there. One of the traits I'm most proud to have installed in AJ was his personal running challenges.

I find that by writing it down, sharing it aloud, and working out the details, I'm most likely to do it. It's not as hard as it may seem. I tell myself, "You can do it. You CAN do it!" Figure out what your travel goals are and aim to burst them.

Newly pregnant, still nursing my baby, and taking care of two other kids, that red-eye blew the top off me like Costa Rica's Arenal Volcano. With our room being cleaned, I collapsed on a couch in the hotel lobby while exhausted three-year-old Ella slept on my chest. I have no idea how much later I awoke, disoriented and still tired. An afternoon barefoot walk along the soft beach sand at Porto Pim helped. The aura of salt in the air tickled our noses as mists of water from breaking waves sprayed our faces. Brooklyn and Ella followed me like obedient ducklings, then would cling like possums to AJ when they needed a break.

At the far side of the beach, we ascended Monte da Guia. The hike worked wonders for my girls, tiring them out but distracting them enough that they didn't notice. Atop the mountain, a breathtaking, yet unexpected, view beckoned. Volcanos had formed two bays thousands of years ago, both craters visible on opposing sides. The first, ringed by the beach where we had walked and sheltered from the ocean, formed a near-perfect circle. The second seems to challenge the sea, looking outward from the circular peninsula. From the cone, we could see both craters that had been filled with water and cracked open to the deep. The volcanos, so raw and so new, reminded me of my two daughters. One seemed comfortable and secure, striking and calm. The other appeared challenging and wild with courage and beauty bursting forth. Both were perfect.

Before embarking on our trip, we knew it was important to be in top condition so we could climb to the tops of old volcanos for breathtaking views along the ocean. For the couple of months before our trip, AJ and I decided to train ourselves, similar to the preparation he does before marathons. We carried Lucas and Ella to strengthen our backs with five-year-old Brooklyn walking beside.

Since we live near Maryland's Rock Creek Park, we would drive ten minutes to hike a four-mile loop around Lake Frank in Montgomery County. It is pretty ideal for training and has something for everyone—winding trails through the woods, an immense eagle's nest, a paved path, meadows with no real trail, a giant dam, and water-crossings.

During one of our training hikes, I decided it would be prudent to remove my shoes to keep them dry since the water level was a bit high. "Hold on," I called to AJ as I balanced against a tree.

"What are you doing?" he asked.

"I don't want my shoes to get wet," I explained as if to one of my kids. I bound the laces, and before he could respond, heaved them across the river.

Well, most of the way. A thin branch nine feet up snagged them out of the air before they could hit the other side. AJ and I used to point out shoes dangling from a power line or from a branch and wonder how they got there. Now we knew.

First there was a moment of disbelief, of stunned horror and confusion. Brooklyn, near the end of one of her first long hikes, sought advice in her reaction. Clearly this was a bad thing, Mommy had no shoes. Instead, I keeled over in laughter. I roared at my stupidity, poor aim, and misfortune of snagging that branch. I laughed the hardest I had in years. Probably since the shrimp incident in the Outer Banks. They all joined in, and we laughed so hard, we cried. Then poor Daddy had to figure out how to get the shoes down.

Fast forward two years to when the poppy-seed sized fetus from Azores, was now my little Sienna and I cleared AJ to run ahead as I hiked with all four kids. "Are you sure?" he said, not wanting the real answer.

"We'll have fun," I replied. "It will be easy," I lied. Easy wouldn't accurately describe the approaching dogs, snacks to be strategically meted out, minor arguments to resolve, and a cold breeze that made me regret not pushing for that extra layer. It was fun though, especially finding large Osage oranges and kicking them like soccer balls. It was tiring too, great for approaching nap time. Most importantly, it was fantastic bonding—my older two running ahead to the bend and my son holding his sister's hand. Baby Sienna walked only partway, but four kids in, I happily carried her.

AJ met up with us a half mile from the car after he had run ten miles to our three. The river crossing just below the parking lot was swollen that day, making it a sure thing our feet would get wet. Falling in wouldn't have been a disaster, as it's still quite shallow, but I still wanted to avoid it. I kept my shoes on. When AJ and six-year-old Brooklyn were partway across, a man appeared on the opposite bank. He smiled good-naturedly so we continued. We had, after all, arrived first. AJ came back to help Lucas, then I stepped down with Sienna securely on my back. I reached back for Ella and worked my way across with her. The man watched until we finished.

"It's all yours," I offered with a big wave of my arm.

"I'm not crossing," he replied. "Are you guys training for something?"

"Nope. Just out here hiking," I replied.

"Wow," he said and continued on his walk along the opposing shore. "Wow," he repeated as he shook his head.

Back in the Azores, my dad rented a car for our first unscheduled day, and we fell into our roles—I directed from the passenger seat, AJ zoned out, and my mom entertained the kids. The spectrum of blues and greens delighted our eyes, the scenery out of this world.

We had planned to all hike around the Cabeco Gordo Volcano rim. Brooklyn struggled at the start since rain had turned the large uphill into a mud bath and she quickly became frustrated. My mom offered to stay back with her since the others were safely tucked into backpack carriers. Halfway around the caldera, when we edged close to the cliffs, I breathed a sigh of relief at that decision.

From the top of the circular ring, we could see the entire island and across the water to Mount Pico, ringed with clouds at twice the altitude. The kids waved at the cows grazing a few yards away. Toward the end of the mile and a half hike, we heard birds shrieking, over a thousand feet below in the center, invisible to us, but living amongst the marshes and thickets.

We visited an abandoned whaling village that had been covered by Capelinhos Volcano. The kids loved running across the dusty paths, covering their clothes in so much dirt. That was a surreal experience, seeing relatively modern buildings covered with ash from 1957. That year and the next, in a series of eruptions, the island expanded by nearly a square mile. That served as an even closer-to-home example of our place within nature. Earth will have the final say. With that sobering thought, we ordered some Papa's Pizza carryout to eat along the harbor.

With the jetlag finally diminishing on our second day, my mom and I took Brooklyn for a whale tour. My body had thwarted any effort to go the day prior, instead colluding with my brain to sleep in. So instead of going out that first day, that afternoon we walked to the marina to schedule our excursion. That same morning, the tour had encountered a blue whale. We had just missed it.

The cute seaside town of Horta offers fish and chips, snazzy little souvenir shops, and a world-class view of Mount Pico on the next island over. Although it's a small town of just 7,000 people, the Marina has incredible historic significance. Founded in the mid-fifteenth century, it has functioned as a foothold in the Atlantic and in the whaling industry. The marina sat across the street from "The Peter," a café and sports bar, and center of town.

The Peter itself has been around for over 100 years. In the past, it served as a post office, currency exchange, and, of course, a pub. It also was the place I was directed to when, surprise, surprise, I had to use the toilet. It's amazing how that pregnancy symptom presents before just about any others. Sailors across the world have used it as a home base, especially before the Internet. Ironically, neither the original nor future owners were named Peter. The name was penned by an American soldier during WWII who thought the young owner looked like his son, Peter. The owner's name was Henrique.

We set off in a little dinghy, er, zodiac. The twenty-five-foot long boat holds eighteen and was actually their biggest boat. We were packed like sardines—appropriate for a seaside voyage, plus warm and tight for our little girl. After three hours, Brooklyn fell asleep in that position, the water rocking her the way I had for the first two years of her life.

Although the zodiacs appear feeble, I felt at ease in the low, fast, compact boat. It hugged the waves as tight as I hug my kids every morning. We bounced and splashed along. Then, word came of a Fin Whale nearby. Fin Whales are the second largest species in the world, at 72 to 82 feet long and 100,000 pounds. When we did encounter the massive water mammals, the zodiac allowed us to get much closer than we could have in a large boat. It was incredibly personal—with some incredible views. Better yet, I could watch it myself, then see that awe again through the eyes of my daughter.

Back at the apartment, Ella and Lucas were playing on little bikes on the patio while AJ watched.

"Is my dad back?" I asked. My dad had left quite early that morning to attempt a summit of the volcano, Mount Pico. It should have been an all-day event.

"He just got back and is napping," AJ explained. "He said he took the ferry to Pico Island. But when he got there, he got lost on the way up and it was raining and foggy. To get down, he had to jog, then hitchhike in the back of a tractor." AJ looked at me before adding, "I see where you get it."

We flew out the next morning to Angro de Hermoisa on Terceira. We rented a car to offset the spread-out terrain, driving along the coast and to visit three inland volcanoes. I learned more about volcanos that day than I had ever known I wanted to.

We hiked along a short tunnel and entered the chimney of the Algar do Carvão volcano, before descending over 200 slippery steps to the bottom. It forms a rare intact cone, one of only two in the world that allows tourists. Inside gleamed a series of contradictions.

Hanging stalactites and rising stalagmites lined the walls that surrounded a lake fed from dripping waters. Rainbows of color painted the walls and glowed as prisms. Three-hundred feet above us, peering in like a giant child, was a sliver of light so narrow yet so clear, it shone down as if from Heaven. It was entirely magical, and one of the most surreal environments I have ever encountered. Photos can't do it justice—disappointing since looking at them is how my children's memories will be formed. Perhaps, as my embarrassing moment did for me at International Night, it will come back to them one day in a flash, as they travel with children of their own to the one other intact cone.

We stretched our legs at Furnas de Enxofre in the center of the island. I should clarify: the adults stretched our legs—the littles were pinned to our backs, and Brooklyn was held in the iron grip of my hand. This was not a place to run loose. Although it was a much smaller scale than, say, Yellowstone or Furnas, which we would be seeing in a few days, the steam and hydrogen sulfide emissions breaking through the earth were quite dangerous. The kids enjoyed the scent of rotten eggs in the air and giggling at the gas.

Our last volcano, Gruta do Natal, or the Christmas Cave, consisted of a series of deep lava tubes over 2,000 feet long. We pulled up to a small house in the middle of Terceira Island, built as protection over them. The house sat right off the main roadway near the Lagoa do Negro, like a cheap roadside attraction. We arrived a few minutes before closing, rushing to complete the trifecta.

"Put on these helmets," the guides directed us. When he saw me, he added, "And move your baby to your front."

"Why?" I inquired for no real reason other than I was curious.

"There are a lot of sharp rocks. If you turn quickly…" The man paused and demonstrated hitting a protruding rock. Lucas would get a thumping.

As we walked deep into the earth and the girls crawled through the bowels, we saw the formations up close—more stalactites and stalagmites, along with the lava formations. I had not expected the guide to teach us so much. The kids loved the adventure.

During the drive, we encountered the picturesque countryside. "Watch out for the cows!" I called to my dad as we veered onto a narrow one-lane bridge going up the mountain. We had gotten a bit lost earlier as we left the city, but we were finally on track.

"I see them," he muttered back, crouched over the wheel. He didn't see the thirty goats, however, and slammed on the brakes to avoid them. Like a flood, the roadway suddenly filled with a menagerie of animals. A dozen milking cows plodded along behind their babies in the back of a pickup. This would be a trip highlight for my kids—except that all three were asleep.

"You have got to be kidding me," I said. "This has never happened before." Even Never-Sleep.

"Don't hit them," I warned, as a cow stepped in front of the path. My dad slowed again, cursing to himself in his grumpy old man voice. For the most part, he's easy-going, but when he's tired or wants his way, all bets are off. We drove along behind them, down the peaceful country road. Up ahead was an intersection, and the cows were going straight. "You can go left," I volunteered.

"Look at that one," came my excited husband's voice from the back seat. A rogue cow had gone right at the stop sign. She abandoned her calf, sensing freedom to the east.

"Yehee!" shouted my dad, rooting for the underdog. A cowboy leapt out of the truck to join his pal on the road. A chase ensued. Back and forth, Daisy the Cow went, searching for a break, but eventually she was wrangled. We certainly enjoyed cheering her on.

That wasn't the case when we happened upon a true bullfight in town. We had arrived in the sleepy fishing village with what seemed like half the island population. A local invited us up onto her patio to watch. For the "fight," men would hold the bull with a lengthy rope as he stomped through the town. Young men ran away from him, antagonizing him the whole way. If it sounds cruel, well, it was. We were trapped since there was a loose bull in the streets, but we left as soon as we could, trying to ease away the memory over dessert.

Hotel Caracol came recommended, so we booked a comfortable two-bedroom suite for a steal. The hotel overlooked the water with a great view of the historic Angra do Heroísmo. With Lucas napping, I took the girls swimming in a poor, rather dark pool. After twenty minutes, an exercise class kicked us out. All dressed up with nowhere to go, I let them splash to their hearts content in the frigid sea water. Since it was only May, the water had not yet reached a remotely optimal temperature. Clearly, that wouldn't stop me. When the excitement caused them to promptly fall asleep afterward, so did I.

In the afternoon, we walked to the city. Along the way, we ran into my parents and Lucas who had ventured out earlier. My son seemed overjoyed thinking that I was saving him from his kidnappers. He was actually just hungry. As I fed the baby, AJ laid down on a crisp white wall, Ella still strapped to his back.

"Where did you go?" I asked my parents. The city really was amazing with picturesque mountains on the water, narrow roads that wound through delightful little shops, and sparse traffic.

"You have to go to the café we found. It had melt-in-your-mouth animal cookies and fresh cappuccino." Ice cream, too, Brooklyn would discover. "See the cathedral?" How could we not? The largest temple in the archipelago stood impressive; tall, imposing, and white with red piping on the two pillars in the distance. "It's past there."

Once they gave us plans for the next two hours, came the inevitable, "What do you guys want to do about dinner?" My parents shared the restaurant they had visited the night before at the eternally late hour of seven o'clock.

Per usual, my dad gave in-depth directions based on memory. "It's only a ten-minute walk from the hotel. You take the road going north out of the roundabout. Not the one we did to see the bull, but the next one over. Take that about half a mile, pass the turn, and it's about a hundred feet past the roundabout. Got it?" Then he added, "It's kind of hidden so keep your eyes open." We agreed on a time.

Horrified at the directions, AJ sat up quickly. The front of his shirt was covered with white paint.

"I wondered why the wall looked so clean," I admired. And off we went to replicate my parents' morning.

We concluded with a trip to Monte Brasil. At the base of the mountain, an extensive, colorful playground greeted us. The park ran at least a half mile along the water and older folks ran along the looping paths. Brooklyn and Ella burned their energy playing pirate on the wooden boat and traipsing among foreign swings and slides. Then, we climbed the mountain, past an old fort and through plush overgrowth, emerging near a small free zoo with deer and birds. The kids ran around some more amongst panoramic harbor and city views. But, alas, the girls were hungry, and I missed my little boy.

We hiked down for dinner, following the intricate path, and met up with the rest of my heart. The restaurant had a fun and surprisingly safe playground over rubber—an upscale McDonald's play place. Though the kids had fun, being overtired made them stop listening. Then, like a light switch, we were out.

Our last puddle-jumper arrived in Sao Miguel under a cloudy sky and dense, moist air. We headed straight to Lagoa do Fogo, a huge blue lake filling an extinct crater from just 350 years ago. We wound up the high mountains on a wide, newly paved road through the clouds until we emerged victorious in the clear skies above it all. Surrounded by thick vegetation, many consider Lagoa do Fogo the most beautiful attraction on the island. Unfortunately, there would be no views that day. If the weather had cooperated, we would have hiked some of the eight-mile path around. My dad and AJ planned to run ahead and move the car so the rest of us could do half.

We parked near another car at the overlook. The inhabitants were making their way back up the dirt steps, seemingly appearing from the clouds below. They looked quite happy, so I figured we could give it a shot. My mother was horrified with that idea.

"It's called Fog Lake, what do you expect?" I joked. It's not actually. Fogos translates to Fire. The clouds rising from the lake resemble smoke, but today it had settled to appear as a blanket of cotton balls resting on the lake.

"You're going to wander off the path and never make it back. It happens all the time."

"It does not happen all the time. The path is very clearly marked."

"Your dad and I are not going."

"Then can Lucas stay?" His face showed peaceful contentment as he slept, and I hated to wake him.

"Katie, that is not funny."

"Remember, you're his guardian if anything happens to us."

"I can't believe you're doing this." I loaded Ella onto AJ's back and held Brooklyn's hand. When the futile battle had been lost, my mom shouted after us, "Take lots of pictures!"

I'll admit that during my pre-children vacation days, I would convince AJ to do some borderline dangerous things. In the Dominican Republic, I had found a cheaper, most authentic snorkeling option, promoted by my guidebook, by driving to Playa Dominicus and renting a boat to see their esteemed Parque Nacional Del Este, fifty miles or so away. Always up for exploring and saving a buck, I was in. The fact that we would see one of my favorite animals, the flamingo, added to the thrill. We left our barricaded enclosure and drove off with a stranger to the middle of nowhere.

When we arrived, the driver happened to know someone with a boat who could take us out. I know we didn't pay as good a price as we could have, but I also knew my Spanish was subpar and it wasn't worth haggling. A few yards into the water, I glanced around.

"Where do you keep the snorkel gear?" I asked.

The driver looked confused. "You want to snorkel?"

He returned to the dock to borrow gear from a friend. We paid ten more dollars. My guy and I exchanged looks about whether this would be worth it. It was.

I had limited experience seeing the Caribbean Sea and this trip, in early May, offered picture perfect weather. Photos show the water to be turquoise. In person, it appeared crystal clear. We swam in secluded coral reefs and relaxed on a private beach, buying snacks from a small shack. That afternoon was one of the most pleasant of my life. Relaxed exhilaration.

Jamaica offered even more sketchiness, three years later and newly married. To avoid the huge resort taxi surcharge, we booked a tour to the Luminous Lagoon through our sailing guide. A cab arrived as the sky was darkening to purple. After a twenty-minute jaunt, the driver released us with a boat operator, who dropped us off at night in the warm, dark water.

The lagoon holds millions of dinoflagellates, a microorganism that glistens a fluorescent light into the water. Before we eased into the water (because who knew how deep it was), we looked at each other. What if the driver took off and left us in the dark water? The large mangroves hugging the shore hid the shoreline from our eyes. Were there crocodiles or other creatures that could hurt us? Bandits?

The water of the lagoon glowed reassuringly as we moved our arms and legs throughout the water. This place claims to be the largest and most brilliant of only four bioluminescent lagoons in the world. Crowded tour boats visit the lagoon most nights, but that night, we were alone. Both adventures were amazing. Neither are one I would do with my children, small or big.

I could see why my mom was skeptical, but Fogos Lake provided none of those concerns. The trip to the lake and back was just over a mile, and we returned within an hour. At the water's edge, we let our daughters feel the cold, fresh water before marching Brooklyn back up. We could hardly see ten feet in front of us, much less the other shore.

With some extra time, a cheap Plan B option, Caldeira Velha, came up from the reserves and performed like an all-star. My dad, Brooklyn, Ella, and I quickly changed into our swimsuits and stretched out in the warm thermal pools as the skies opened. I felt at peace sitting with my sweet girls, feeling the rain stream through my hair and the hot springs swirling around our legs and chests. From his spot in the rain, Ever-Hungry husband joked while eating his daily ice cream ration, "You should check out the cold pool." I looked at the dainty mountain waterfall. No thank you.

The rain took it out of Ella, and she felt asleep en route to the hotel. I gladly stayed in the car, reading a book and watching her little chest rise and fall, while the others ate.

The spectacular Terra Nostra Garden Hotel greeted us. The hotel has won many awards and is considered to be the best in the Azores. It is not typically my family's fare—we're not quite motel folks, though I do like a good Holiday Inn—but it was only three nights, so we decided it was worth the splurge. With no suites, Brooklyn bunked up on a little cot with her grandparents. Worth every penny. The hotel coexisted beautifully within the exotic, foggy mountainous locale.

The storm blew over, and we were blessed with clear blue skies for two of the next three days, allowing us to take separate drives to the opposing coasts. To the west are the beautiful island views and the ocean along with the classic photo used in all advertising. We drove along the coast, stopping at sites high above the sea and watching fruitfully for whales.

We then veered down a narrow path to Mosteiros Beach, a rough inlet surrounded by boulders. It was amazing, watching the torrential waves sculpting the landforms out in the Atlantic Ocean. The water ballet offered an expedited lesson on water erosion. After our short stop, we headed back to finish our drive to the three-mile wide former volcano (what else?), Sete Cidades. This Island of the Seven Tribes holds volcanic structures and four lakes. Legend has it that two of the lakes were formed with the forced separation of a princess and her shepherd lover. The tears from their blue and green eyes formed the disparate lakes that sit together in eternity.

We hiked around the top, passing more cow pastures. "Look at the views these cows have," I said. It rivaled most all in the world. The road edged the rim of the volcano, dipped into it, and meandered between the green and blue lakes in the center. Like Ireland, gorgeous.

That day contrasted with a drive to Nordeste, literally the 'northeast.' Though one of the least visited parts of the Azores, it boasts incredible steep cliffs, farms, and sleepy villages. It also holds the oldest functioning tea estate in Europe.

We started with a long drive to the southeast coast and a beautiful long, peaceful walk through the jungle. My mother was not a fan of the minor cliffs and held Brooklyn's hand tight the entire way. The other kids bounced along on our backs.

I had read that the eastern cliffs were breathtaking fjords, like those in Norway, albeit on a smaller scale. We quickly discovered the one risk of winding along massive cliffs in a car—the likelihood of someone related to me getting sick. Poor Ella drew the short straw, losing her lunch for the first time in her life, ironically right before we actually stopped to eat.

We were bummed when the persistent rain came, but it actually encouraged us to relax at Terre Nostra. The highlight of my kids' trips were the hours spent splashing in the pool. We explored the famous gardens and gave the kids one-on-one time at the hot springs. During the day, busloads of tourists came to the hot springs for the day, including old ladies who loved children. Though relatively shallow, my children wore life vests and I held them in a vise since the water lurked a murky brown. Without the bright yellow vests, I had nightmares of an incident from our past. When my oldest was three, she had fallen through the cover of a pool and into the dirty water beneath. AJ ran across the yard and jumped through the hole into the water below before my brain even grasped what my eyes had seen. Since she had only been under for maybe a nano-second, she wasn't scared. But I shudder to think what would have happened if neither of us had been there.

As the rain continued, we passed the Caldeiras das Furnas before dinner. Those holes of steam terrified me, so I gave my kids about twenty seconds to look, then released them to my parents to sample fresh-cooked sweet corn steamed in the caldeiras. And ice cream. Always ice cream.

"Look, Mom! A bubble!" Ella shrieked to me after dinner. She was stirring her chocolate milk and a pocket of air formed between the milk and the side of the cup. She was higher than the massive mountain from Moana.

In the Azores, we saw the wonder of nature that had formed the archipelago. We watched as bubbles formed in the hot caldeiras, dissipating as steam or gas and warming our surroundings. Another volcano will erupt, and the land will change again.

My kids enjoyed this since they love bubbles of all sorts—floating soapy ones magically transformed from water stretched taut across a wand, massive pink ones formed with wads of chewing gum, bubble baths, and the ones that fizzle in your pop. Breaking the bubbles brings the greatest happiness, testing the limits that physics holds on that sphere. My baby fights to shatter them, releasing the air inside from its trap. The splat of gum on my daughter's face makes them all laugh.

Most of us live our entirety in a bubble—within our family cocoon when young, our communities when growing up, then friendships while adults.

Bubbles give us the comfort and protection we need when scared to see what else is out there. However, they aren't sustainable; in the end, they always pop. Life, after all, is not forever.

We can all take an example from that chubby baby hand. Sometimes it's important to burst that bubble and see what happens. Trying something new can lead to amazing and unexpected adventures in the world beyond.

Third Trimester

THEY'LL BE WAITING IN HELSINKI

I WAS NOT SURPRISED when one of my children started showing signs of obsessive-compulsive disorder. My own family had been a bit obsessive with checking things off lists or counting miles or calculating rates. My dad used to record every movie he watched and track every mile he ran. Seeing a kid sorting things or lining up their toys in pairs seemed reasonable until the pediatrician shared that it's not quite normal. Personally, I try to internalize my obsessiveness. My compulsions aren't particularly productive—adding letters in my head, putting every little thing away, and reading every article in the newspaper before recycling it—so that's probably for the best.

"Can you put down a bad book?" my career advisor at Stern had asked when helping to craft my 'pitch.' I had just stated my strengths to be finisher, responsible, and doer.

"I don't think so," I replied. Then I thought about it on my two-mile walk home and remembered a saga I owned that I hadn't completed. I promised myself I would finish it before graduation.

My brother, Bryn, embraces his eccentricities and has devoted himself to reading the entire Marvel comic series (apparently over 32,000 comics) and identifying as many species of birds as possible. He's seen 3,657, along with 360 mammal and over 1,000 random other animal species, as of the end of 2020. He led a birding trip to Borneo with likeminded people before meeting up with the rest of my family in Vietnam.

"Um...no," AJ confirmed when I asked if our kids were ready for a fifteen-hour flight.

"Yeah," I agreed, "probably not Baby Sienna." Or three-year-old Lucas. Or five-year-old Ella. Perhaps I should have just shipped off seven-year-old Brooklyn with a kiss and a prayer.

I had negotiated the right to consider it by agreeing to go to Disney over a school holiday in January, coincidentally over my daughter's birthday. Seeing Cinderella at that age is pretty much the best thing you can do. I also secured a solo Happy Birthday serenade from a singing Mickey Mouse—apparently a hard thing to do—when scrolling through the last-minute FastPasses. We have just set the bar too high. Perhaps next year, I can buy her a unicorn. My parents joined us, so with four adults and four kids, we were able to take in a lot of rides and enjoy ourselves with only the usual Disney stress. In exchange for my sacrifice, I got to choose an exotic destination.

I started eyeing up the travel deals, planning a caviar trip on our hamburger budget. I stuck to my rules from Italy: the shorter, the better with a ten-hour limit and some place new. I liked Scandinavia and Eastern Europe. I had already visited the homelands of both in-laws, so it would be nice to see the realm of my ancestors. My paternal grandmother (of garlic bread fame) came from Bohemia in the Czech Republic.

A Copenhagen deal appeared with a free stopover in Iceland. I dreamed about spending a day in Reykjavik with my kids. I calculated airfares and visited the Blue Lagoon's webpage to research their rules for children and was poised to book.

But oops, I forgot to mention it to AJ until after a tiring weekend with the kids. At that point, he couldn't imagine going to the grocery store with them, much less Europe. We argued. In the end, we put off until tomorrow what we couldn't agree on today. The next day, the deal disappeared, and the fare had doubled in price. I was crushed.

"Next time, tell me sooner," he requested. "Let me know when you find it, not when you have the whole thing planned in your head." A month went by, then two until I feared I had missed our chance at Europe. Even my 100,000 credit card airmiles were useless in August with five tickets and an infant.

And then…a deal appeared on SAS Airlines. Kids fly free to any major city in Scandinavia. I have four children. Four kids fly free with two adults. Using the transitive theory, it's like I had not given birth four times.

I shared my find with AJ before calling the airline to book a multi-leg flight. Rather than a typical airline agent, I had stumbled upon a personal concierge.

"I'd like to see Stockholm, Helsinki, and Copenhagen," I proclaimed.

"I'm so sorry," the man on the end of the line effused. "You can't do that with the Kids Fly Free deal." I felt as if the air had been punched out of me, similar to when my three-year-old unexpectedly launched himself onto my stomach in a moment of rest. The concierge continued, "Have you heard of the ferry from Helsinki to Stockholm? It is one of the most beautiful ferries in the world and sails past Archipelagos in Finland and Sweden. Your kids would love it."

I was speechless. Did an airline rep just tell me not to fly and take a boat instead?

"The boat is overnight," he continued. "Everyone loves it. Why don't you fly into Helsinki, take the ferry to Sweden, and then continue on from there?"

"Can you plan my entire trip?" I wanted to say. I didn't really—at least I don't think I did. I very well may have since I make a habit of sticking my foot in my mouth. Then I found a marathon for AJ to run in Helsinki. Our itinerary was planned.

I called my parents. They were coming back from Asia via Switzerland, and the dates fit into their schedule. They claimed they had booked their flight home a few days prior.

"Non-cancellable," they said.

"Four kids too many," they thought.

AJ and I were on our own for ten days. How would we pull this off?

The answer: social media.

Now, I don't care for posting to social media. I may placate my mom on her birthday and congratulate my husband when he finishes another race, but I primarily use it for the one thing most people do: stalking. Well, that and looking at cute photos.

LESSON LEARNED

I am exceedingly-particular about packing, diligent to avoid forgetting anything. Perhaps my mom wearing her Bart Simpson pajama shirt nearly every day of a two-week trek when my parents left her bag at home influenced my thinking.

Therefore, when traveling with my family, I build a list two weeks out. I record as each item goes in the suitcase, placing a check next to that child's initials and consolidating it in as little luggage as possible. Socks—Check. Check. Check. Check. Underwear—Same. Obsessive perhaps, but it works.

For this trip, we brought one fifty-pound suitcase (the maximum weight without paying extra), a large duffel bag, a backpack diaper bag, and the two Minnie suitcases. Our stroller shuttles one kid plus nearly everything but the suitcase. Pushing it, I feel like a contestant on my favorite old gameshow, Supermarket Sweep.

Our airplane carry-on carries a little bit of everything to satisfy the needs of a long flight. I amaze my family with what I can pull out. For this last trip, it contained games, snacks, a set of clothes for each kid (pajamas for the overnight flight), a sweatshirt and socks for me, pacifiers, a laptop, headphones, a book that won't get read, candy, and diapers. ChapStick too for the dry air, and a refillable water bottle. Once they're four or so, our older kids manage a small suitcase or carry-on backpack. That bag holds their chosen objects plus some of the above items fit into the hidden niches. Not the passports or tickets, though. Those, along with our money, go in a small bag carried close to my heart. The keys go somewhere so secret that we inevitably panic upon arrival back home.

Clothing is grouped by kid, the piles rotating through the suitcase like a clock. Brooklyn's items sit at 11:00, then Lucas's, Ella's,

Sienna's. Food items and the sound machine serve as dividers between each pile and the clothes cushion more fragile items. Their clothes generally squish down to the size of a Tickle Me Elmo doll, but I do roll bulkier items to conserve space.

Like at home, we try to minimize chores at stressful times, like mornings before we've eaten. I lay out their clothes in advance, with the help of a certain, fashion-conscious five-year-old, to get us out the door quicker in the morning.

Liquid toiletries are taped closed and put into a baggie placed in their own compartment of the suitcase. Other disposable items, like diapers, reserve suitcase space that can repurposed for souvenirs on the flight home. Assuming ten diapers a day, that saves suitcase space to bring home that set of handcrafted bowls (or case of wine).

Until joining Facebook years after everyone else, I would send an email, "Hey, remember me?" and cross my fingers that the AOL address still worked. With social media, I can now contact people after not talking to them for fifteen years since we are "friends." On the flip side, I've been solicited through chat for everything from advice on improving credit to helping their wife increase their milk supply. (And yes, that was the same person for both.)

For Scandinavia, I turned to my former adversaries for court space at Davidson College. The basketball team may have only churned out one mega-NBA star (and what a star he is) but it's possible we send the most abroad. My distant cousin (perhaps), a super-friendly giant from the Czech Republic, played in Germany. My first ever college date, a funny, chill guy and the Stephen Curry of my time, retired after over a dozen years playing across Europe. Our former point guard lives in Stockholm with his college sweetheart and kids. Another player became mayor of a small town in Finland. My small school churns out some awesome people.

I spent the next three months planning for this monstrosity of a trip using their insights, the Internet, and guidebooks from the library. In the end, I brought one guidebook and then promptly lost it during transit. A broken zipper on my daughter's Minnie suitcase let it slip from that hole into the abyss of the Copenhagen airport.

All four kids were angels on our seven-hour red-eye flight and troopers when we arrived for our layover in Copenhagen. Though I had feared the worst, everyone had slept. Baby Sienna snoozed in the bassinet, and the others sprawled like puppies over us and the seats.

Since there was nowhere to sit for most of those two-and-a-half hours, we marched the corridor like nomads. When a bench appeared like a mirage in the dessert, I feared I would doze off and a child would disappear. Ella rhythmically pet the pelt of a reindeer at the store like she twists her curls when falling asleep. When they called our flight, we finally joined the cattle class down the escalators to the airport bus.

Chapter Eleven

TANTRUMS IN TALLINN

FTER THE WILDS of camping for the Davidson College orientation trip, Jessica and another friend went to the other extreme by transferring to New York University. Which meant that to see them, I would be visiting the Big Apple for the first time on my own.

My friends showed me New York City and took me to my first real club. Hundreds of zombie-like raving teens and early-twenty-somethings enveloped us. Perhaps that's not what they were doing, I was quite naïve after all, but I didn't like it all the same. When my friends saw my shell-shocked face—I'm terrible at poker—they quickly ushered me to the hip-hop room. There I came alive, dancing and chatting with the locals. People of all ethnicities moved to the beat of the music, dressed in the colorful styles of the day. The guys wore baggy jeans and I had my cool, back pocket-less jeans and lacy top.

"Where are you from?" a young man asked. I shared that I was from Michigan, went to school in North Carolina, and was visiting friends at NYU. I probably gave him my social security number as well.

"What about you?" I inquired.

"I live on Staten Island," he responded. I thought he was pulling my leg.

"No one lives on Staten Island," I replied.

"I do," the guy retorted.

"No…" And so, our discussion continued. With my limited knowledge of the region, I had confused it with Ellis Island. I only understood years later when I took the (free) ferry to watch the Staten Island Yankees and set foot on the island for the first time.

That's how the old fortress, Suomenlinna, appeared to me at first glance. I thought we would be visiting a massive UNESCO defensive structure. Spanning six islands, it had been constructed while part of Sweden nearly three hundred years ago. However, we also found museums, restaurants, a zoo, and surprisingly, homes. Around eight hundred residents reside there. The site, about fifteen minutes off the coast of Helsinki, welcomed us on our first Scandinavian expenditure like Ellis Island. I had chosen the island for a first day trip since it seemed a short, easy trip; a way to stretch our legs while still seeing something historic.

Getting there had been rough, as it tends to be those first few hours after a red-eye with kids. The Helsinki airport is roughly half an hour outside town but thanks to my research before the guidebook became lost forever, I knew a cab would be the cheapest option—and of course the direct service was a boon to our sleep-deprived selves.

Throughout our trip, we engaged with some of the nicest hotel staff and Airbnb hosts we'd ever met. In Helsinki, though only one room was available, the staff let us check in early to a room with a beautiful view of the Gulf of

Finland from the West Harbor. AJ and I laid back on the queen bed in our tiny room with kids bouncing all over before that restless energy drove us to get them outside. That's the contradiction in kids—exhausted, yet full of energy when someplace new.

With no firm plans but plenty of time that first day, we ambled the mile to the main harbor. I had figured we could catch a ferry to an island. Sienna quickly dozed off in her carrier.

The bustling excitement of the city met us as we approached the harbor. The lush parks bled into the city center, and the water reflected the cloudless sky. Finnish food abounded; fresh fish on ice, meat pies, pea soup, and some savory-looking cinnamon rolls with a spicy-sweet smell that tickled our noses. My kids quickly discovered the creperie, and I found the fruit stands. We purchased fresh berries and spinach feta and banana/Nutella crepes.

To save time, I bought our ferry tickets to Suomenlinna while AJ waited for the hot crepes. I stood on the dock, baby on my back and clinging to the hands of my three other children, literally one step away from the boat.

"Last call!" the ticket taker shouted, looking directly at me.

Time slowed, but the perfection of crepes took one minute too long. The ticket taker placed her second foot aboard. Seconds later, we watched them drift away as AJ came running up the dock.

"Why is the boat leaving?" Lucas asked sadly. Missing our first ferry of the trip, not a big deal yet since another would come in thirty minutes, we instead enjoyed our picnic dinner on the waterfront, watching the locals mix with the tourists. People of all types (well, blonde good-looking Scandinavians of all ages) milled around. A wall of tall, stoic evergreens stood guard, watching as cruise ship passengers were replaced by local businesspeople as the afternoon moved on.

When we did join the ferry, we were happy, full, and my kids ready to amuse the other guests. They danced around the boat, smiling for the camera. Lucas excitedly waved to the sailboats—and anyone else with a hand, wing, or flipper.

I felt a slight breeze permeating down from the deep blue sky. It was just the ambience to put my kids at ease and lull them into a peaceful, easy ride. And like the Staten Island Ferry, the ride gave us a landscape view of the city. We passed the large, colorful government buildings that sat behind the market—yellow, pale blue, mint green, orange, and red, all humbled by the large white church overlooking from the hilltop. I was shocked at its grace and how the most foreign place my baby had ever seen could feel like home, simply because of who I was with.

"God bless you," people came up to us to say in Finnish. Or perhaps, "you idiots." The language barrier can be challenging sometimes. We noticed more than one group counting our children on their fingers, and others asked to take our photo.

Released into their Eden at Suomenlinna after an eight-hour flight, the kids finally ran to their heart's content. Foreign playgrounds are awesome and a must-do on trips. In addition to the fresh air they'd get back home, the kids also meet local kids who speak another language. It's entertaining to see what contraptions the crazy foreigners devise, too. My kids crashed loose in a fraught playground. Ella and Sienna went high on a double-seated swing before Ella catapulted herself across cement. Brooklyn nearly flung herself off a rocking lion spring rider while Lucas climbed on former cannons shouting, "Pew pew!" After an hour, we returned for an early bedtime.

Our second hotel room was now ready, nowhere near the first. AJ took two while I settled in with Sienna and Ella. About fifteen minutes later, I heard a knock at the door. Lucas, quite attached to Mommy at that age, came for the night. Big sister Ella diligently accepted the trade. Thankfully he hadn't bitten her that day.

Our day started off similar to how the previous one had ended—full of missed connections and poorly managed time. Yet, with a positive attitude, those misses brought spontaneity and made the day all the more enjoyable. First was the missing of the bleep-bleep of my cell phone alarm. My inner clock screamed middle-of-the-night when it was in fact half past nine.

LESSON LEARNED

Timing can be a science with small children. I'd love to say, yes, get to places as early as possible, but arriving too early can negatively impact kids' moods or cause boredom. We pre-board airplanes but twiddle our thumbs (or suck it in the case of the baby) while everyone else gets on. Therefore, we generally aim to leave an extra thirty minutes early. That way, when the kids have gone to the bathroom and had their snack, loaded on coats and shoes, we still arrive with time to spare.

Additionally, if there is something important—a marathon, a crucial boat or flight to catch—we use multiple alarms. The clock, my phone, a wake-up call, AJ's phone. I do also recognize that the first day is the hardest, so there's nothing essential that can't be made up later. That's why, on this specific day, we had only used one alarm. If we missed it, we'd adjust our day.

"We're late!" I yelled into the hotel phone to AJ in a room at the other side of the hotel. I threw on my clothes, then Sienna's, while I put my son on the toilet. The girls arrived dressed with their dad (thank goodness I'm so absurd about laying everything out the night before), then let AJ dress Lucas while I brushed my teeth. I felt for our passports and closed our laptop into the safe. I strapped Sienna onto my back, and AJ loaded the diaper bag onto his. He grabbed Lucas's hand and we ran out the hotel door in an astonishing twenty minutes, high-fiving in the elevator, for the ferry to Tallinn, Estonia.

Though I generally prefer avoiding big excursions on our first day, this timing would allow AJ to "rest" his legs the next day before the marathon.

Thanks to the vicinity, affordable Euro, cheap tickets, and kids under-seven sailing free, Tallinn is an easy add-on.

AJ counted our children—twice to be sure we didn't pull a Home Alone—and waited for an extra-large cab for the short trip to the ferry while I grabbed as much food as humanly possible. We had paid the bed-and-breakfast rate, so I wanted that buffet. It's also really hard for me to change the routine.

At the terminal, I jumped out of the cab and rushed to the ticket office with kids on my heels. "Two adult tickets, one child, and three under sevens please," I gasped.

"What time?" the woman behind the counter asked.

"Ten-thirty," I responded.

"I'm sorry, but we're no longer selling tickets," she stated.

"Please," I begged. "We missed our alarm but need to get on that ship. Is there anything you can do?" I sounded like a mad woman, and she seemed to feel genuinely bad. She leaned over and spoke to her counterpart at the next kiosk.

"We no longer sell tickets after ten." I looked at the clock; it was five past. "There is a ferry at one-thirty. Would you like a ticket for that?"

Then I went through the five stages of grief, starting with denial. "No, absolutely not."

Anger. "You are terrible. Do you really think I can wander around with them for three hours?"

Bargaining. "Which kid can I offer you in exchange for making this ferry?" I felt depressed that I had ruined everything as I walked wistfully away from the women.

Time for acceptance as the aroma emanating from the bench enticed me. We weren't on the ferry or sitting in the cushioned lounge chairs that overlooked the water. We were not where we hoped to be, we were not even at a table, but my kids were happy. We enjoyed our scrumptious breakfast seated on a hard-backed bench—one that is uncomfortable no matter how you sit—in the sparse lobby, eating from the to-go boxes I received from the hotel maître de. Ella danced around, and Brooklyn sang about Scandinavia. That extra hour of sleep had helped them tremendously. As I stuffed my face with a flaky chocolate croissant, AJ and I planned our day.

AJ and I agreed to find an activity for the next few hours and get a room on the next ferry. Since the sailing coincided with naptime, whoever was tired (ahem, me) could rest. The original itinerary had us trolleying around the next day, so I hoped it would be a good way to pass time. Lucas gazed wide-eyed at the prospect of riding the big green and yellow trolley. Simple pleasures.

Helsinki offers a reasonably-priced twenty-four-hour public transportation pass. Kids six-and-under are free. It may seem odd to get one two hours before leaving the country, but we could also use it the next morning. Plus, I really didn't want to calculate how many times we'd hop on and off just to save a dollar or two. We hadn't brought the stroller for Tallinn, so Sienna rode on my back.

Helsinki is the most northern city to host a summer Olympic Games, so we stopped at their stadium on a similar crisp, cool August day. The stadium was built in the mid-1930s for the 1940 Summer Olympics. Those were, of course, cancelled during World War II. There weren't too many countries who could have attended, and Finland wasn't exactly a prime location, just across the sea from all of the fighting and misery. There had been an Olympics in 1948 but, due to a difficult economic climate and rationings, they were little known and usually a sidebar.

By 1952, the world was booming again, and Helsinki hosted the Summer Games. The new world order showed with thirteen new nations making their Olympic debut—the Soviet Union, the People's Republic of China, Indonesia, Israel, Thailand, and Saarland. A third of them are no longer in existence, just sixty odd years later. In addition, this was the only Games for Saar (East Germany) and China's only until 1984. Japan and Germany were even allowed, and the Soviet Union hadn't yet started boycotting. In total, a record sixty-nine countries participated, ten more than the Games before, and nearly 5,000 athletes. The athletes also broke the greatest number of world records until 2008. They were the first big-time games.

My parents had shared that the stadium was under construction when they visited so I was surprised, but not really, to see it still closed more than two years later. It was like they were building the Taj Mahal or, in my community, redoing a little-used one-lane bridge. Though Lucas may disagree, I guess three years isn't that long in the scheme of things. As it was, we could see the rings.

I noticed a statue of Paavo Nurmi. "Wow! Look at that! Go stand in front of Paavo!" I urged AJ excitedly.

My husband, the runner who watches documentaries on the Barkley Marathons for fun, hadn't heard of him. I was stunned. I wouldn't have been more surprised if he shared that we had a fifth child.

"You don't know the Flying Finn? He's the founder of middle and long-distance running. I can't remember all of it, but he influenced Roger Bannister and the American and Australian he raced against, along with those other runner guys in the books we read." He looked at me curiously. Why had I let him convince me to read so many running books? Am I really that big of a nerd? I don't even really care for running.

I'm terrible with names, but of course AJ knew about the race I was referring to and those other men. Paavo's training methods and style influenced the runners in every one of those books I mentioned, Wes Santee (the American), John Landy (the Australian), Bart Yasso. It could be said that Paavo was the best runner ever. He dominated distance running in his time, setting twenty-two official world records, winning nine gold medals and three silver ones in twelve events. At his peak, he ran undefeated for 121 races at 800 meters and up. He was unbeaten in his career in cross country events and the 10,000 meters. He introduced pacing and is credited with making running a major international sport. His work laid the groundwork for AJ's major life goal.

How could my husband not know him? Was my whole marriage a lie?

We then walked to their seemingly amazing amusement park, Linnanmaki. Even the trolley on their web site bounced up and down and blew colorful bubbles, and rays of light beamed around the cartoon sun. Though the larger and more centralized Tivoli Gardens in Copenhagen was a must visit, this could serve as a quick forty-five-minute stop.

Like everything in Finland, the park offered an additional perk. Kids could go on multiple rides for free—the pirate ship, motorcycle ride, carousel, and Ferris wheel, among others. Like, totally free. A couple of weeks earlier, I had reviewed the times tables and tentatively penciled it in for Friday afternoon. My kids would love it.

As we passed under the central train lines and eased up the elevation to the remote part of Helsinki on a weekday morning, a sinking feeling crept in my stomach. The park appeared, but the rides loomed silent. The gates were locked. School had started and the park wasn't open on a Thursday.

Suddenly, all of my planning did not seem to be enough. I had already made three silly mistakes. I felt like an idiot. I was trying to do too much. Looking back, most add-ons seem easy. You feel you can fit in one more thing until it topples over like the Jenga blocks when the baby joins the game.

As I berated myself, I noticed boulders lining the path and climbed to the top of the largest. Brooklyn joined, then Ella. AJ climbed further down with the littler ones. On top of Helsinki, the air was clear, and we could see the sea.

Things happen. Planning a trip from 4,300 miles away is nearly impossible to get exactly right. It didn't matter that the Olympic Stadium was closed; AJ learned something huge about running history, his biggest passion. (Well, aside from his family!) Our side-trip to Linnanmaki may have wasted hours on our only day in Helsinki, but it was tolerable as a filler.

"We should head out," I called to AJ as a trolley approached. On that trolley, we somehow overlooked our transfer (mistake four) and wasted another thirty minutes before barely missing yet another. We finally boarded our last trolley less than an hour before our 1:30 ferry departure. We were in nearly the same predicament as before.

As we settled in for that last short ride, we chatted with a young blonde man with a baby that Sienna immediately befriended. Finland is known as the happiest country on earth, largely in part to the fantastic benefits endowed to new parents. Each newborn receives a special box containing baby clothes and other necessities like bedding, diapers, books, etc., and a mattress. The box can then be used as a bassinet for the newborn baby. Mothers earn over 100 paid working days and fathers get half of that. They also receive another twenty-six weeks of paid leave to be split between both parents.

"All public buses and trams are free for anyone with a pram," the man shared. That explained all of the strollers around town. Finland is also the only developed country where fathers, like the one we met, spend more time with their children than mothers. I am blessed to raise my kids with a hands-on husband, but that stat? Though we both worked full-time before that trip, I probably saw my kids two hours more a day since I had a home office.

As I finally started to relax, a small group of transit officers jumped on the trolley, half a dozen stops from the cruise terminal. It looked like our bad luck was returning.

"They're searching for people without tickets," our dad friend shared.

A man in our cabin did not have one. Of course.

I nervously checked the time as the trolley idled. When we finally arrived at the ferry terminal, I ran ahead to get the tickets. The attendant escorted us onboard as the doors sealed behind us. We finally got lucky. That's the key. Make whatever situation you're in the best it can be. Then you will always feel blessed.

I splurged for the €30 cabin. That was the best, and probably only, money I've spent for a nap. Ella the champion napper, Sienna, and I dozed off while the others explored. When we reached land, I had to shake my sleeping beauties awake for the next phase in the journey.

I had three goals in our short three-and-a-half hours in Tallinn: see the Old Town, climb something tall, and get a good, low-priced meal. Old Town led the charge, an authentic walled, medieval city. Estonia also boasted being the most affordable of our destinations.

I did know it would be a long walk; most estimates showed Old Town at least half a mile from the D-Terminal. Adding to that was unexpected terminal construction that spit us out in some alley. This, along with my poor recollections from the missing map of the lost guidebook, meant we set ourselves up to walk well over a mile to get there. That's half an hour in kid time.

"We should have grabbed one of those," I said to AJ after we passed a couple of pedi-cabs driven by young, strong men and women.

"What?" he said incredulously. "I didn't know you'd do that." As if I was a glutton for punishment. I was exhausted.

"Too late now," I said. "Plus, we're probably almost there." We slogged on, Sienna riding bareback while the others pushed on. Brooklyn and Ella are great walkers, making the trek to and from school every day. Lucas just loved holding my hand.

Outside of the town wall, I approached someone for directions. "Do you speak English? Can you help us?"

The woman became visibly excited. It didn't seem like every day that she got to speak to a crazy American with a gaggle of kids. "I'm from Germany," she said proudly. "I just moved here six months ago. It's much cheaper here."

I got straight to the point. "How do we get in?" I asked pointing at the nearly two-story wall facing us. Nearly two kilometers of the original city wall and twenty tower walls still stand. The city's appeal is one of Europe's best-preserved fortifications from the medieval ages. Climbing over didn't seem to be the solution. It had been ages since AJ had hoisted me over a wall.

"It's pretty far," the woman said, pointing off into the distance. A streetcar whizzed by. "You should take that; it's about three stops to Central Station. It really is far away." I wasn't surprised since I had known it was a walk, but we were already tired. The woman paused before continuing, "Or you can go through this alley with us and walk through the rear. It's just not as lovely."

"Right here?" Pretty enough for me. We walked together through a parking lot, then a small former guard sentry. We were inside the wall but not near the sites. She then pointed up a steep hill.

"Take this to St. Olav's Church. To the left is Pikk Street. That's our Fifth Avenue." She seemed quite proud of this city of just over 425,000 people. I thanked her, and we headed up the cobblestone alleyway, past the cute old stone storefronts toward the church.

Built in 1267 and named for King Olaf II of Norway, the Gothic church originally served Scandinavian merchants. Upon completion and for seventy-five years in the sixteenth century, the church topped the world. No matter that the 159-meter spire served as a lightning rod and burned down multiple times due to its outrageous height. Now it stands a mere 124-meters. Time to climb.

After walking around the church interior, I realized I should take Sienna to the toilet. Darn potty-training. I was directed outside to an auxiliary church building. My daughter suspiciously eyed the line of public toilets. Then, up by the window, I spotted a small baby potty. Her face lit up when I placed it on the floor for her. I could not believe our luck.

In the United States, parents potty train their children later and later. I remember an older coworker stressing about training her three-year-old toddler before starting preschool. In 1947, sixty percent of kids were trained by 18 months. By 2003, the average age increased to 36.8 months, according to the literature review in the Jornel de Pediatria. My colleague was not alone.

Since we used cloth diapers, it thrilled me to end the excess laundry before my daughter's second birthday. That cut our laundry to every other day. However, after changing our laundry routine, I learned that I had only two pairs of socks. With that discovery, I succumbed to buying more at my next grocery shop. Yes, Safeway sells white socks.

I convinced AJ to invest in cloth diapers when we lived in New York City. With a non-working wife and six figures of student loans, he liked the saving money aspect. I did it almost entirely for the environment. Disposable diapers are the third largest consumer item in landfills. That's a lot of plastic!

My views put me closer in alignment to the European philosophy. It's not Kenya, where parents employ the elimination method and truly start training at four months or China, where the kids wear split pants, but it is significantly earlier than back home. In Finland and other Scandinavian countries, training starts in infancy, with babies fully trained by two.

Along with asking if we wanted a baby crib (um, yeah), when reserving our room on the overnight ferry, the online form asked if we needed a baby pot. What sounded like some legalized drugs was, in fact, her own little chamber pot. With a more homogenous population, people do it at the same time and in the same way. These Scandinavians really cater to young parents, making it easy to have children.

When we returned, the girls climbed the tight, winding stone tower staircase— Brooklyn racing ahead and Ella plodding along before me. Sienna rode on my back like a miniature jockey. AJ declined to porter an additional thirty pounds up the 237 steps and instead followed slowly, holding Lucas's little hand.

The views at the top were worth a million bucks. Old Town and Toompea Hill hypnotized us, the warm breeze washing over us as we stared across the water and the port area. I slowly walked around the narrow edge with my daughters. I felt safe behind the quite-high railings. AJ swayed side-to-side, paralyzed from his fear of heights, trying not to look out at the drop.

Once safely back on the ground, we hiked up to reach the true top of the city. We passed through the gray stone Long Leg Gate tower on Pikk Jalg, passing artisans selling their paintings and old buildings as we cleared the nave of the city. At the precipice of Tallinn, we took in another view of the sea. Seven hundred years ago, soldiers stood there watching invaders coming from all areas of the Baltic. I prepped for my own future battles about lollipops or who would get to hold my hand on the walk down.

With its strategic location in the Baltic Sea between the East and the West, Estonia lobbed like a ping pong ball between Denmark, Germany, Russia, Sweden, and Poland. The citizens finally freed themselves from Russia in 1918 for just a couple of decades before World War II. After regaining independence again in 1991, they joined the European Union. Only time will tell if freedom will reign or be another short-lived peace.

From above, the copper-red pitched roofs rendered the buildings inside the wall nearly identical. We wandered that labyrinth of streets looking for dinner. Suddenly, the buildings opened up and we entered the picturesque Town Hall Square. The bright yellow, pink, and blue buildings with intricate white sculptures displayed their individuality. We had found the action—unfortunately quite late in the day. We paused for a moment to appreciate it and breathe in the aroma of roasting nuts. Then, after a day of searching for a cheap, delicious meal, we ordered pizza from a hole-in-the-wall joint.

While AJ waited, I sat outside within the confines of a stone alleyway reminiscent of the Middle Ages, and Lucas loudly slurped a pineapple milkshake. I heard a woman snicker.

"Mine too," she said stiltedly and pointed down at the small child in her lap.

"How old?" I asked.

She froze. "My English not so good." I figured that was the end our conversation, but she clearly wanted to continue. "Where are you from?" she asked.

I struggle with this question while abroad. When I say, 'the United States,' I sometimes hear, 'no kidding.' Usually, I say my state or nearest city. Except when I lived in Connecticut. This time, I held my breath and said, "The United States."

She could not believe it. A big "oooh!" escaped her lips and her face lit up. "You're from USA? How did you get here?" She stared at my children, even though I only had two at the moment. (The kids have learned that divide and conquer is the best way to get attention so those who didn't care for pineapple shake were inside begging their dad for something else.)

"We flew to Helsinki," I explained. "Then we took the ferry here." The calm, quiet woman I passed when I sat down suddenly had the energy of a Golden Retriever puppy.

"Do you have family here?" There had to be a reason.

"No, just visiting." I smiled. She couldn't quite grasp that I would fly a quarter of the way around the world to come to this small city. She explained that she hadn't really left Tallinn, much less Estonia. The woman was beyond thrilled to practice her English with a native speaker.

She shared that the pizza was good. "You can pick the toppings," she added solemnly. I hoped we had stumbled on a local hidden gem of pizza, but that comment gave me pause.

AJ rushed out the door with our hot pizza, so I gave a quick goodbye. We had forty-five minutes, and so for the third time that day, we ran for the ferry. We jogged out Viru Gate, part of the original wall of Tallinn city, built in the fourteenth century. Parts of the wall had been bulldozed, but the towers were preserved. It was a beautiful site to pass through, as if entering a fairytale. Exiting it gave a different experience, like the end of a movie where the lights come on and you're back in a crowded theater with popcorn on the floor after a unique experience.

We did not have enough time to walk on the actual wall in Tallinn, and for that I was secretly relieved. The railing looked frightfully low. I would have been weak-kneed wrangling my kids the entire walk, fearful that they would walk too close to the edge.

In life, I clearly have some irrational fears. I like to think it's normal, like how people are scared of swimming in the ocean since there are sharks when in reality, less than ten people die each year. Since I keep these concerns to myself, I don't know if they're normal. For instance, I have this fear that if I have to pee and there's a fire in my house, I will go in my pants. I get the peeing part since I birthed four kids, but still, not rational. There is also a black snake that frequents my office window. (Well, I saw him slink across the windowsill one time.) I'm concerned that one day, I will accidentally squish him when I cut across my backyard to pick up my kids from school.

I don't really fear snakes; I just don't want to be surprised by one. When I first arrived to study in Australia, I had done a short hiking orientation in the beautiful mountains of Binna Burra. The first morning, I woke before sunrise since it seemed like sunset back home and decided to wander around the bush. Alone. I held little fear because, in the words of my guide, "Ninety-nine percent of snakes are scared of humans here." Then I encountered the one percent.

I was in my oblivious world, hiking alone in a new country, squealing inside as I spotted a couple of miniature kangaroos (or as my brother would say, pademelons), when I nearly stepped on a three-foot-long snake. In Australia. Dangerous Australia. (Of course, three-foot-long is not really that big for a snake. The next day we discovered a three-METER one living under someone's cabin. My own cabin merely housed a large lizard.)

I stopped quickly and hyperventilated like AJ must have in Costa Rica when we saw the peccaries. I waited for the snake to move, but when he didn't, I hightailed it off the trail and sprinted back to the cabin. On the way, I passed the burrow of a funnel web spider, the world's most venomous. The night before, our nature guide pointed to the silk trip-lines that radiated from the entrance. The story went, if I had been bitten and ran back to the cabin, I would be dead before I arrived back. Which means I wouldn't have made it back to the cabin at all. That was something to fear!

"Just a python," the guide assured me when I returned. I was breathless and terrified. "He was probably waiting for prey to strangle." The guide went on, "Pythons hold little venom, especially one that size. He wasn't dangerous." Not dangerous? Come on now. I wasn't an idiot.

We left the bustling Old Town behind. I hustled along, with Sienna on my back and a pizza on my front, AJ carrying Lucas, and the girls keeping pace. We ran down the long road and turned at the entrance from earlier.

The girls were champions. Brooklyn is a little running star at school with her thin strong legs, but Ella also did her part. At the end, she tripped on the escalator but soldiered through with the promise of a band-aid on her red (but not bleeding) knee. We made it again, just barely in time for the second time that day.

With no open rooms, we wandered the ferry like vagrants, relaxing where we could find space. That was not really too hard, considering the ship had a large mall, a giant play area, and a decent food court. I disagreed with the tastes of my Estonian friend. Although AJ claimed it was the best margarita pizza he'd ever eaten (really?), I thought it too doughy or cheesy or maybe just plain bad. I hadn't found a good meal in Estonia but found an inexpensive open-faced smoked salmon and avocado sandwich on the boat that exceeded my expectations.

I settled into a cushioned portal window of the boat's play area. Feet up, I watched as my little two rode push cars, Ella colored, and Brooklyn climbed around like a monkey. After a bit, Brooklyn and Lucas joined AJ at the food court Burger King.

A character who looked suspiciously like Minnie Mouse came to make balloon creations. With a flower balloon in hand, Ella proudly went to flaunt it to the others.

As soon as Brooklyn saw that (and slurped up the last bite of fake ice cream), she asked if she and Lucas could get their own. We watched the interaction in real-time through the cruise ship's video monitor. Example 991 on how the Finns cater to parents. Brooklyn returned with two balloon creatures for herself.

"How did you get two?" I probed.

"I asked."

"But why? Now your sister will want two." I could see troubling brewing with her impulsive sister. There would be tantrums in Tallinn.

A memory from freshman English class has stuck with me—when I was still new to the high school and didn't know many people. Thankfully I did have one friend in that class, so we joined forces for a speech on the poem of our choice. I've long forgotten the name of the poem, but it was on creating wine or vineyards. I do remember it was a good poem.

My partner and I developed a strong half-hour presentation. Before our turn, we had a little chat. "I know you've seen this, but (we'll call him Kevin) always has his hand up in class," I stated. Kevin had broken his arm and kept his bright cast elevated at all times. The neon cast drew the eye, and he looked as though he was constantly raising his hand with a question.

"Of course, I have," she responded. He was called on during literally every other presentation. He would say the same thing. "I'm not raising my hand," in confused indignation every single time. He never had a funny or witty response; he just honestly could not figure out why he was called on. My friend and I found his monotone response much funnier than it probably actually was and would giggle uncontrollably. We were fourteen.

"Whatever you do," I commanded her, "do not call on Kevin. He is not asking a question. He never asks them, and we both know this."

"Yeah, yeah," she replied. She wasn't an idiot.

"I'm serious. I don't think I'll be able to not laugh if you do." She promised she wouldn't.

We planned to share a two-minute clip from the movie, *A Walk in the Clouds*, to demonstrate our premise. (Wineries? Grape crushing? California?) The movie starred a *gorgeous* Keanu Reeves and an equally attractive Napa Valley landscape. Before showing the video, we had submitted the cassette for teacher approval. Being the 90's, I had fast-forwarded to our scene for his review.

The day of the presentation, we inserted the video and gave the first half of our presentation. Then, I directed the class to the TV. It was not the grape crushing scene. Keanu and the actress were in bed. My partner and I exchanged mortified glances. I frantically blocked the television and tried to fast-forward/rewind to the right spot while she fielded questions. Except that nobody had questions.

Guess who she called on.

She couldn't help it the same way my five-year-old couldn't help her outbursts. Like my friend had to call on Kevin when she was under pressure, my daughter's urges get the best of her. Nearly every time. When Brooklyn came back with two balloon animals, Ella immediately left the table on her way back to the playroom. Although Brooklyn could walk alone for two minutes on an enclosed boat, this one did not get that same privilege. I called after her to stop but, at that point, she was in her own world and on the verge of a meltdown. I rushed to catch her.

"But Brookie has two!" Ella screamed at the top of her lungs when I tried to stop her. The corners of my mouth turned up, and I almost laughed at the absurdity. I couldn't help it but stopped as I noticed the faces of strangers looking our way. Ella's face had turned as red as Lucas's fire trucks and the wails sounded just the same.

A man approached as my daughter laid prone on the floor. "We've all been through this," he comforted. That's nice to hear but doesn't help when a child is running around shrieking, about to lose her cool. I knew that with this kid, if I didn't stop this quickly, it could turn into an hour-long affair. She excelled at ignoring distractions. When she hit the full throes of a meltdown, she would alternate between kicking and screaming and becoming unresponsive and inconsolable.

I caught her quick this time. I hugged and comforted before she completely lost her cool. This time she would calm herself (with a second balloon, I'm not proud to admit) and we would resolve it. Sometimes it takes an hour; thankfully, this one was only a few minutes.

This is the story of my daughter's life—constantly comparing herself and wanting what her sister has. As the kid-sister of a super athlete, I get it. My own sister considers herself a mini-celebrity back home, second only to Derek Jeter (whom my dad refereed). Geno Auriemma from UConn's women's basketball program came to my house for goodness sake. I'm just happy that I can teach them (whether in my own home or abroad) how to share, how to get along with others, and that sometimes things aren't equal. With four kids, some days one may see another as a competitor—for time, for resources, for recognition. My hopes are that, more often, they see that there is always a friend.

Chapter Twelve

STROLLERS AND FINNISH SAUNAS

"**E**LSA! ELSA! WAKE up!" Lucas, acting the part of Princess Anna, cried as he shook Brooklyn's shoulder. "Come play," he said.

Ella had been slotted for that role in our home video of Frozen, but an ill-timed tantrum brought in the gleeful understudy. From games to sleeping arrangements, being included is Lucas's only requirement. For the first three years of life, he was easy-going—the one who eats what he's given, plays with whatever toy is in front of him, watches whatever his sisters have selected. His sisters could carry him around or dress him up. Therefore, when filming their version of *Frozen*, Lucas serves the role of Everyman—Anna in the first scene, Kristoff, Hans, Olaf, even Marshmallow the Ice Monster.

My parents reiterate that they have no favorites. Not me. Lucas is my favorite child. Not only is he sweet and thoughtful with a fun personality, he's also a momma's boy. Baby sister, Sienna, also earns that honor. How could she not with her delicious baby thighs, chirpy voice, and inherited blast of curls?

Yes, they're both my favorites, along my studious and hardworking Brooklyn—the kid who taught me about love—and my fierce, thoughtful, and sleep-happy Ella.

I credit one of my best local friends with this philosophy. "Growing up, we each believed we were Dad's favorite," she shared about her deceased father. "I know, for a fact, he liked me best. And I guarantee my sister and brothers think the same thing."

Every person deserves to be the center of someone's universe, someone's favorite in the world. I'm raising my kids to think I love them more than any other person in the world. I want them to feel that unconditional love.

Alone among three girls, at times, Lucas may feel overlooked, a seed hidden within the family apple. It's hard being one of four, I'm sure. Finding your place and getting individual time with Mommy and Daddy. He looks to his sisters to lead, doesn't cry out for attention as much the other middle child, and is not the baby. When he gets solo time with one of us, he takes it in. We started a new tradition of allocating ten minutes a night where he chooses the activity. For the most part, it's trucks—of course. Or books about trucks. He's finding his place, making his way to the surface like that apple seed does before exploding into a tree.

Lucas hopped right on the stroller the next morning opposite his baby sister to avoid a big sister stealing his seat on our way to the outdoor museum, Seurasaari. After two stress and excitement-filled days, we looked forward to some relaxed exhilaration in Helsinki. The girls gamely walked along, examining the graffiti under the bridges and finding impromptu balance beams to traverse. We used our transportation passes to catch a local bus after walking about a kilometer or so along one of their 1,200 kilometers of bike paths. That's 750 miles—the distance from Washington, D.C. to Orlando, Florida, or less than four months of running to AJ.

The Finns embrace a 500-year-old national concept called Sisu, or inner strength. This roughly translates to grit, fortitude, or perseverance. Finns are known as the happiest people on earth, partially since they derive pleasure from uncomfortable things like jumping into holes in frozen lakes and spending time outdoors every day. As with the other Nordic countries, their babies nap outside every day, even—especially—in cold weather. In AJ's home state south of the Mason Dixon Line, where I now reside, I was considered 'very hardy' for walking my kids to school every day, even when below freezing or, gasp, in the teens.

The bus took us through parkland and along the picturesque river to Seurasaari. The island became a park in 1890 and an open-air museum in 1909. It contains eighty-seven mainly wooden buildings, relocated from all over Finland. The island itself contains a beautiful, peaceful dense forest and picturesque walking trails. The kids cost nothing. Due to the trolley and ferry tours the day before, I thought it would be relaxing to enjoy the mild weather and clear blue skies in a park atmosphere. It turns out that my (lack of) preparation paid off.

I'd only seen one museum like this—a much more modest version near my brother's Michigan home. I had used that, with about a dozen buildings spread over a dozen acres, as the frame of reference for AJ. Apparently, he had quite enjoyed that little excursion. Each Scandinavian country has some different variation of this. Sweden's Skansen (which we planned to visit in a few days) dwarves Seurasaari in scope. Although similarly sized (sixty-four vs. seventy-five acres), Skansen boasts the world's oldest open-air museum and includes nearly twice as many old buildings. It also includes a zoo as well with moose, reindeer, and other native Nordic animals. Dense with attractions, it felt like an amusement park. AJ preferred the peaceful and remote feeling of Seurasaari. We tasted Finnish history and their countryside as the kids ran around.

Baby Sienna squawked with excitement at the ducks, geese, and swans hanging out by the surprisingly busy ice cream stand. To a toddling nineteen-month-old, it was a small slice of heaven to be free. At the large southern manor, Brooklyn and Ella played their first game of croquet. They climbed on sawhorses for a mock race over obstacles and around the massive, lush lawn. Lucas tried to join in but couldn't quite jump over the foot-high obstacles and instead ran around like footloose three-year-old.

As we discussed the route back to Helsinki, I spotted a sign with a picture of a boat. I remembered some kind of ferry, but two days from my guidebook, those memories were fading fast. Google maps had suggested the bus. The makeshift sign seemed to show the ferry leaving on the half hour—and it was about ten minutes past. We walked to the small harbor by the 'bathing house.' I was bummed about missing that, but after learning it was a nudist beach, that was probably for the best.

"Do you know if a ferry comes here?" I asked a man on a bike. He didn't but pointed to a café at the top of a hill, probably a quarter-mile away.

"You can ask there," he said. I channeled my former athlete, running the stairs like I was doing a stadium drill.

At the top, out of breath and feeling my age, I gasped to the clerk, "Is there a ferry?" She looked up from scooping an ice cream cone to look at me oddly. Her English was terrible and my Finnish nonexistent. Fingers crossed, I retraced my steps, much slower this time and holding the railing on my way back to the dock. A moment later, a small boat appeared on the horizon.

Ella sat on the boat deck with me, the wind flowing through her hair as she chattered about in her incomprehensible logic. The others stayed below, peering out the port windows and eating goldfish crackers. The boat ride took us directly to the harbor. We floated along the waterfront, past our hotel, the massive cruise ships at the ferry terminal, and a plethora of restaurants overlooking the coast. We saw workers hoisting tents and makeshift barriers to corral the runners as we passed the start point of tomorrow's marathon. It was awesome and unexpected—luck of our making was shining on us. Ever-Hungry was stirring and didn't realize I had a trick up my sleeve.

On the two-week basketball tournament years earlier, my dad and I had gone to a steakhouse on the last night with my sister's team. Before you continue, please remember that a) we were not well-off, b) my dad was cheap, c) we don't like waste.

My dad boxed up half of his T-bone for the next day at Hershey Park in Pennsylvania. Then, when my sister's skinny teammates saw this, they offered up their leftovers too. This was the summer I gave up red meat for good.

At Hershey Park, I begged for countless treats, starving the way only a kid can. Each time my dad would pull a steak out of his pocket to my indignant refusal. Upon seeing each ice cream or pizza stand, the cycle would repeat, and he'd show me pockets stuffed with cow. Over the next two days in Helsinki, I did the same for Ever-Hungry husband with his self-proclaimed 'best pizza ever.' I'd pull the leftover pizza out like a magician. We had been married for ten years—I could see his hunger signs a mile away.

While Ever-Hungry ate the pizza, the rest of us devoured crepes on the patio of the Allas Sea Pools. Nutella melted onto Brooklyn's fingers as she picked apart the crepe while smidges of chocolate donned the corner of Lucas's lips. The weather was perfect, the temperature in the mid-eighties and the sky bluer than that whale we missed in the Azores.

The Allas Sea Pools sit in the heart of the city, on the harbor overlooking the Market Square, across from the main port and the important city buildings. It contains a lap pool, a large toddler pool, and a sea pool, in addition to the multiple saunas. It also had showers to wash the kids like farm animals, helping us cut out another bath time. With four kids, that's always a perk.

Imagine that you are holding a pig. A small one, like Babe or Wilbur when he met Charlotte, one you can hold in your arms or in a blanket. He is skinny for a pig, but still has chubby, edible rolls and soft, smooth cherub skin, not scratchy like a peccary. Though he's squirmy, he's also pretty stinking cute. A little ham. Now imagine he's greased up and slippery, trapped in a pen of water. You pour bubbles on his head, and he squeals. The creature wriggles since he doesn't want to be held, twisting to get away, his legs kicking back-and-forth fruitlessly like a dog over a swimming pool. That is bath time with my son.

In the mornings, he'll need to get dressed. Put a shirt on the wiggly boar, underwear, some pants, socks, and shoes. Perhaps a coat, mittens, and a hat. Some mornings, he doesn't want to get dressed. On those days, the only rule is that each item must go on one more time than it comes off. To fix that, we change the routine. For now, if he gets himself dressed, he gets to pick out breakfast. We try to invest in positive parenting, aiming to teach them what they can do themselves. The alternative is too much like crisp bacon—hard.

Utopia emerged behind the strollers and Finnish saunas. The older three waded into the toddler pool while Sienna snoozed on me. Finnish mothers nursed their babies poolside while their other children napped on giant beanbags speckling the landscape. I couldn't remember the last time I had experienced days like the past three. I could not imagine a more pleasant place to be then right there at that moment.

When Sienna awoke, we spent the next couple hours hopping between the two pools and the gender-separated saunas. I embraced my inner Sisu and convinced Brooklyn to jump in the sea water one with me. We were shocked by the 12C (54F) water. Growing up in Michigan and swimming in our name-sake lake in May and June, I thought I was prepared. Even so, it chilled me. I convinced Ella and Lucas to jump (or climb) in. Since they are so trusting, I felt just a little evil, but it's part of their heritage, after all.

"Ulos! Ulos!" shouted the lifeguard, waving his arms as he spoke in fast Finnish. "Pissaa uima-altaasa." We stared at him like idiots though it was pretty obvious what he wanted, even before he switched to English. Out of the pool. There had been an accident, and the pool would be closed for the next three hours. I cursed the Finns and their early potty training. I grabbed Sienna and Brooklyn for a trip to relieve our stress in the sauna. That ended our pool experience.

The Finns love their saunas. Though there are only five million residents, there are three million saunas. They relax in saunas with their families and friends. Back home it's a luxury, but the sauna exists as an intricacy of daily life for the Finns. As a person who is just a little too interested in birthing stories, I enjoyed learning that Finnish mothers used to almost exclusively give birth in saunas before the rise of modern medicine. It takes homebirth to a whole new level.

A small baby, less than six months, nursed on the lowest level. Sienna happily climbed up the steps to earn her sauna badge. My baby was way too curious to nurse though, happy to snuggle in my sweaty arms. When we needed a break, AJ visited the men's sauna, and the kids entertained themselves on some outdoor gym equipment.

In the US, I see similar equipment at parks though rarely, if ever, used. In China, I noticed lines ten deep to similar equipment. Here in Helsinki, my kids moved among the elliptical, monkey bars, and balance beam. That's probably not what they were but that's how my kids used them. Eventually we headed to the giant Ferris wheel overlooking the harbor. I had promised my oldest I'd take her. In line, I discovered it cost fifty euro. I was not about to pay that much for a view. The whining began.

"It's really not that exciting," I said.

"But I want to go," Brooklyn griped. "You said we could." AJ and I looked at each other, neither of us really is inclined to go up and around, each abhorring one of those.

"How about if we take the money we were going to spend, and you can each pick something out?" I asked, resorting to bribery. I gestured at the array of tourist shops lining the waterfront. Brooklyn seemed suspicious until I added, "We can get ice cream, too."

Brooklyn and Lucas picked out stuffed reindeers in knit sweaters that said things like, "Make Helsinki Great Again." No, I did not buy a very fine moose, but they did sell them. I asked the stall owner to direct us to the site of the summit between our President and Russia's. He pointed to a non-descript government building, the Presidential Palace, just down the way. We walked past it just to say we did—as I just did—and continued our tour.

We passed through Senate Square. This looked like something I had read about one of the walking tours, though I wasn't quite sure exactly what. Story of my life sometimes. It seemed a pretty historic and appealing place to people-watch.

Brooklyn and Ella immediately raced up the fifty-plus steep steps to the base of Helsinki Cathedral when I turned my back to read a plaque. People watched as I chased behind them with a sleeping baby on my back. As soon as the girls broke the plane, they were no longer visible. Meaning, I actually had to climb all the way up. AJ lagged behind to conserve energy for the dreaded marathon the next day.

The Senate Square sits in the oldest part of central Helsinki. Along with the Cathedral, the Government Palace, Sederholm House—the oldest building in central Helsinki, and the main building of the University of Helsinki surround it. AJ became disjointed by a mob of students in togas who had flooded the steps after us for some university orientation events.

Therefore, Lucas was shuttled in easily to a little Italian restaurant AJ had found, Ristorante il Siciliano. I quickly backed out for a little, allowing Brooklyn to come along too. Ella raced out the door after us. Unfortunately, my five-year-old was on the brink of her second big meltdown of the trip. Screech Owl was back.

A pleasant Asian woman with two children, the only non-blonde people for blocks, stopped Ella. "What's wrong little girl?" she asked to calm my heaving, sobbing mess. The woman talked kindly to Ella. In short, being the thoughtful, understanding person I would like to be. My daughter was momentarily stunned by the attention but resumed her screaming and crying, no cohesive words, just tired tears and fear at the injustices of life. I felt Sienna wriggling in her sleep, bringing me back to reality of my busy life. A man popped out of the café across the street and rushed over to us.

With my son's blonde hair and blue eyes, the traits he got from his dad are more than skin deep. "What do you want for a snack?" my parents asked him, on a trip to Wisconsin as he awoke from a nap. "Eggs? Peanut butter and jelly?" Lucas, barely two at the time, did not answer. Instead, he brought my dad his shoes.

"What do you want?"

"Restaurant," Lucas responded.

People ask what we do about food on trips. What about those picky eaters? Clearly, not all of my children willingly eat whatever is in front of them, so we need planning to ensure we are all taken care of nutritionally. This entails a few things. As mentioned earlier, we fill up on inclusive breakfast. Then we aim for a solid early dinner. That can be carryout or sitting down to eat. It completely depends on the mood of the group.

For lunch, we eat the staples. We usually bring a jar of peanut butter in our luggage (it's considered a liquid), cereal, granola bars, and crackers. Barring the peanut butter, you can buy those items upon arrival, but I find it much cheaper back home, plus the extra space in the suitcase is awesome for souvenirs. (See Packing tip.)

We buy the perishable items at a local shop—milk, fruit, bread, cheese, yogurt, and eggs (if we have a stovetop). Like peanut butter, boiled eggs are great to take along on daytrips for the picky eater. The kids also enjoy visiting a local grocery shop and comparing it to what they see back home.

The last advice I have is not to worry. Bring some comfort from home for your peace of mind, but give your kids a chance to explore. My kids enjoyed daily crepes, and Lucas shocked me with his love of smoked salmon. Smaklig måltid!

"Don't cry," he said smoothly. He handed Brooklyn and Ella each a juice box. Uh…what was going on? Before I could say anything, a random older man appeared. Not to be outdone, he stopped and said soothing words in Finnish. He reached into his pocket and handed them each a small bag of gummy bears. We were in some kind of happy-ending Hansel and Gretel. People giving candy to children, strange men talking to little kids.

The gummy bears did it though, along with Sienna waking up. Dinner was saved and followed by an uneventful evening. We wandered a bit to find AJ's marathon bib, failed at finding an ice cream shop, avoided a meltdown over previously promised ice cream, and got scoops at our hotel. Only a parent calls that uneventful. We also finally got our new room, just a couple doors down from the first.

When we had been married just a year and a half, AJ and I stood toe to toe at the start line of a 5K race. As we waited for the crack of a gun to release us, I thought about that morning's conversation.

"You don't mind if I leave you, do you?" he asked in his offhanded leading way of giving the answer he wanted in the perceived question.

"No," I replied. "I want you to do the best you can." He had just started running, trying to lose the twenty-five pounds he'd put on since we married. He felt like he was finally back on track. I fully supported him doing what he needed to do to feel good. AJ wore all black—one of my cotton, extra-large volleyball warm-up shirts and mesh warm-up pants.

When the gun erupted, he sprinted ahead like a cannon. Still young, a former athlete, and reasonably fit, I went ahead at the relaxed, easy jog of a fast tortoise. I walked to and from school daily, about four miles roundtrip, plus jogged a little on the weekends along the East River in NYC.

After about a half mile, I caught up to AJ and we ran together for a bit. I pushed the pace a little, thinking he would keep up. He fell behind a few feet, then a few yards, then he was out of sight. I finished the race in a respectable time, just over twenty-five minutes. I felt beyond thrilled, considering I hadn't trained.

It mortified AJ that I had beaten him. He couldn't believe it. At that moment, he vowed he was going to truly get in shape and run a marathon that spring. He decided he was going to be a true runner, and I wouldn't beat him again. That is why, on a bright, cold morning in a foreign country, I was on the sidelines supporting him with four small children.

The day passed in a blur as we followed him around the course, something like this:

9:00 Wake kids up and get them ready. Clothes laid out the night before.
9:30 See Daddy running out hotel window at Mile Three. Thankfully staying at race hotel. Daddy looks great.
10:00 Eat breakfast—basically walking back and forth from table to buffet like a waitress until the kids are full.
10:20 Meet Daddy outside. He looks great, about ten miles in. Big smiles, waves, and high-fives.
10:30 Turned away from hotel sauna since it's closed during the middle of the day. Is this a joke? Finish packing up room and drop off bags in the lobby.
11:15 Wait for Daddy to come by at Mile 16.
11:45 Still waiting.
11:50 Daddy arrives late, limping while he runs. "I'm done," he says since his ankle hurts. As I push two kids in the stroller and have one on my back, I give him a look like, "Are you kidding me?" Instead, I say, "You can do it!" AJ looks at me skeptically. He only wants to hear, "I still love you if you quit." I would, but he knows those words will not cross my lips.
12:00 We follow the racers along the path on grass. Stop at a pleasant playground for a break. Kids run around as if they'd escaped from the zoo.
12:15 Bribe children with malted milk balls to leave playground. Congratulate myself for carrying candy in pocket. Follow racers again.
12:30 Turn around when I realize I left the passports at the hotel. Short-term memory failing again. I had reminded myself at least a half-dozen times that morning and the night before. Don't want to burden an exhausted AJ with remembering when he picks up the luggage before our ferry.

12:45 Pick up passports at hotel. Three kids crying now, respectfully taking turns so there is only one or two doing at a time. They all want to be in the stroller. They all want to hold the Tallinn ferry balloons. Why did I have so many children, and why did I let Brookie get two?

1:15 Finally arrive at the finish line. No idea as to AJ's whereabouts but people walking are coming in now. I hope my husband finishes.

1:25 More people walking. I hope my husband is still alive.

1:30 We see AJ running along the water, if you could call his hobbled gait that. A few minutes later, we watch him cross the finish line. The kids cheer. AJ wants to collapse and die. I try to hand off two kids to take when he showers and gets our luggage. He agrees to bring one as we eat free bizarre protein ice cream sandwiches.

1:45 The girls amuse themselves at a playground. My baby tries to climb through another child's urine at the top of a slide. We leave abruptly.

3:30 Baby falls asleep and girls race the fun run—half a mile. They receive the same medal AJ got for 26.2 miles.

4:00 Meet the boys at the ferry terminal. Drop off my kids so I can run the half mile down to the waterfront and buy one last banana Nutella crepe and fresh raspberries. I try to claim our family's fourth Helsinki Marathon medal for my effort.

5:00 Cruise ship departs. I served as a family pack mule since AJ can hardly walk with his injured ankle. For once, we make it with time to spare.

We had just one more hurdle before entering the back half of our trip, when time would accelerate like my son's Marble Madness tube. As the youngest child, I used to show patience. I could spend hours reading, playing with my Barbies, or watching my sister's practices and games. And as an adult, I value that trait in my children—waiting their turn in line, letting others go ahead, and appreciating the smaller moments in life. Unfortunately, that doesn't always happen.

I had studied the Stanford marshmallow study in college and grad school, the experiment where a child is offered one marshmallow now or two in five minutes. Those who were able to wait tend to have better life outcomes. My problem with it is the lack of variables. How about, yes, you get the two marshmallows, but you must also wait until your three-year-old brother finishes his hamburger. During the wait, you must stare at the marshmallow while Mommy feeds a baby. Ella's marshmallow was a flip sequin heart pillow she had seen during the boarding madness.

We had spent the past hour in the vast playroom, AJ (finally!) eating the last of his pizza and the kids diving into germ-infested ball pits and hiding from the massive Moomin characters. The Finnish creatures were indeterminable—I had thought they were some large white mammal, but they are actually a family of white and roundish trolls. That was probably the last thing I would have guessed after Big Foot and the Easter Bunny.

The kids were now eating hamburgers as they faced the bin of pillows. "Can I have it?" Ella begged.

"Sure," I demurred. "But after dinner."

To her, she'd already delayed her gratification once when her siblings got their MHGA moose. "I want it now!" she erupted. She burst from the table, unable to wait any longer. Unless she's an outlier in the experiment, this didn't seem to bode well for life outcome.

We dragged her (and everyone else, of course) up the elevator to our room. She screamed and cried. As did I.

"I need some time to myself," I said to AJ. Since 'myself' rarely means alone, I ambled across the hall to a large picture window with Brooklyn. Out the window, we could see that were sailing across the Baltic Sea, through the Archipelago Sea. Though the islands are small, using sheer numbers, many consider the Archipelago Sea the largest island group in the world. We watched the changing landscape, island after island of rugged landscapes. The peaceful water soothed my nerves as I experienced the paradise with (at least one of) my children. Like the thousands of islands in the distance, the rewards are out there, sometimes a little difficult to see.

A while later, I climbed into the twin bed under Screech Owl's bunk, careful not to wake the others in our small room. Lucas would soon creep out of his futon to cuddle. At home, he would wake during the night. I'd hear a bump in his room as his feet hit the floor, then a soft latch as he closed the door to avoid waking the baby. A few seconds later there would be a pitter-patter down the hallway, the low creak of our door opening, and the bump as it swung closed. He would tiptoe across our rug and heave himself onto the foot of our bed. Then he'd crawl up toward the pillow, settling under the covers between his dad and me in our warm bed. On bad nights, the girls would scream after a nightmare or to use the bathroom. This kid? He came to us. That night I slept much better than I would have thought possible, the waves rocking me to sleep.

My first memories in life are abstract, nightmares from when I was younger than two of the kids on that trip. In one, I wandered around lost and in tears, searching in vain for my mom. In another, I scoured the dark, scary subbasement of our split-level home looking for missing puppies. I awoke in tears from both.

Sometimes, life seems rough, but it's really not so bad in hindsight. You missed the ferry. So, what? Sometimes, you're caught waiting out a thunderstorm in the cold. Sometimes, you're running beyond exhaustion. Sometimes, you're at the funeral of an older family member you'd like to see one more time.

Through their Sisu, the Finns have it right. The bad won't last forever, so I try to find the blessing, however small it may be. Appreciate the sun when it peeks out from behind a cloud, feel the runner's high, acknowledge a long life, and smile with family members you haven't seen in years.

Then, appreciate the memories. I laugh when I think of standing in the cold, standing outside the closed amusement park, how the night gets longer in AJ's running story, and that dog stealing our supply of snacks for the entire trip. As AJ aptly quipped, "The more miserable, the more memorable."

I hope to reach an age where I can sit on a porch and reflect on my long life. Those memories, of travel and expanding my mind, miserable or not, will live with me forever. I will remember that cruise ride. AJ will remember the Helsinki Marathon. And that is great.

Chapter Thirteen

CAR SEATS TO SWEDISH CASTLES

MY FAMILY WOULD pile in the car over the summer, driving to see Uncle Jerry in San Francisco, to the Wisconsin Dells for yet another basketball tournament, or south to Florida for fun. We would maneuver through a snow squall in Canada, or we'd occasionally fly, taking that discount inclusive trip to Jamaica for $99 a person during hurricane season. We weren't rich, but my mom could certainly find a bargain. Plus, the hurricane didn't come to fruition. At least not when we were there.

One such trip wound through the Great Smoky Mountains on the Tennessee/North Carolina border on our way to an aunt's South Carolina beach house. We had visited the cheap amusements of Gatlinburg and were driving our full-size, tiny-engined Buick through narrow woods on dirt roads. At one point, my dad directed us on a shortcut through the mountains. We were ignorant that a shortcut in the mountains is quite different than one in glacially-flat Michigan, driving down a weather-ravaged two-track dirt logging road, crossing a slightly swollen creek beneath an awning of green, and emerging on the other side. We then drove up the parallel mountain, tree branches crashing into us as my older brother pretended to call for black bears out the windows that had been opened to counteract the over-heating of the car. We were in the middle of nowhere, trapped in a swampy Bermuda Triangle. With all of the cliffs and trees, the road was too narrow to turn around, and we hadn't seen another person or car for seemingly hours.

Eventually we happened upon a small clapboard church at the top of the mountain. A man, a quite heavy gentleman, stood outside. My mom left the car.

"Excuse me, sir, could you tell us how we can get back to the main road?" she asked. The guy looked her up and down, chewing a piece of grass sticking out of his teeth. The pause was deafening. Though quite warm, my mother shivered a little.

"I once had a pair of overalls that fit," was all he said. I really don't recall if we made our way through or had to backtrack. I do remember that my dad floored the gas and didn't look back.

My parents have been there for the moments in my life, the travels, the good and the bad. Even though that particular trip was crazy and a bit absurd, they protected and took care of me. We spent a lot of time together in the car. My own little family was about to do the same in Sweden after a short thirty-six hours in the city.

We awoke in the Stockholm Archipelago, a mere 3,000 islands that make up the city and surrounding areas. During breakfast we watched the natural, tree-covered islands fade as the city outskirts came into view. My little ones exclaimed their joy watching the fishing boats and kayaks out on the water. Loaded down with people and belongings, we prepared to join the second wave of busses leaving the ship, leaving just twenty minutes after the first. I was pleased with my thinking, happy to avoid the lemmings crowding the galley floor, pushing to exit first.

Busses lined the vast terminal. We passed a full bus and stopped at the second. "Does this go to City Center?" I asked. The driver seemed to grunt in agreement. We enjoyed the twenty-minute ride into town, calm, peaceful and new, past football fields and buildings onto Djurgården, a massive island garden in the middle of the city. A few people got off along the way. In front of Skansen, our driver turned to look at the half-full bus.

"Why are you still on?" he queried. We all chuckled good-naturedly at his joke. His deadpan humor was spot on. But then he repeated himself. AJ and I locked eyes. Was this Swedish humor or were we missing something?

I spoke for the group. "We're going to City Center." The severe expression on our driver's face conveyed that we were not.

"What should we do?" another woman asked.

"Go back to the terminal and catch another bus," he said. The woman sat down in resignation.

Our hotel was less than two miles away. There was no way I would settle for that. I was the pushy American after all. My mom would have wooed the bus and started a chant like she had at my volleyball games. I tried a more pragmatic approach.

"How far can you take us? Can you drop us any closer to the City Center? We can take a taxi from there." We had less than two days in Stockholm, and we weren't about to waste it. The driver considered my request and agreed. Ten minutes and twenty dollars later we were checking into our hotel, Radisson Blu Waterfront, across the street from the Central Station. We were on a roll.

The blue sky shown down on us as we crossed the river that morning on our way to Gamla Stan, the Old Town. The neighborhood, dating from around 1000 AD, is one of the largest and best-preserved medieval city centers in Europe. Now, museums, restaurants, cafes, and shops fill the space. We ambled through the tight cobblestone streets among gold-colored buildings, looking in windows and sampling fresh waffles whose aromas permeate the air. We glimpsed the crowded entrance to Mårten Trotzigs, an alley less than three feet wide. Following a group of tourists, we arrived at the Nobel Prize Museum and Stortorget Square, Stockholm's oldest.

I knew that the Stockholm Palace, and the changing of the guard, was nearby. We wandered around in circles looking for it—like our Costa Rican hike with the stray dogs, we were lost literally twenty-five yards from our destination. Thinking we were late, we quickly peeked at the chapel before heading to the courtyard. I had thought the event was on the hour, and with some guards visible, I assumed it would be just a few more minutes. Then a few more minutes. Then some more. Eventually, the guards corralled us to the side and lined the path with temporary barriers. The kids and I pushed up against them as people filled in around and behind us. Sienna showed surprising patience—the hours watching gymnastics classes and soccer practices have built that tolerance.

With all the excitement, my sweet baby gave in to her need for a nap. AJ snuck Ella and Lucas into a pizzeria where they could watch the chef roll the dough while I stayed outside.

"Come here, B," I whispered. "I need to walk with Sienna. Want to get a treat?" We meandered to the ice cream shop with the waffle aroma and split an ice cream and hot fudge-topped Belgian waffle. We laughed as we scooped up the dripping ice cream while the baby incredulously napped on my back. After our contrasting snacks, my family reunited to walk through the islands and their fantastic architecture.

My dad's father had instilled travel in his own family, through car trips with his five children. Since my grandpa was a high school principal, over summer breaks they also would drive across the country (and Canada!), seeing all fifty states and the National Parks, camping where possible.

My dad recalls a time when he and his sister, the two youngest, were fighting in the backseat. As was common at the time, my grandpa would turn around and swat at the kids. "Pipe down!" he'd yell.

Inevitably, the fighting continued until my grandpa stopped the car. "Get out, both of you." After some arguing, the kids did as they were told. Then my grandpa did something apparently common back then: he stepped on the gas and drove away. He came back, sure, but not until my aunt was crying as she chased the car. Grandpa wanted them to know that he was the boss.

My sister, Kylie, and I, however, were the apples of his eye. Growing up down the street from him, he loved watching our sports and bragging about our endeavors. I won't deny that we both benefitted from some moneyed handshakes after games.

His relationship with Bryn and our cousin was different. Grandpa would order them around and demand that they get him things. He did not age gracefully. When the boys were in high school, they drove fifteen hours with him in his Buick Roadmaster to a wedding for our oldest cousin.

Pulling up to the drive-thru window at McDonald's, my grandpa said, "Four plain hamburgers."

"Can I have cheese on mine?" my cousin quipped. "How about fries?"

"Four plain hamburgers," my grandpa repeated, more sternly this time. His word was as final as death.

Although I had gotten the travel bug from my grandpa, we weren't quite that strict. After exhausting themselves in Gamla Stan, Ever-Hungry indulged the kids with McDonald's. I never buy it for my kids, making it their restaurant of choice.

"I'd like two cheeseburgers with nothing on them," he ordered for Ella and Lucas, since they disliked pickles and sauces. He placed the tray down. Lucas's face dropped as he opened his wrapper to an empty bun.

After resolving the missing hamburger situation, AJ took Lucas for an early bedtime while I swam with the girls at our sister hotel, Radisson Blu Viking Hotel. Sienna loved jumping in toward me as her sisters raced across the pool.

Ella had just learned to swim a couple of months earlier. People are absolutely crazy about the sport in Maryland. Parents start their kids early and swim year-round. It's too much for me personally, but it seemed to work for Michael Phelps and Katie Ledecky. In Michigan, we don't even have to swim fast to avoid sharks.

I signed my daughter up for the local swim team—pre-team, actually, since the kids aren't exactly proficient. My daughter was an expert at that. Being non-proficient, that is. Ella's initial swimming involved alternating between hopping in the shallow end and refusing to put her head under water. The coaches, looking like they were about twelve, were good-natured and patient with her. After about two weeks, it clicked, and she was swimming like a champ, roughly three paddles before stopping. It didn't matter; she could now visit the diving board and slide. Our pool days then involved the little two playing on the steps while I watched Ella alternate between the two options in her little three-foot frame.

At the end of the season, Brooklyn and Ella competed in a popsicle swim meet. Swim a lap, get some ice cream. Brooklyn had done it previously, winning the kickboard event. It was a great coup since she's built like a runner or gymnast, tenth percentile for weight and fiftieth for height, hardly buoyant. Ella, however, put forth her best effort as she kicked across the pool in over two minutes—at least thirty seconds behind her closest competitor.

"Ella! Ella!" chanted the crowd on the pool deck. She could not have made it further. I could not have been any prouder.

When I saw the girls racing across the Swedish pool, my analytical side came out to equalize the race. "Start halfway!" I'd shout to Ella. "Count to five before you jump in," I'd coach Brooklyn. I eventually moved to the hot tub and let my baby stick her feet in. I was all-in to the Nordic lifestyle.

"We're all done," I said to Sienna as I got out.

"Not on your life," she answered in baby language, flinging herself into the pool.

Not again, I thought, as I leapt after her into the cold water. I offered a compromise—she could jump to Brooklyn to be carried back to the ladder. They did that about a hundred times until I convinced them to join me in the long-anticipated sauna. We stripped down and relaxed in the hot room. Even Ella came in.

That night, I went on the computer for the first time of the trip. As I signed on to social media, I saw a familiar scene. A friend from business school was posing on the bridge we had crossed just a few hours earlier. I hadn't talked to him in years. Now he was staying just a few streets away. Like our time in the Dominican Republic and the Vatican, home had a way of following us.

The next day came our whirlwind tour of Stockholm. We had exactly eight hours to explore before the car rental agency closed. I had mapped it out to the minute. There were so many great things to see and so little time.

"We could have seen more had we not stayed in Helsinki that extra day," I told AJ. Limping next to me, he didn't crack a smile. We had also seen a group of men running some sort of marathon the day before. "You could have done both," I also joked. That didn't amuse him either.

We walked first to Djurgarden, site of the ill-fated ferry bus. Without luggage, it was pleasant, just over a mile and a half through the city shopping area and along the waterfront. We passed through tidy gardens with old statues. I gave a nod to the mama bear with her cubs. We saw bands of preschool kids sporting uniforms of fluorescent vests and milk mustaches, holding hands as they engaged in some outing around the city. The independence that Scandinavian parents give their children is quite amazing. My daughters don't go outside for recess when there's a drop of rain.

We crossed the bridge to the lush island and headed to the Vasa Museum, Scandinavia's most visited. In 1628, shortly after leaving on its maiden journey, the Vasa capsized in the harbor and sank to the seabed. Over 300 years later, rescuers brought the amazing 226-foot-long and 155-foot-high warship to the surface and secured it at this site. The price seemed reasonable, especially since all four kids (up to eighteen years, actually) were free.

We then walked around a wide lawn to Junibacken, or as we called it, the Pippi Longstocking museum. We couldn't cross the lawn since a wagon-sized machine slowly crept across the grass.

"What do you think that is?" I asked AJ. "A lawnmower?" My guess seemed reasonable considering the linear trajectory, but he thought it was ridiculous. I do put forth absurd ideas quite often. Based on the law of probabilities, I occasionally am right, which reinforces even more silliness. I'm like a cousin-conspiracy theorist. Mine are mundane usually, like, if I combine pears and blueberries into a cobbler, will it be yummy? It must be lovely to live with.

I get this trait from my mom. On a trip with my family to Missouri, my dad could not start the rental car after my mom parked it. He tried everything for the next ten minutes—or so we thought.

"Are you out of gas?" AJ asked, a reasonable question.

"Oh my God, I bet someone siphoned it," my mom responded. It was a 'rough' part of Branson—the mini golf parking lot, sight of high school gangs practicing their putting and flirting.

"Wait, what? Who would do that? And why?" we reacted.

"Hold on," my dad said. "I just need to put the car in Park."

All four kids loved Junibacken, running loose in the large Storybook Square among settings from (I'm guessing) popular Swedish characters and books, like the (beloved?) Max, Alfie Atkins, and Mulle Meck. They scampered around the cobblestone streets, stopping to play on the motorcycle, in the kitchen, or in the workshop. Brooklyn ran around a hamster wheel, and Ella drank imaginary tea from the café. Lucas liked the airplane, and Sienna climbed her first ladder, nearly giving me a heart attack.

We hopped aboard the train at Vimmerby Railway Station to enter the magical land of red-haired, pigtailed, Pippi Longstocking. I was pleasantly surprised. It seemed wholly foreign to me, in that simple, understated way that alien places often do. The train lifted us past diorama-like scenes reconstructed from simple materials and dolls featuring Astrid Lingren's characters like Simon Small, the dragon Katla, Festus, and Alfie Atkins. There was the simple thunder soundtrack of thunder in Robberland, and we heard narrated stories like the one where a boy died saving his orphaned brother from a fire and came back to him later in life as some kind of spirit.

When we arrived in Pippi's home, Villa Villekulla, my kids ran to play in her two-story house, slipping down the large slide, and climbing on her large horse, Old Man. AJ and I sat by the tall, open windows, taking in the majestic, colorful buildings across the river. The view gave a peaceful air to the whole experience.

Thirty minutes later than planned, we finally moved on to the rest of the place. Brooklyn and Ella posed for photos in the upside-down room and hid in the toadstools. Since we were rushing to Skansen, we missed the multiple daily performances and more.

The Papa Bear park was overwhelming since our Goldilocks family had visited the smaller, just-right version in Finland. We did eat delicious food—an open-air pan cooked wrap for me and pizza for the others—and the kids enjoyed the petting zoo, scratching the heads of the goats on display. I looked at the time and noted that we had just thirty minutes to catch our 4:30 boat.

We walked quickly to the public dock by their amusement park and the chatter followed.

"Can we go there?"

"Look at those rides."

"Mommy, I want cotton candy."

I had the wrong dock.

"Go down to Vasa Museum," someone advised. I ran along the water with Sienna on my back, the girls keeping up and Daddy following with Lucas. Another firm, "Not here," until we finally reached our destination. The boat pulled in, and we climbed aboard. Whew.

I sat up top with Brooklyn and Lucas, watching the beautiful city views fade as we crossed the channel. The air held that crisp, clean feeling now expected in Scandinavia. We were the only foreigners, joining the locals on their commute home from work.

LESSON LEARNED

But how can we afford it? For most people, paying for the trip seems the hardest part. Flying your family to Europe may sound as expensive as rocketing to the moon. I'll be honest—we made decent money and hadn't yet encountered the burden of paying for six international flights. We took full advantage of kids under two flying free in our laps. That is part of the reason we've been able to make it work. With multiple kids, they're like puppies in a crate; they don't actually need a full-sized adult seat and can share with their one-year-old sister when needed. For our flight to California, we had two lap babies. Airlines are usually accommodating on space if there is any (and usually there is).

Learning from my mom who could stretch fifty cents to a buck, I scour discount sites and set up flight alerts. We fly slightly off-season, having gone to Italy in May and Scandinavia in late August before our kids returned to school (and after the kids there did!). For that, we were rewarded with 'Kids fly free' vouchers. We paid $1,500 for our family of six.

In the post-pandemic world, airlines may offer fantastic deals for those willing to take them and some even leave an open middle seat. Families will return to flying at their own pace, but deals can be found for those willing to look.

When parking, we typically find off-site deals at nearby hotels for half the price of the airport. Some places even offer free, delicious cookies. For early flights, we consider an overnight stay since many hotels offer up to a week of free parking.

There is a lot of pricing flexibility in accommodations. With four children, we now struggle to fit our sanity and family in one room. That's why we mix up hotels with rentals. The hotels provide amenities, breakfast, and a pool while the rentals have great prices and space. With some well-timed snack and lunch purchases, our food does not have to cost significantly more than at home. With some searching and flexibility, our Scandinavian adventure cost about a third of what a friend paid to visit Disneyworld. (And most parents will have Disney on their list at some point!)

Of course, there may be expenses for museums or transport or whatever you want to see. Many cities offer multiple day passes—and many of those include children under seven for free. This is important to us so, similar to what I did when I made a pittance after first graduating college, I save a portion of each paycheck so we can make these trips. Sharing the world is important to my husband and me.

Sometimes there are minor inconveniences to save a few hundred dollars. We had to pick up our car a mile or so outside town since the inner-city rental office charged about $400 more for a minivan. When we landed at the docks, I got my bearings among kids running around to begin the .8-mile walk to the rental agency. Since we had caught the ferry, we had an hour or so until pickup closed. We let the kids run around at one of the four playgrounds along the way. As we approached the town center, we suddenly encountered a giant fence. It ran as far left as I could see. The same to the right. Peering through, I could see a massive complex going up, something at least six city blocks long and multiple blocks wide. There was no way through. Our short walk suddenly became much, much longer as we made our way around the obstruction. We passed blocks of empty lots, fenced car dealerships, and even our designated address.

After the long day, we had one kid whining, then two, then three. And then…the rain began. Just a dribble, then a hard, steady falling of droplets from the sky. I ran into a second dealership. It was BMW, a sharp place with clean, expensive cars. I felt like a drowned rat.

"Is there a Hertz rental agency here?" I asked. The cultured man behind the desk pointed backwards, past where we had come. It was in the (other) car dealership.

I should have known the Swedes would be efficient. We were just picking up a car after all—what more did that need than a few parking spots? As we headed back, the skies opened up, and we ran safely inside. What an adventure!

The actual counter had been closed for about two hours, but a woman at the dealership helped me navigate the kiosk. My credit card was declined. Ditto with the second. We had forgotten to tell the card companies I was going abroad. They wouldn't work without identification. Panic began to set in. I gave it one last shot with the debit card. Bingo.

We piled into our Ford minivan, an imaginary car back home that I only can drive abroad and navigated our way back to the hotel. It was only a couple of miles, but since the city sits on two levels, it was tricky to ensure we were on the right one. I missed our exit but found a way by cutting through the bus depot with questionable legality.

Brooklyn and Ella helped me grab our luggage while AJ secured dinner. Grabbing luggage entailed the kids needing the restroom and wanting complementary cookies, chocolates, and candy. They didn't actually know about the chocolates, but I fancied one and pocketed a few for future bribes. I wasn't quite sure how I was going to finagle the kids and carry our large suitcase, duffel bag, stroller, and backpack.

Thankfully, a tall, strong, striking Viking warrior came to the rescue. The pretty woman hoisted the bag on her shoulder and pulled the suitcase. "Would you like me to put the suitcase in the back?" she asked. I held my baby in my arms while my son clutched my leg. The girls were in sight.

"Sure." She lifted the fifty pounds with ease before placing the stroller on top. Since the door inevitably wouldn't close, she displayed her strength, quickly removing everything and following my detailed reloading instructions.

"Tell me where to go!" I hollered to AJ. We were off to our next destination, three hours south, and cars choked by me on both sides as we swam through rush hour traffic.

He threw up his hands. "You know I hate directions." No English on the signs and a Finnish GPS didn't help. I zoomed the map out in hopes it would help. The dashboard showed our dot drifting along the eastern coast, further and further from our destination on the E4/E20.

"Maybe we can just get off at the next exit and cut over. What do you think?" Although we had missed our exit, I really didn't want to go back into the traffic of the city and risk overlooking it again. The sun was slowly edging toward the horizon, still quite light, at seven o'clock.

"Why not?" AJ said as he zoomed out the map further. The roads appeared to meet up in some distant universe. We had rented a car for the adventure, not just to get between two points.

Our little sojourn took us past the suburbs of Agesta and Huddinge, through multiple roundabouts, and past cute homes. At every roundabout, I inevitably uttered, "Why can't we have more of these in the US?" One of my biggest pet peeves is sitting at a stoplight with no oncoming traffic. The book, *Delayed Response*, describes the art of waiting. Citing examples throughout history, including Civil War letters, text messages, and planetary discovery, the author emphasizes the importance of patience to help reduce stress. He asks you to contrive, "Who benefits from my waiting?" As I sit at empty traffic lights and fritter away my life, I simply answer, "Nobody. Nobody benefits from this. A roundabout would be so much better."

We arrived late at our little Airbnb, tucked away in the small village of Granna. Brooklyn, Ella, and Lucas stirred to life, excitedly running around a home that wasn't theirs that they could treat as if it were. Our hosts, a native Swede and her British husband, greeted us with open arms.

Our core traits emerged the next morning after AJ poured bowls of plain Rice Krispies.

The kids (yes, all of them) promptly covered their cereal with salt, thinking it was sugar. At home, the condiments are safely stored away from their curious fingers. I rinsed each bowl and convinced each child no salt remained before finding the sugar.

Sienna promptly napped within two hours of waking.

Brooklyn, Ella, and Lucas gleefully discovered the small indoor pool.

AJ engaged in another marathon, this time of laundry. The machine took two hours to wash and another two to dry, similar to his pace limping through Helsinki. I compared our machine at home to US marathon star Meb Keflezighi, finishing in 2:08:37 on a good day. Time didn't matter to AJ, just the fact that our laundry got clean. I didn't have that patience. I much preferred obsessively selecting clothes for the day and repacking the suitcase. After more than half a working day of laundry, we dragged the wet second load out to put in the car. I had meticulously plotted out our drive through Sweden to find our stops. We had to get going.

Along the way, the computer system in the car would sporadically flutter. A red icon would pop up, blinking and buzzing along with a few words, as though we were in grave danger. We were in the middle of nowhere, it seemed, but I wondered if we should pull over.

"What if it's the oil light?" I'd say. "Or could we be overheating?" He quickly dismissed those concerns.

"It looks kind of like a coffee cup," I added, back in conspiracy mode. "What if it's some kind of sign I'm not driving well?" It seemed to have occurred while changing lanes on the highway, and I may not have used my indicator. The third time it happened, he took a photo for me to translate that night. "Fika," it said. Basically, take a break. The word Fika is a Swedish tradition of coffee and sweet baked goods to clear the brain. I could buy into that one.

I looked up the American version of the product and not surprisingly, it is the 'Lane Keeping System and Driver Alert.' We always find a way to take the fun out of a serious topic. The system learns the habits of the driver and serves as a smart advisor. Pretty cool, but it needed some help if it would call me drowsy for skipping a turn signal on a barren highway.

The trucks on the road fascinated Lucas. More than anything, he loves trucks. On road trips, he shouted, "Truck, Ella, truck!" After days of new sights in Scandinavia, he had found his Zen on those foreign highways.

He will play with his cars for hours, lining them up or rolling them back and forth along the ground, the wheels spinning like the stories through his head, as he imagines them along the highways, the bridges, the terrain. One day, shortly after becoming a big brother, he constructed a highway on my sleeping father in our sunroom. Papa has long legs, a fantastic road for an imaginative boy.

Sienna threw up for the second time of the leg. We stopped at Lake Vattern, the second largest lake in Sweden and sixth in Europe, to clean her up. Then, after our second hour of driving, we passed through the Swedish great woods. The tall trees were magnificent, looming over our car. Large reservoirs and farmhouses dotted the path. I felt more resemblance to my home state. No wonder Swedish immigrants settled in the Great Lakes region.

We entered Store Mosse National Park, a beautiful and calm park, open with massive bogs. At the visitor's center, guests removed their shoes, donned complementary slippers, and drank free coffee out of ceramic mugs. Not us. With our jamboree of kids, we did not fit the Zen participants having fika. After happily paying no entrance fee, we wandered the paths through the woods and across the bogs. The kids found a mini ropes course to go between trees and hidden fairies and frogs. We climbed a lookout probably four stories high and gazed out at the wide-open expanse. It was a mystical, magical park. Ever-Hungry husband even found a hot dog truck to suit himself and his mini-me, Lucas.

After all of that adventure, Sienna fell asleep on the way to Smalandet Wildlife and Safari Park, or "the moose sanctuary." According to their website, you can "take a fascinating train ride through the Kingdom of the Moose." Guides provide branches of the moose's favorite food, and you're nearly guaranteed some spectacular encounters.

"Can I get tickets for the shuttle?" I said breathlessly to the young woman selling tickets.

"The last shuttle just left," she responded. It was five minutes after four o'clock. I had gotten lost at the exit. "But you can take your own car." As if sensing why I was bummed, she added. "You can feed the animals. They like apples and any other fruit you may have."

I looked in the bottomless backpack of snacks—four apples from the tree of our Airbnb hosts.

"Keep your eyes peeled," I said to the kids as I pulled in.

"I see a big one," Brooklyn shouted a few minutes later. A herd of bull moose stood on top of the hill, far from the car.

"I saw them first," Ella promptly followed.

I spotted some females (cows) near a watering hole on the other side and pulled toward it. A calf came closer as she eyed the apple in my hand. She crammed her head through the window while her protective momma stood guard. Ella shrieked delightedly as the animals ate from her hand next. Inevitably, Ella dropped the apple, seemingly lost forever. The moose glared at her. We broke apart the apples, feeding the cows and petting their big snouts. The calves even devoured our Ritz crackers. The kids giggled approvingly. Sienna clung to her daddy.

We then crossed a grate to enter the Bison exhibit, a short loop to see the giants of American prairie land. The kids appropriately oohed and aahed. Then, as we were leaving, we heard a snort. Sienna nearly jumped out of her skin, a look of sheer terror on her face at the noise.

Back through the park we drove on a parallel path until we encountered the earlier bull moose. I pulled over and searched intently for the lost apple. Once found, I split it so we could take turns feeding those large mammals. I pet the velvety antlers, soft as moss.

"Which way do you want to go?" I asked AJ when we were back on the road. There were two options for us to get to Denmark—the massive, five-mile long Oresund bridge from Malmo to Copenhagen, or the shorter route by ferry from Helsinborg to Helsingor. My directions suggested the bridge, but the ferry seemed much more interesting.

The car ferry crossed Oresund, the strait between Sweden and Denmark. The strait serves as a border between the salty oceanic water and our previously visited Baltic Sea. The location has been strategic for thousands of years since; at only four miles, it is the closest meeting points of the two countries. The Danish collected tolls here for 400 years in early Europe. That led to the creation of Kronborg (i.e. Hamlet's) Castle and its now-gone foe on the Swedish side.

That spot, with so much history, and so much strategic importance, was a short twenty-minute jaunt for us. Seeing their Gibraltar, I remembered how my dad had forgotten his passport when we visited there. He would have loved the significance of Kronborg. I had a high happiness level after another magical, unexpectedly perfect drive, but I missed my parents. They would have loved the day.

Brooklyn, Ella, and Lucas ran around the deck while I took Sienna up to the top deck for the imposing castle view. She loved the cool breeze on her face from the warmth of her mommy's arms. When we exited the ferry, we hopped back on the E4 for the last leg of the day's journey.

People tend to have a baseline level of happiness. Whether they win a million dollars or lose it all, they will revert to some central sense of balance. The base level for some people is to be miserable—Les Miserables, as AJ says. Easily dissatisfied, they complain about everything and find the negatives—the pulp in orange juice. Even when you are actively resolving their issue, they will literally complain about something else. Not me; I hate to hold a grudge.

My goal is to try to be a creator, not a complainer. I want to make the lemonade. I believe that things tend to work out. And when they don't, I count to ten or a thousand until I return to status quo. That's what I learned at the beginning of a slow shift as a cashier at the grocery store during college breaks at least. When I'm impatient about traffic lights, I try to be grateful I'm in my warm car. Or I at least try to be productive through my forehead Kegels.

In that time while we waited for the next ferry, I asked my kids for their day's highlight.

"The trucks," Lucas announced.

"The moose," said Brooklyn.

"That's what I was going to say," came Ella. Sienna smiled contentedly, included in the fun. She had, apparently, forgotten about the two times she had gotten sick, thanks to inheriting my motion sickness gene.

We arrived later than anticipated in Hillerod at Annete's Airbnb. The home backed to the park and was stunning—multiple levels with loads of stairs, glass sculptures, and classic artwork. As lovely as her home, Annete graciously offered it all to us, tired parents and starving children piling out of the car like the burgers from Pop! the Pig game. We dried our clothes and put the kids to bed in three separate rooms on the upper level. We had as much bedroom space as at home, with candies adorned on the pillows to boot. Our host prepared a warm, custom breakfast in the morning with fresh croissants and fruit. She gave my kids toys to play with so AJ and I (and the baby, as always) could sleep in. Even though my parents hadn't traveled with us this time, we felt as if they had for that one night.

Chapter Fourteen

SLEEPING LIKE DANISH BABIES

ONE DAY, WHILE sitting on the couch, big and pregnant, I became distracted with a social media diversion. "Type your name plus 'meme' into Google." My name? Nothing memorable. When I entered AJ's info, I laughed out loud. To myself. I think I snorted.

A photo of the comedian James Gaffigan appeared with the quote, "You know what it's like having a fourth kid? Imagine you're drowning, then someone hands you a baby." The baby in my belly, my fourth, kicked in agreement.

Having four kids is tough, he is certainly right about that. I struggle for balance—getting enough sleep, eating healthy (enough), exercising, peeing alone. Even more so than after the other three, everything changed. The neighborhood moms were God-sends, making meals and letting my kindergartener follow them home from school.

Sienna, however, arrived as a ray of sunshine. She was the baby I needed at that point in my life. She is my smiley kid—always happy to be included and curious to see what's going on. While Lucas acted the numerous parts in our *Frozen* extravaganza, she served as extra extraordinaire. She stole scenes, singing and pulling the blanket off our 'monsters.' Sienna gets excited about the little things and lets us know.

She's difficult not because she's challenging. She's actually quite easy. Her first word was "Yeah." She's difficult because four is challenging.

For a person like me that overanalyzes things, a baby changed the equation. With four kids, I can't be on top of every decision or stress about the little things. That's why, when we actually do date nights, I prefer AJ choosing the restaurant. I'm happy to avoid weighing the pros and cons of simple choices. I'm even overanalyzing whether this is the appropriate story to include.

This trait was taken to the extreme during an informational interview I had set up with a coworker to learn more about her team. I worked in corporate America, the dream of few but provider of many. It was not an interview, per company policy, and I hadn't yet decided if I was going to apply. I prepared for the talk by researching the person I was speaking with. That's it. I like to know what to expect and for things to follow a proper order.

My call started pleasantly enough. I remembered her name. I didn't say I wanted to spank anybody. I asked thoughtful questions and bantered appropriately. Suddenly, she dove into an interview, throwing me in the deep end. I felt as if pushed into the water, flailing and forgetting how to swim. My mind churned. Do I answer? Do I remind her this isn't allowed?

"What is your biggest weakness?" she asked. You may think, duh, of course she's going to ask you questions. Not me. I had conducted a dozen similar info sessions, thousands in the words of my father-in-law.

I froze. Like completely froze. I could sense myself slowing, sinking deeper toward the drain. I blurt out inappropriate things, not sit in silence. So, I laughed. Well, kind of, I'm sure. "This is supposed to be an informational interview. I haven't told my manager that I'm interviewing." She didn't have my resume for goodness sake.

That didn't deter her. She was unforgiving, not exactly the type of manager I wanted anyway. "What's your greatest weakness?" she repeated.

An ocean of silence flooded the line. The interview, informational and actual, was over. I had bombed. I have a slew of answers—I overanalyze everything, I'm not the best at quick responses, I can't turn down a dessert—but at that moment, I was silent.

To combat this in real life, I ironically schedule spontaneity into my life. I consciously enter situations where flexibility is necessary, where limits don't exist. That happens with travel and raising four unique kids. I am grateful to have found a partner who this comes naturally to for help on this path. There's a lot to be said about organization but sometimes the best moments in life come without a plan.

As we set off on the final leg of our journey on my birthday the next day, I awoke a year older and much, much wiser. Not smart enough to avoid another action-packed day, I'm pleased to say, but clever enough to purchase a seventy-two-hour pass for the last three days in Scandinavia. The passes are good for over eighty attractions and include all public transportation. The biggest benefit would be reduced decision-making on my part.

Our host, Annette, directed us to a path through her back garden that led to the signature gardens of the largest Renaissance castle in Scandinavia. When I chose Frederiksborg Castle as our official castle experience, the gardens had drawn me in, nicknamed the Danish Versailles.

Tall trees fell over us, mostly shading us from the busy rail-line shadowing the path as we crossed the threshold into a fairytale ambling along the gravel path. Mostly, I say, because Lucas would perk up when he heard an approaching train. We'd stop and peer through the branches as it sped by. Thatched roofs caressed the homes on the other side. Birds chirped, wildflowers blossomed, and wild berries grew by the side of the path.

As we approached the garden from the north, I freed Sienna so she could join the walk. After a few moments, she stopped in excited bewilderment to watch a red squirrel chasing another round and round a tree. Her siblings slowed to her pace, pulled into her world, seeing the animals skitter around the giant trunk.

The garden had four different terraces, descending down toward the moat of the castle. The hedges were meticulously trimmed, and the grass sloped as if carved with a knife. They reflect the ideals of that age, similar to Versailles, where man portended to control nature.

In 1599, a young King Christian IV tore down the existing building to create this majestic castle to house the royal family, it ended up, for over a hundred years. Now, the magnificent museum houses period furniture, coats of arms, and inspiring artwork. By the time we entered the top floor, after just over an hour, tired and ready to go, I spotted an Andy Warhol hanging discreetly on the wall. It was pretty amazing.

As we were leaving, I took Sienna to the basement prison for a bathroom break. She held onto the bars overlooking the base of the moat, reflecting what I'm sure was the last outdoor view of some prisoners of long past. Then, AJ took the kids to cavort at the castle playground while I ran a couple of miles through the village to pick up our car before our trip to Roskilde along pleasant farmland. My dad would have been proud of my resourcefulness in fitting in a jog on my birthday.

Ella becomes excited about simple things. I mean, that's normal for her age, but she wears her emotions on her sleeve. She is challenging sometimes, oh man, is she hard, but this kid can melt even the toughest heart. Her big, expressive eyes show her exact sentiments.

When my kid feels an emotion, it overpowers everything. Her joy is all-encompassing. It draws the sad person up, makes the grumpy old man snicker, and elicits roaring laughter in her siblings. It's a powerful tool; challenging, but when used right, it can change the world.

Perhaps I'm being a little dramatic in this next segue, but just trying to give a glimpse into life with my child. Every year, we'd drive a few times to see my family in Michigan or Ohio, passing through hundreds of miles of farms, mountains, and over famous rivers. After we drove through the Allegheny Mountain tunnel on our approach to Somerset, Pennsylvania, we'd would pass a mountain dotted with huge wind turbines. The first time we passed them, I had to roll down the car windows to let out her shrieks.

"Dancers! Dancers!" Ella called. She was flaying her arms about the car pointing in all directions, looking like a dancing spider herself.

"Um, what?" I asked.

"Dancers!" she repeated. I should add that her speech was slurred, not uncommon at this age. For whatever reason, she pronounces the letter 'a' with a British accent. My words carry the nasally harshness of a Midwestern, but for her, a word like hands holds a stretched 'a.' Marsh-a-mallow. The graceful dance of the turbines whipping around fascinated her. Then, every time she saw them, the shriek and call for them would return.

This came to a head in Denmark, land of the windmills, producing over forty percent of their energy. Over 6,000 of them exist in this country between the size of Maryland and West Virginia. Granted, most are offshore and visible to us when our airplane landed, but still pretty amazing. They appeared again that day, dotting the hilly, bucolic countryside.

"I see a dancer," Ella alerted us in her British accent.

"It's called a windmill," Brooklyn stated. Close enough, I wasn't going to correct her.

"It's a dancer!" That time the 'a' lasted about three seconds.

"Windmill."

"Da-a-a-a-a-ancer." You get the drift.

"How about this side has windmills and those out your window are dancers?" I compromised. They both agreed. Then we saw another.

"Windmill!" shouted Brooklyn, triumphant. I heard a whisper, covered by Ella's hands. I'll let you guess what she said.

Soon enough, I saw the cathedral at Roskilde on the horizon. With its beautiful twin spires, the cathedral overwhelms the skyline. It is entirely too large for a city that size and like my kids in the car, seems to be bursting to escape its environment. It also had no parking.

"I see a spot," I called out as we started descending the hilly, narrow road.

"It looks kind of small," said my husband. I decided to try it anyway. I pulled forward on the uneven cobblestone road, easing beside the preceding car. As I slowly eased my way back, I heard a low screech from the side.

"Oh, fuuu…." Eight piercing eyes stared at me in the rearview mirror. "Fudgesicles!" I muttered.

"We're getting ice cream," Brooklyn stated matter-of-factly to her siblings.

"We're getting out of here," I muttered. "Is that car fine?" I asked AJ. No damage to them, thank goodness.

We detoured instead to the waterfront for the Viking ship museum. The weather was peaceful that afternoon, warm with a cool breeze, the grass green and lush. Dogs wandered the grounds with their owners, a perfect little park on the water.

Like his ancestors, my grandfather had been a sailor, so I always assumed he liked swimming. On our last visit with him, he shared how he had nearly drowned in a pool.

"How can you be a sailor in the Navy, work on Lake Michigan, descended from the first people to cross the Atlantic, and NOT be a good swimmer?" I asked incredulously.

He looked me in the eye and replied, "I was a *great* sailor. The goal was to not go in the water."

In 1962, five Viking ships that had been deliberately sunk nearly 1,000 years earlier were pulled up from the watery deeps. The Skuldelev ships, each had a different original purpose—one a cargo ship, another a warship, and others in between. The large ships had been filled with stones to block the channel and protect the city from an attack. I took the girls to the Viking ship hall while AJ grabbed food with my son.

"Where are the boats?" Ella asked on entry. Five fairly disintegrated boats sat in the sparse atrium. The gray sea rolled in behind a large picturesque window. The remains for each ship varied in complexity. Some were just a few long boards of oak, twenty-five percent of original, while others of pine, birch, and oak nearly filled the iron frame in which it sat. The great long ship spanned thirty meters, while the fishing vessel was only eleven. Seventy people could ride the long ship off to war at high speed. Some explored the North Atlantic and covered the North and Baltic Seas, by sails or oars.

My girls appeased me for a few minutes but excitedly ran to the other indoor activities. Ella colored drawing after drawing of ships while the other girls climbed aboard a play ship in full costume. They acted like Vikings, pulling up something deep within them.

I tend to think of the Vikings as Norwegian, but the ships had also been constructed in Denmark and Ireland. The Vikings settled in Ireland in 800 AD and one of those bases formed the origins of Dublin. The museum also taught me volumes about my ancestors. For instance, the men were quite the catch. Well before electricity or running water, they were fastidious about cleanliness. Viking men combed their hair every day and bathed once a week. Women of respectable families would leave their arranged marriages to become concubines for them. Imagine that—one shower a week, and you get the cream of the crop.

Beyond the ships, the museum includes fabulously reviewed replica tours, a toy boat station, a live building demonstration, lawn games, and more. We couldn't do the tours since Lucas and Sienna were too small. Instead, the boys relaxed on the waterfront, Lucas eating a snack while AJ sampled a local beer, and the girls and I strolled over to the lawn games.

"How do I play this?" Brooklyn asked as she held a large wooden mallet. The games all seemed to be some variation of throwing a stick at wooden objects—giant heads, other sticks, a ring toss. This one involved aiming a mallet at three heads (yes, heads!) about ten yards away. Brooklyn and Ella loved repeatedly chucking it the two feet they could heave.

"Can I try this?" Ella asked at an intricate labyrinth in the grass before embarking on a fitness routine I need to replicate at home. Basically, the girls ran the equivalent of a lap around the track, give or take, within a plot of land the size of our one-car garage.

Eventually, we had to head to Copenhagen. In rush-hour traffic, the bikes surrounded our rental car like the mosquitos of Belize. Their designated lanes ran next to us for most of the trip and their numbers overwhelmed the cars. Parents loaded two or three kids onto the front, or they carried their whole lives including the kitchen sink in the back. I imagined myself riding with my broad—one on each the front and back of my bike and one with AJ while Brooklyn rode alongside. I love to participate in local activities, but we'd have to pass on that for this trip.

Our room was in a fantastic location, right on Nyhavn, the historic waterfront and canal district with colorful townhomes from the seventeenth and eighteenth century, some dating back to 1681. Nyhavn used to be the main port of Copenhagen, hosting ships from across Europe and the world. Hans Christian Andersen even lived there for over twenty years while writing some of his masterpieces, including *The Princess and the Pea*. I imagine it served a seedier purpose back then with lots of sailors, pubs, and whatnot, but now it's just food, music, and relaxation.

When I arrived after dropping off the car, AJ snatched me into a doorway ninety degrees from the bodega. "Are they still not here?" I asked, assuming that he hadn't yet gotten the key. "Where are the kids?" Inside. I had not expected to stay ground level, three feet from a bodega, with a bus stopping directly in front of our window. With the shotgun style home with long, narrow rooms and a tiny bedroom, AJ wanted to leave on the spot.

However, like an ad in a travel magazine, the view from our stoop displayed the photo that had attracted us to Copenhagen originally. It couldn't have been more centrally located. Plus, it was dramatically less expensive than the small hotel rooms available for over $400 each. I wondered where Alanis Morrissette would be performing.

A crib greeted us in the middle of the living room with a sign: "Do not move." Clearly, the owner had never put a baby to bed. With the wisdom of four kids, I quickly took it apart to put in the tiny bedroom off our larger room. Both of these bedrooms would have fit into our own relatively small master bedroom. We squeezed the crib perpendicular to the bunk beds, against the window—showing the room's exact width of three and a half feet. We were unable to fully open the door (a fire hazard if anyone slightly larger than a post-partum, once-a-week exercising mom needed through), and there were about four-square feet of open floor space. I am anything but inefficient.

Sweating from furniture Tetris, we departed for my birthday dinner. Dozens of appetizing options—pizza, seafood, Chinese, Italian, an old-fashioned ice cream parlor with homemade waffle cones—lined the waterfront. The long dinner caused us to miss that last one, unfortunately.

We chose a fantastically located, tastefully acceptable, and incredibly slow restaurant. The kids' cheese pizza and my appetizer, smoked salmon with avocado, came out quickly. The first piece of salmon melted in my mouth as I noticed the other two disappearing into my son's. The things we give up as parents. My salmon pasta came an hour later, by which time we had lost all control of the kids and they were running the cobblestone streets between the restaurants. Brooklyn and Ella started it, but then Lucas joined, and after forty-five-minutes, we acquiesced to let Sienna partake. Another twenty minutes later, they brought out crème brûlée. At home, we traditionally bake a homemade cake. AJ finally caught on to the traditional part after about three years of me leaving cake mix and frosting out, along with the eggs, butter, mixing bowls, and a pan. Crème brûlée was not my ideal birthday cake, but free is. We dug in.

We slept quite well on that noisy street corner, like Danish babies. I couldn't hear a peep.

Unfortunately, the dreary northern Europe weather caught up to us the next day. During our Airbnb stay in Sweden, our hosts had shared that the weather was generally like England in the summer and Russia in the winter. Since that dreadful weather had arrived, we had to postpone our outdoor plans.

"What should we do?" I appealed to Brooklyn.

"Amusement park!" she shouted.

I pointed out the back window. "It's raining," I reminded her.

"Aquarium?" she asked.

Loaded up with snacks, extra clothes, and water, we stepped out the front door to discover that the bodega guy had locked us in. AJ tried the keys and pulled to no avail. We were trapped on the stoop like dogs in a cage. I was relieved I hadn't discovered it the night before; I can't imagine the nightmares my claustrophobia would have induced.

Before climbing out a back window to escape, I concocted a more intricate plan. "There's a door in the bathroom to the playground. We can go out that door and lock the bathroom from the inside. That way, if anyone breaks in, they'd only get into there, not the apartment." I looked around. "But first, let's move our toothbrushes. I don't want anyone using these."

That logic wasn't sound, but AJ went along. Only when we returned did we find the instructions on how to break down the wall, or rather the bodega gate.

The National Aquarium, Blue Planet, in the Copenhagen suburb of Kastrup was quite lovely—and like everything the day before, included in the seventy-two-hour pass. We walked a few blocks to a central station, Kongens Nytorv, and boarded a direct train to the site just as they opened at ten. We planned to stay for two hours so Sienna and Lucas could nap, but like most things there, we could have spent a whole day. The creatures enthralled the kids, big and small. I was happy to learn that the building reduces energy consumption by using seawater from Oresund.

The Blue Planet contains seven million liters of water, divided among five main sections. We passed beneath sharks and rays on a path surrounded by four million liters of sea water. We witnessed a colorful coral reef and a rainforest with butterflies, birds, and bats flying around. At that time, the bats were hanging upside-down sleeping more than flying for us.

When Ever-Hungry husband, I mean the kids, was ready for a snack, we dropped into the delightful café overlooking the water. The sea was grey and angry that day as rain spit-balled fearlessly, but we were snug inside eating our cookies, brownies, and warm/hot cocoa and coffee. That is, until we went to watch the otter feeding outside. The cold weather helped drive away hordes of fans, so it was just us and a school of deaf children. Although there was a guide who spoke English, it was the third language of the performance. We watched the guide use Danish sign language, the other guide repeat it in Danish, then wait for the rushed, poor English translation at the end. It was, surprisingly, a fun experience, the damp cold aside. The otters swam around, putting on a show, effortlessly cracking the crab claws open and using their large, fat bellies as dining trays.

The kids explored the touch exhibit—starfish, crabs, and the like—showing the déjà vu of every similar place: Sienna screams in excitement and fear, Brooklyn pretends to act mature but freaks out at the last second, Ella wants to do the same, and Lucas cuddles behind me. Every single time.

I squinted at a terrible map in my hands, hoping to find the start of the Train Tours, the fifth activity on the pass for Brooklyn, Ella, and me. Blurry Danish marked the roads and were non-existent in person. We walked through the spitting rain, looking for any signs of a train around the main square. I should not have relied on the map that came with my Copenhagen card. Finally, I approached a kiosk at Ved Stranden.

A man stood behind a long table at the information booth. I stepped under the wide roof to speak to him. "Do you know where we can catch the train?" I asked.

"It's closed. The train stopped working." The rain started picking up, so I huddled further under the roof.

"Do you sell tickets for the boat tour? They're included in the Copenhagen Pass, right?"

"Yes."

LESSON LEARNED

Like "What to Expect" when, you know, expecting, maps are instrumental while traveling. For me especially, since I have cheap cell service and can't always get service outside the US. Upon arrival, I ask the front desk for a map with directions and advice on the areas of town we may want to avoid. Sometimes those things that take five minutes save us hours of time.

With kids, we try to do what we can before leaving. I bring a guidebook with map or snap a few photos of a recommended waking tour. I research the public transportation options to confirm what is included in the city pass. There are some areas of planning where you can skimp. I rarely research restaurants in advance. We don't do detailed itineraries in advance since our days may be influenced by the kids' moods. I am, however, a firm believer in a good map to help get around. Each night, I plot our next adventure via Google maps and snap a few screenshots. It's one thing to get lost, but before setting out with kids, I want at least a general lay of the land.

"Is the boat covered?" The man pointed down toward the water at a long, wide, shallow, open-topped boat. Not in the least. Brooklyn and Ella nodded eagerly that they wanted to go, their hair wet but their cheeks rosy and happy. "When does it leave?"

We had about thirty minutes, so after reserving our tickets, we searched for food. I turned to my little troopers and said, "What should we do?" The rain slowly started dropping down as if in buckets.

I remembered a tall building we had passed, some kind of city hall or church. The building, Nikolaj Kunsthal, it turns out, saved us from the unending rain, so we didn't really care what it was. I asked the guy behind the corner at the former church, a funky-looking man with spiky hair and a nose ring, if we could climb it. Three Euro or fifteen, I couldn't say. Since it cost something, the price didn't matter. We only had fifteen minutes.

As we turned to leave, he waved at the adjoining room. "The art exhibit is included in Copenhagen pass."

I am not artsy. I don't take my children to galleries and have a limited knowledge of that realm, especially modern art. The things I remember most are what my fifth-grade art teacher, Mr. Hammond, taught us about Roy Lichtenstein and Alexander Calder. That is the extent of it. It was a new experience, free and convenient at that, so we headed in.

We entered into the cartoon universe, colorful and cheery by the Danish artist, or former graffiti genius, HuskMitNavn. The pictures proved absurd and thought-provoking, more than just a little bit off. Brooklyn liked the character whose shadow had a mind of its own. Ella was concerned by the man spilling paint and actual paint going off the canvas onto the real floor. I could feel the emotions as if I was part of the cartoon. We spent a solid ten minutes in the small exhibit before heading back on our way.

The Canal Boats website states the boats are covered and heated in the winter. Not in summer. The captain handed us red ponchos as we stepped down onto the boat and seated ourselves.

The boat ride was cold, miserable, and incredibly fun. Wearing the ponchos was an experience in and of itself for the girls. They couldn't believe that there were disposable coats and that they would keep us dry. Ella giggled at how ridiculous they looked. They laughed far more than I would have even thought was possible.

Although it rained the entire ride, we got an amazing guided tour around the harbor and through the canals. We saw the Old Stock Exchange, navigated through the hip Christianshavn neighborhood, and, the girls' favorite, the Little Mermaid statue. I learned that the centrally located Opera building was a poor compromise of two contrasting architectural styles. Though it was the signature achievement of the architect, Henning Larsen, he considered it his "greatest failure." It looked like a toaster. On our idyllic cruise through the canals, we saw churches like Our Saviours, Amalienborg Palace, castles, old homes, and more.

The massive aluminum Amager Bakke Plant in the distance completely amazed and flabbergasted me. This facility was developed to be a sustainable CO2-neutral incinerator. The trash will be converted to energy to power the city's grid. In addition to its stated function, it will also house recreational facilities, including a ski slope and the world's tallest artificial climbing wall. It is amazingly forward-thinking and environmentally friendly.

Then we got to walk the mile back to the hotel in the pouring rain. It was magical and delightful, precisely because I saw it through my kids' eyes. We were drenched and a little cold, but we were warmed with memories and fun. And not just because my daughter ate her first Magnum ice cream. Or maybe it was...

After warming up with hot showers, I steered AJ and the ducklings back out to tour the Royal Palace. Much like our confusing drive out of Sweden, unfortunately we found ourselves instead ascending an old elevator with a group of twenty people to the lookout point. It wasn't what we were expecting, but why not? The guide shared that the tower previously had an open-air patio that had been infiltrated by pigeons. Now there are stone pigeon statues and cooing noises channeled in. I thought it was a bit weird, but the kids loved it. Weird can be interesting and memorable.

As we exited out a second door, we passed the entrance to the Royal Kitchen and Palace—right at closing. We were on our way to the round tower, Rundetaarn, the oldest functioning observatory in Europe, when I walked hard into a metal block sticking out of the middle of the doorway, doubling over from surprise and pain. My foot throbbed from the force and my head reminded me that though I used to be an athlete, I had always been a clumsy one.

At one of my high school volleyball tournaments, I repeatedly fell in the nets that separated our court from its neighbor. Like, literally four to five times.

I'd go out of bounds to start my approach to spike the ball and boom, I'd be lying on my face. The setter passed me the ball as I watched from my prone position on the floor. In college, I ran after an errant ball and flattened another player's father after plowing into him. I'm disappointed I can't recall if I actually got the save.

As our state's best player, my friend Kim from the "Spank the football team" speech had been recruited to the top volleyball programs. Kim and I visited my sister, Kylie's school when they played National Champion Penn State. After the game, we climbed down the bleachers to say hello to a girl we knew. Or rather, she climbed down. I galloped like a horse, racing her for God knows what reason, and I ended up foot over head in the middle of a patch of stairs. I dusted myself off good-heartedly and continued the walk.

"Oh, my God!" an Amazonian woman towering over me gasped. "Are you okay?" She had her hand pressed to her heart and the genuine fear in her eyes contrasted her strong build.

"Oh yes," I said. "I'm just fine." Just a little bruised pride, I thought. I stretched my neck, looking for our former high school rival.

The tall girl shook her head seriously. "That was the most awkward fall I've ever seen. I'm surprised you aren't hurt."

Well, thank you for your concern. For the most part, though, these falls haven't really resulted in injuries yet. Oh sure, I've sprained my ankle multiple times from landing on another girl's foot and jammed my finger playing basketball. I tore open the skin on my knees, elbows, and hips diving after the ball in drills and reemerged from the training room wrapped like a mummy. In college, I even dislocated my kneecap when it hit the ground digging a line drive down the line. Yes, *digging* it. Although my scream pierced louder than the referee's whistle, and I had to be carried off the court, that ball did not hit the ground. Those injuries weren't from being clumsy, thank goodness. Those injuries had real causes.

With my clumsily caused injury, I hobbled along Kobmagergade, avoiding the puddles on the cobblestone street, annoyed at the flip flops I had to wear since my shoes were sopping wet.

We entered the round tower, and Sienna took off. With no stairs, she took to the spiral ramp winding up, orbiting the center. I found varying accounts of length, but the official website says 281 meters on the outside but only about a third of that in the middle. I made her stay near the windows with less pitch, only about ten degrees. I could envision Sienna tripping and rolling down like a little log.

In addition to the exciting ramp, the kids found niches in the center, perfect little alcoves where they could hide and jump out to scare the life out of their dad. At the end of the walk, one led to a floating glass floor above a bottomless pit. Or at least that's how it appeared to me. The glass stands eighty-two feet over nothing but is a couple of inches thick and can hold quite a bit of weight, even a family of six.

The old toilet near the top intrigued me. The privy allowed researchers and astronomers in the seventeenth century to relieve themselves into a space leading down to the bottom floor. There was no way to empty or ventilate it, so it was an early attempt at a septic tank. Over the course of hundreds of years, the stench built up and became overpowering. In 1902, the toilet was replaced, but the pit was not actually emptied until 1921. It is truly amazing that this is the same country that developed the Amager Bakke Plant. The astronomers were some of the smartest people in the world, but they thought using human waste as insulation would be prudent.

It's the same in the U.S., of course. We put interstates through the center of cities and reduce walkability, add twenty billion disposable diapers to landfills a year, and think it's best to ship eggs or other products across the country rather than eat local. I hope that in 400 years, people are saying, "Wow, these Americans are building the first zero emission spacecraft to Mars. Can you believe they threw away two trillion diapers in the twenty-first century?"

Speaking of toilets, we took a pit stop in the same location that had hosted Hans Christian Andersen. Brooklyn giggled upon learning the author of *The Little Mermaid* had peed there. This one was halfway up, near the Library, and had modern plumbing.

At the top was the actual observatory that had been used for over two hundred years. The scientists left 150 years ago for better equipment and to avoid encroaching light pollution, but it is still used by amateur astronomers and visitors. Encircling that is an outdoor platform with another good view. At only 136 feet tall, it wasn't spectacular, but did offer a unique view of the old city.

The windows along the slope offered an interesting perspective. We'd walk about thirty steps and see the same view as before, just ten or so feet higher. Thirty more, and we'd see the same thing. My eye always seemed to catch the sign for Joe & the Juice, a juice shop, started in Denmark in 2002. I was disappointed that after seeing it eight times on the way up, we didn't end up trying it. My kids needed a real meal, so we instead tried out their fast-food joint, Max Burger. (A bit over-priced but the kids liked the milkshakes and chalk board to draw on.) Back home, I was surprised to find that Joe & the Juice is actually a small chain of about 200 locations, and one was just a few miles from my in-laws.

As it was early and the kids were fed and had napped, Brooklyn and Ella were drawn to the stupidest museum I've ever seen, The Guinness Book of World Records and Ripley's Believe it or Not. I'd never visited one, but we had free passes.

"Want to try it out?" I asked AJ.

He looked at me suspiciously. "You hate places like this."

"I do," I conceded. "But it's free, and it's raining. Let's go in for fifteen minutes." It was as bad as I anticipated, but the kids enjoyed it. They liked seeing video of the world's tallest man (272 centimeters) and a doll proportioned to the world's smallest woman. We saw silly records like most dominos falling over at 1,382,101 (unlike those dominos, that record has stood for over thirty years), and eating contest results, along with most baby pigs born to a sow (twenty-seven), and the tallest buildings in the world. I like facts and figures so it may seem like a fun museum, but the décor and cheesiness were ridiculous.

I had forgotten that years earlier, a friend had convinced me to join her at the 'Great Cloth Diaper Change.' At the event, I contributed two babies toward the 8,331 counting toward our World Record. I'm always game for a friendly challenge.

When I was a kid, my dad purchased a pig puzzle—an easy, one hundred pieces of a portly but cute fellow. It wasn't meant to be challenging; we competed to see who could do it fastest. My parents, siblings, and I raced against the stopwatch, trying to break the five-minute barrier, then three. We kept personal and house records. It was completely absurd but a boondoggle in our home. We would challenge our friends when they came over.

This past summer, my dad shared the electronic birthday card his brother, Uncle Jerry, had given him—'Find the hidden objects.' They had competed growing up on the ping pong court with Grandma cheering, "Go Jer!" My family exacted out turns at the card, seeing how quickly we could find the hidden dog and frog, turtle and umbrella. We first broke twenty seconds, then ten. I switched from using the mouse to touch screen to save two seconds. Then Brooklyn joined me to record seven seconds.

"Cheaters," my sister cursed.

The night before our last day, I decided we needed one last trip to a sauna. I wanted to experience a morning like the locals. I also told AJ I wanted to put a sauna in our mild-climate Maryland home. He agreed to both ideas. I turned to a trusty search engine for help. But for what? Kid sauna? No hits. Kid spa? Nothing good.

Eventually, I found a place by looking for the "Best pool in Copenhagen." I could not imagine a decent pool in Scandinavia without a good sauna. Valby Vandkulturhus. Now that's a mouthful. It certainly was a neighborhood find, located in an industrial area among a Sports Complex facility, a golf course, a massive Building Supplies company, and at least two schools. When we arrived on the train at 9:30, it seemed a hotbed of activity. The biggest struggle for the American bumpkins entailed crossing the massive train line between us and the pool with no one who spoke English. After about ten minutes, I finally solved the riddle—climb up to the eastbound tracks, then go down the opposing stairs.

I had desired a spa, but this had no frills. Since it was off-hours, the tickets were insanely cheap, twenty Danish Krone for adult and ten per children. The first child under seven is free so half our brood was covered. That came out to a whopping nine dollars total, the same as AJ's airport coffee. The site did not translate to English well, but price and hours did, along with rave reviews and good photos.

My kids sprang out of our arms as we piled out of the locker rooms. Sweet Sienna waddled over to the steps in her puffy cloth swim diaper, grabbed the large handrail, and lowered herself backwards onto the first step. Brooklyn and Ella jumped right in and swam toward the cave (yes, a cave!), and Lucas ran over to hold my hand.

Almost immediately, a guard hustled over, speaking quick Danish. Yikes. Had my kids been running? I can never tell if my baby is following the rules. Is waddling fast the same as running? I mean, she'll slip and fall just as easily waddling, and she couldn't quite run.

The guard spoke slower, pointing at Sienna. He paused for a moment as he searched for the right English words. "No diaper." Sienna was splashing on the first step and shrieking with glee.

"This is a swim diaper," I explained. I lifted her out and pointed to the silky white swim diaper.

"No. It must go down the thigh." He pointed midway down his own thighs as if he needed one himself. He could tell I wasn't going to go easily so he curled his finger and directed me over to the one-foot depth baby pool to a young couple playing peacefully and happily with their young baby, maybe ten months old. He spoke rapidly in Danish to them and they brought the child out.

"Your baby needs a diaper like this one." He asked the mother to show her baby's swim diaper. It was a disposable version of mine. This embarrassed and infuriated the guard. We were both in trouble. He called over his manager, a woman a bit more proficient in English, to resolve the situation.

"Children who are not toilet-trained need to wear tight pants over their swim diaper. The city is very strict, and we'd have to close all pools for seventy-two hours for an accident." I don't know if she was pulling my leg; three days sounds extreme. In Helsinki, the pool had closed a couple of hours. Regardless, it was a big deal.

The other woman sadly conceded and took her baby to the locker room. Although it wasn't my fault, I wanted to shout after her, "I am so sorry. I did not ask to see your baby's diaper."

I was not about to give in to the lifeguards, loud American that I am. "Do you sell any of those pants or is there a place nearby that does?" The woman shook her head no. "Well, here's the thing," I started. "My daughter is toilet-trained. I put her in a diaper to give you piece of mind since that's what people prefer in the U.S. If you'd rather her wear no diaper, no problem. I just thought you would rather her wear one."

The woman looked me up and down. I was not lying. The head guard concurred.

"Baby, do not let me down," I whispered to Sienna. I forced her on the toilet and reluctantly removed that shield between her skin and her swimsuit. We returned, sans diaper and with an eye on the clock to return every fifteen minutes. I was not about to lose that bet.

After that incident, and truthfully during since AJ had resumed swimming with the older ones, confident I would resolve it, the kids had a blast. Lucas and Sienna wore foam Danish swimmies on their arms as they floated around. The kids played in the baby pool before making their way to the slide. The guards were rigid about kids under seven not going on the slides alone, so AJ and I alternated going up the stairs and sliding down with Ella, Lucas, and Sienna. When the age suddenly jumped to eight with the next rotation of lifeguards, I was out. Four kids each needing a personal chaperone was my limit.

I grabbed Sienna and Brooklyn to explore the sauna. Who knew there were so many different types? Wet, dry, infrared, scented… We hobbled across a 'wellness' or, as I preferred, 'death to delicate feet' mat, complete with spiky rocks that tore into my high arches. Brooklyn and I quite enjoyed daring the others to try the miserable experience.

Outside there was more gym equipment, like in Helsinki, including three in-ground trampolines. Brooklyn, Ella, and Lucas ran around and bounced like Tigger, forgetting they were wiped out from a morning of swimming.

We had experienced the most relaxing two hours of our entire trip. Sure, I got into an argument with the lifeguard. And yes, it's not easy to supervise four kids in a place where eyes are constantly required. But their smiles and the fun they experienced truly made the trip. It was just a pool, a nice one granted, but we were together, trying something new as a family.

For one of the rare times on the trip, we were not just tourists, but enjoying the amazing ordinariness of Danish life. I showered in the locker room with the local women. We all had put on some weight or carried stretch marks from birthing children. This was life. That was remarkable.

We had reached our trip finale and the apex for the kids, Tivoli Gardens. Opened in the 1843, it's the most-visited theme park in Scandinavia and located right in the center of the city. We crossed the street from the Central Station, got our free wrist bands to walk around for the day (only one entry per Copenhagen pass is allowed), and bought a couple unlimited ride passes. Sienna had reprised her role of easy-baby by this point, long asleep after crashing on my back as we walked to the train station from the spa.

"Hey Brooklyn, want some sushi?" I said as I spotted a 'Kids eat free' deal at Letz Sushi, the sustainably sourced Danish chain. When there's a sleeping baby, splitting up helps ensure she stay that way. Ever-Hungry took the rambunctious middle kids to nearby Burger House. I sat sideways in the restaurant due to a massive baby, but that's a small price to pay for a peaceful meal overlooking the central pond of the world's second-oldest operating amusement park.

"This is yummy," Brooklyn said as she slurped down the salmon sashimi she had peeled off her rice. The timing worked well as Sienna had just emerged from dream world. I could pawn the rice into her greedy hands. The only thing she wanted more than a nap after a two-hour swim and sauna excursion was carbs. Brooklyn's eyes shown with glee when she discovered the silver fish with her meal was filled with chocolate.

Tivoli Gardens has much stricter rules about kids riding solo than we have back home, so each of my kids needed an adult on every ride. I'm used to American parks where Brooklyn can serve as Sienna's 'parent' or we can watch from a distance. Additionally, perhaps due to the park's compactness within the middle of an expensive city, the coasters are short in length. That means rides do multiple loops. Don't get me wrong, I am all for getting value for money. But to me, as a motion-sickness-prone mother of four children who needed an adult companion, the rides got old fast. I once became sick swimming in the water. Imagine riding a roller coaster as it goes around three or four (or seven!) times. And then doing it for your second or third kid!

However sick they made us, the coasters held great appeal, including the ancient, wooden Rutschebanen. Built in 1914, the ride required an operator to pull a manual brake to control the speed as it careened down the hills. After riding twice (six loops total to AJ's three), I added this to the list of jobs I would never be able to do, along with single-use plastics manufacturer or big tobacco advertiser.

"Brooklyn, I need something different," I said. AJ looked green after his triple-stint on the Galley Ship, a ride that rapidly undulates around a circle while going up and down a hill. "Choose something else."

She looked up and pointed high in the sky. Twice as tall as the round tower where astronomers originally mapped the stars, stood the aptly named Star Flyer, one of the world's tallest swing rides. AJ shook his head, a solid no. Heights terrified him.

I loved the idea of it and thoroughly enjoyed the slow ascension to 260 feet, proudly pointing out Nyhavn to Brooklyn. I loved the panoramic view. But spinning around more than a dozen times? Worse than childbirth for me.

Beyond those rides, the atmosphere was fantastical. Beautiful gardens and old trees lined the paths set among the City of Spires with its beautiful towers.

"Look," cried Ella. She watched mesmerized as a giant stuffed bear in red trousers and a blue hat performed near the children's play area. The others pulled me toward a large, lopsided ship with wobbly slides and cargo nets nestled among the trees. Ella didn't move.

"Daddy, can I go hug him?" Ella, sweet thing she is, asked after the show finished. An eye still on the others as they teetered along an obstacle course together, I watched her slacken into the arms of that huge carnivore. It melted my heart. After watching her for a few seconds, then nearly a minute, however, the warmth melted to a cool sadness as I realized how clearly my daughter needed that embrace…and she'd turned to a bear for that love.

"Oh," I thought, sad and a little embarrassed. At that moment, I realized that I needed to improve focusing on each of my children's individual needs. It is so incredibly challenging with four children who have contrasting personalities, but on days I accomplish it, I win the lotto.

Ella and I tightly holding hands, my family veered toward the far side of the central pond. There, we encountered Sienna's favorite—the ducks. I don't recall my other children loving birds that much at this age, but they captivate my baby. Perhaps she'll be a birder like my brother and identify thousands in her lifetime. She'll travel to Borneo to see the helmeted hornbill and Australia to see the emu. Perhaps, she'll seek out the quetzal in Costa Rica. Or maybe, since she's a baby, she likes how it walks. Who knows how a baby thinks?

"Do you want to feed them?" I asked the kids.

"Yeah, yeah," they all concurred. Even Sienna gave a little "dah," in agreement.

I never do this at home, but I had some Danish Krone pocket change to spend before we left. Otherwise, it was going toward creamer for Ever-Hungry's coffee the next morning.

As four kids surrounded me, I inserted the coin. AJ started the phone recording and cryptically stated, "Last day of vacation in Copenhagen in Tivoli Gardens. Katie and the kids are all feeding the ducks and pigeons. What could go wrong?"

A pigeon cocked its head at the sound of the gears grinding. His Pavlov-instincts kicked in.

"Mommy, are their nails sharp?" Ella inquired. "Momma, are their nails sharp? Mommy?" she repeated. A large handful of small pellets popped out of the machine into my hand. I passed Brooklyn a few.

The bird opened its wings broadly and flapped them a couple times as it jumped onto my back. I felt its scratchy orange claws sink into my shirt and heard it chatter in my ear. One was pecking the pellet from Brooklyn's hand. She tried to pet it with her free hand until it flew away. What had I gotten myself into? I closed my hand tight around the rest of the food and backed away from the machine.

"Are its nails sharp, Mommy?" Ella repeated a third (fourth? tenth?) time. "Can I have some?"

"Ma!" echoed her shadow in her goat-like bleat. Sienna smacked me on the leg, in her manner of asking for some. She didn't know what it was, but if the others wanted it, she knew it must be good. She bent over and tried to feed the ducks pebbles. Lucas hid behind Daddy. I handed Ella some pellets that she immediately threw on the ground to avoid being touched by a bird.

"Why did you do that?" I asked incredulously. Two pigeons were on my arm, one pecking incessantly at my closed fist, trying to worm a pellet out from between my thumb and index finger.

"Mommy's a bird woman," AJ announced.

"Daddy, one fly over me," Lucas responded in turn.

I bent down to show Sienna the birds. As she reached over to pet them, one shot toward the girls. Brooklyn and Ella flew back in surprise, their eyes shining with laughter and glee.

"Bwaaaaah ha ha ha ha ha ha!" Ella laughed diabolically, her deep chuckle penetrating the air. Brooklyn's giggles bubbled up from her chest.

"Mommy, can I have more?" Ella asked without hesitation. When I obliged, she immediately threw the food on the ground as a bird flew toward her. Sienna raised her hands toward me like a poor street urchin.

"Why do they keep coming to you?" AJ asked. I again held three birds and was juggling the task of extricating a couple pellets at a time without giving the pushy pigeon a full-on buffet. I managed to put one in Sienna's hand as a duck opened his large beak near her. The pellet immediately shot out of her hand. A little too close for comfort.

"Lucas, do you want some?" I asked, holding my hand over toward his little frame behind AJ.

"No!!!!" he screamed in terror and jumped away.

I saw that Brooklyn had one on top of her shiny hair. Please don't poop on her, I thought.

"Ah! Aaaah!" Ella continued to shriek as she watched me, alternating between deep, guttural grunts and high-pitched squeaks.

I had morphed into that vagrant woman feeding the pigeons. I'm not sure why they chose me and not the others in the park to jump on. I was sure I had picked up a dozen diseases. At my funeral, AJ would say, "She had naively thought she was smarter than the pigeons. Then suddenly they encircled her. She shouldn't have done it." It did fit the purpose for the trip, though: at least the kids enjoyed it. And I found another job I lacked qualifications for—a professional pigeon-feeder.

And just like that, with the last pellet gone, the birds dissipated. And so, we moseyed on our way. We scarfed European junk food—crepes, ice cream, cotton candy, and Danish-named flavored popcorn.

"What flavors do you guys want?" I asked my three who could talk. Three to a bag, of course they were going to share.

"Caramel," Brooklyn announced.

"Blue," said Lucas.

"I want licorice," Ella selected.

"I don't think you'll like it," I warned. She was expecting a Twizzler, but I had heard Danish licorice could be potent. "Maybe you should try it first."

When the seller obliged with a sample, Ella popped a kernel in her mouth. I could hardly prepare myself for the look of utter disgust as she tasted the ammonium chloride. Her eyes immediately opened wide in shock. Then, almost immediately, her eyes closed to slits, and her little freckled nose wrinkled until the ridge nearly disappeared. The sides of her mouth peeled back toward her ears as her tongue popped out in disgust. She waved her hand rapidly in front of her face and hyperventilated in an effort to, what?, magically say goodbye to the robust, salty flavor?

That look was worth its weight in gold, and my husband and I were able to witness that fun reaction—for free—while avoiding the contamination of mixing that vile taste with the sweet flavors already in the bag.

That night, I treated Brooklyn to the experience I had anticipated for days: an evening stroll around and beyond Nyhavn. That included, just for her, a chance to see the Little Mermaid statue up close. I had gone out nightly in the rain for short jaunts, buying cereal or bananas, but hadn't really explored.

The crisp air and night sky exposed the stars, and most importantly, I had my buddy, while AJ put the younger kids to bed.

"What's this?" my little girl asked while she posed in front of the Marble Church, which boasts the largest dome in Scandinavia.

"Well, the cruise guide said they started building it in the mid-eighteenth century. That's uh, almost 300 years ago. Then they stopped, and it sat in ruins for nearly 150 years."

"What's ruins?"

"It's when things start falling apart. Like our treehouse before we fixed it. It's not really a building or anything. It's like the Colosseum we saw when you were a baby." Construction of the Marble Church finally concluded in 1894. It's certainly beautiful now, with its copper-green, nearly 100-foot-wide dome.

"Who's that guy?" she asked as we followed the brick path into the square of Amalienborg Palace. A large statue of King Frederik V sat in the center, perched on a horse. I had to read the plaque to answer that one.

Denmark has one of the world's oldest monarchies, with the Queen's royal heritage dating back to 900 AD. I was pleasantly surprised to learn that the royal family holds primary residence within the four identical palace buildings that surround the beautiful square and sends their children to public schools. On the other side of the palace is the park, Amaliehaven, with its manicured topiaries and massive fountain that enclose it form the waterfront.

Brooklyn smiled broadly, sans two front teeth, by two Royal Guards, Den Kongelige Livgarde. There's an official daily changing of the guard that's quite popular, though clearly not that late in the evening.

Then we walked along the Kastellet, a star-shaped military fortress surrounded by peaceful water and well-maintained walking paths overlooking the harbor. As the sun set, I wondered if this wasn't my safest idea, but the route only seemed serene and was actually quite popular.

"There she is," I said to Brooklyn as we approached the sculpture by Edvard Eriksen. The bronze and granite statue sat perched on a pile of rocks about ten feet from the shore. The mermaid seemed quite petite but then again, she was the *Little* Mermaid.

Brooklyn's eyes grew wide as she saw one of her fairy tale heroes. The statue was compelling. But, almost immediately she responded, "She's not the real one." She lacked the bright red hair. And clothes.

"She's actually the most real one you'll see," I said. "Her story led to Ariel." Brooklyn thought on that a moment. I don't know if she believed me or wanted to trust her version, so I left it at that. We found a rock to sit on so we could look out at her. We gazed at her as the waves softly crashed against her rock, the setting sun reflecting pink on the water. The cool breeze lifted our hair, and I pulled my little girl tight for a squeeze.

In Hans Christian Andersen's tale, the Little Mermaid swam to the surface and perched on her rock as she stared lovingly toward the shore at the Prince. Now she stares at the state-of-the-art waste facility plant as she welcomes travelers to Copenhagen Harbor and people, like my daughter, stare lovingly at her.

That hour with my eldest, exploring together, safe but out of our element, taught her volumes. I think she saw that Mommy doesn't know everything, but she's always learning. Mommy trusts me to be out in the world. Mommy wants to share life-altering moments. And if she didn't discover those things, at least she saw the Little Mermaid. She will always remember that.

"You clean, I'll pack," I said to AJ on the last day. "When you're done, use the rest of the pigeon Krone at the café, and I'll start walking to the train station with the kids." He scrubbed the floors, cleaned the toilets, and probably power-washed the siding per our host's exacting sixty required minutes of chores that he miraculously squeezed into twenty.

"And you guys go outside," I told our mini-mes (mini-usses?). The locked stoop outside the apartment that had concerned us our first morning served a fantastic barrier. The kids looked like caged zoo animals or prisoners, sticking their arms through the rails.

"Clang, clang, clang!" went the bars as Lucas ran his hand along the length of them.

"Ma! Ma!" shouted Sienna. I heard Ella laugh devilishly.

A contingent of tourists bustled at the bus stop on the other side of the gate, led by a person with a small flag on the top of a stick. One man pointed out my children to his companion. A camera popped out, then a second as the group snapped shot after shot of my 'local' kids. One asked my aptly named Brooklyn if she spoke English.

I laughed as I heard this from the other side of the door. "Say god morgen," I wanted to shout. If these poor people were going to brag about seeing Danish children living on the stoop, she could at least offer a polite greeting.

I shared the story with AJ during our long walk to the train that would take us to the airport for our long flight home. He took the stroller (overloaded with two duffel bags and Lucas) I had been pushing so I could better pull the suitcase while carrying Sienna. I was like the woman in the shoe; I had so many children, I hardly knew what to do. Ever-Hungry AJ carried two hot beverages and six Danishes; he hardly knew what to eat.

"It's amazing," I started. "I overanalyzed and overengineered everything about this trip. Then, we lost our guidebook at the airport, we missed the ferry, had a crazy day in Helsinki and Tallinn, and I sent us to a lot of closed places." I took a breath and nodded my head toward the kids. "Plus, we had a few... uh, struggles." Ella smiled angelically at me, her bright eyes gleaming in excitement and unaltered happiness as she held my semi-free hand.

"We're a little crazy," he said. "But they had so much fun. You did a really good job. Well, other than the marathon. That was awful."

I smiled. "Thank you." Then, I shook my head and added, "I can't believe those people thought our kids were locals. That's awesome." AJ and I had somehow provided our kids that same sense of home and comfort they had in Maryland. It warmed my heart.

With those misses came new opportunities. We found hidden gems and terrible, but memorable, rocks. We paced ourselves to our Screech Owl, I dallied with my oldest, bonded with my son, and expanded our baby's horizons.

I hoped the flight home would be easier than the red-eye there, but my optimism was strongly misplaced. Entertaining wired kids for eight-and-a-half hours is much worse than putting tired ones to sleep on a plane at night. I played countless games of some Pacman-like fish game with Sienna and watched an alphabet baby show at least dozen times. In ten-minute-increments, I watched

Tully, about a mom of three who struggles with raising her newborn and hires a night nurse. Dramatized and excessive, yet oddly familiar, I recognized the tired struggles of a mom with young kids.

I have traveled to beaches where the sole requirement is to relax. I studied abroad in Australia and China to become ingrained in the culture. I learned about giving in Morocco. I camped with soon-to-be-not-strangers, letting go in nature. I've hiked distant trails with scary animals where I faced my fears. Yet it was this trip where my true self came to being.

Plus, an idea came to me on what I could do with my adventures and, for the first time without second guessing myself in a while, I began to write.

Post-Partum

PENCILS AND PARENTING

*D*URING OUR JOURNEYS, we had missed connections, mile-high meltdowns, and miniature cars that rolled under the airplane seats. We had crying kids, cold sea pools, and carsick babies. Sleepless nights. Seatbelt evaders. Sticky, sugary snacks on fingers. We had a Houdini baby breaking free from sleep sacks and another escaping my seemingly iron vise grip. Kids bickered. One really cute kid screamed at the top of her lungs, "Brookie has two!"

It was challenging. Such is raising kids.

Whether hunkering down in Michigan during the longest nights of the year or summering in I-hope-there-are-blackout-curtains Stockholm, it's hard to get them to sleep. It's tough to get them to eat their veggies or pick up their toys. The days drag on—or as the saying goes, "The days are long, the years are short."

Those sixty-hour days are why it's crucial to make life enjoyable. The years are short, so make them memorable. Parenting while traveling may be hard but traveling (as a parent) is fun. And when it's not, I try to reminder two things.

First, wherever I am, whether it's Kalamazoo or the Swedish Moose Zoo, people are mostly kind, empathetic, and helpful.

I've heard, "Cioé, ci siamo passata tutti," in breathtaking Italian.

"Todos já passamos por isso," from a man in thickly accented Portuguese.

And, "We've all been there," in proper Queen's English, that last one while my child lay prone in the middle of a pedestrian path at an exquisite foreign garden with magnificent rose-ringed parakeets. People love to help, even in ways that may be odd back home, like offering a juice box or bag of gummy bears to a crying kid they don't know.

Second, it's important to not be too hard on ourselves. We're all doing the best we can. It may seem others have things under better control. Chances are, they don't. Remember that you are also *that parent* who gets it right, whose kid is the all-star, the "thoughtful" kid, or the one who puts herself to sleep. Each of us has held our own version of a Pinterest perfect pumpkin playdate. My husband and I took our small children on memorable, affordable, and nap-focused trips to places from the Azores to Zuccari's Last Judgment in Rome. I watched my child feed a baby iguana and meet doppelgänger Irish cousins an ocean away. We also dropped that tantrum-soothing pacifier in the toilet.

"You have a very different background from me and others in our (suburban) community," one of my best friends, recently shared. "When we say things or tell stories, you want to learn more about it. You are really open and curious about things that are different."

"Wow!" I said to my thoughtful and overly generous friend. "That is an amazing compliment."

I grew up in middle America, sheltered from foreigners and people who may look or talk differently from me. When a free-spirited Brazilian exchange student came to live with my family, I saw that not all people wear socks and some people drink a lot of water. My mind was blown. I had a lot to learn. There were teammates of different races, college classmates with opposing views, friends who came out.

Four lifetimes ago, I whetted my appetite for travel by living among the locals while studying abroad in Australia. I made friends of different religions and was welcomed into a mixed-race family. Each experience influenced my life and (hopefully) makes me a better, worldlier, and more compassionate person. So, yeah, I want to improve myself, and I want to expand my children's horizons. I want to share my pleasures with them, to live life with the kids, not edit the world for them. I hope they share my awe at seeing something new and they retain their innate curiosity. As parents, we mold our children, and we get to bear witness to their glory. While they live in the moment, we see the path that brought them there, all the dirt and boulders, the volcanos and meltdowns.

Traveling with small children was not and is not an obstacle or a hindrance—but sometimes it's a challenge. And challenges help us grow. They force us to change perception. Some days, I'm the mom who has it all together, and others I've got four screaming messes. I may be sitting in my seat holding a small, sleeping child, but I'm also a tiny speck in an airplane, miles above Earth. Traveling with children presents the opportunity to experience both perspectives at once.

And then, we applied that perspective to a pandemic. We became trapped at home with those kids who were angels and demons when we traveled together. For a few months, our house became our world. This quarter-acre plot turned into a camping adventure, a virtual school, and a 3-star hotel with terrible maid service, poison ivy, and ants. That marathon we traversed the Atlantic for became loops on neighborhood roads and a virtual race across Tennessee. During a pandemic, time is not measured in hours or days but in the length of time until the end of your spouse's conference call.

We learned to slow down and see things differently. We caught frogs and spotted baby owls. We studied our home like we explored the world and addressed issues within our own country and racial history. When it's dark outside, it's easy to forget that the sun will rise soon. The masks will disappear, and we will breathe that fresh clean air again. We will travel again.

When we do, I hope to see others who may have been unsure about taking that leap. When it's safe, take your child to that distant wedding even though she has never been on an airplane. Don't be afraid to take that challenge. Don't be surprised that it isn't nearly the impossible climb you expected. Challenges are not as hard as they initially seem. Whether it's traveling with one kid or four, with confidence, optimism, and a little patience, the rewards can vastly outweigh the worry. As long as we have the necessities—our family, our health, our passports, and their pacifiers—we can see the world.

ACKNOWLEDGEMENTS

SPECIAL THANKS TO all of the educators in my life who supported and encouraged creative writing to this math girl who always had her nose in a book, especially Professor Ann Fox. And to my dad, the best teacher of all (and finder-of-great-deals).

Thank you, Mom, for shaping me into who I am today and for the beautiful photos on each and every trip. Bryn and Kylie, you have always been my biggest heroes. I have been blessed by all of the memories from such an incredible childhood, filled with toys and love. Marcela, my Brazilian sister, thank you for being an amazing godmother. To my grandparents no longer here who supported me in life and helped me to believe in myself. To my nieces and nephews who first introduced me to unconditional love.

Thank you, Mario, for introducing me to my husband and fellow kid-wrangler. Thank you, Kim and Jessica, for your lifelong friendships, and unending optimism and encouragement.

To my college friends and friends since who have expanded my world view, especially Elizabeth who served as my sounding board. Thank you, Erin, for helping make so many of these great memories, at Davidson and in Australia. Christine, thanks for including us for your beautiful wedding which set the stage for Rockabye Reunions. Thanks to the Aussies for making me feel welcome in your country. It was the start of my travels and I am grateful for all of the friendships that trip gave me, especially those of you willing to house me (ahem, Liam) and take an American to Uluru though I couldn't rent a car.

Thank you to my former teammates, coworkers, mentors, and amazing coaches who cared enough to teach me about hard work, being strong, and working together. Thank you to all of you who recommended these beautiful destinations, along with advice, housing, and fun outings while we were there. Thanks to Dorian for sharing the hidden gem of the Azores and the basketball guys for the tips on Scandinavia.

Thank you to my in-laws for raising such a considerate and wonderful son. We're so blessed to have you in our children's lives. Thank you also to Mike and Katherine for all of your help.

Morgan and Elana, thank you for always being there for me and for continuing to push me to improve the world. Abby, much gratitude for reading my first draft and providing thoughtful feedback and for all of your support.

Thank you to my editor, Charlie Knight. I've enjoyed working with you and appreciate you making me a better and more inclusive writer.

Thank you to my cover designer and formatter-extraordinaire, Alice Briggs, for your hard work to make this just right. Love your ability to bring my family to the best light through your creativity.

Much thanks to all of the amazing babysitters who watched my kids, especially Sara, Erica, Tatik, and Carol.

To my book club who reawakened my love of reading and to all the Moms in Olney, for showing me that raising a litter is possible. Thank you, Jenny, for opening my eyes to even more adventure!

Thank you to the Olney Writer's Club—Andrew, Joseph, Bob and Sue, Brian and Mary Lou (especially for the unending enthusiasm), Michele (ditto), Linda, Liza, Emily, Mark, Amy and Weiman, and Caroline. Your recommendations, feedback, and support were critical in polishing my work. Jason, thank you for your encouragement and tips.

Brooklyn, when you were born, my heart moved outside my body. Always remember that you are smart, strong, beautiful, and kind. Have I ever told you that you're amazing?

My dear Ella, my thoughtful and inclusive girl, I love you with all of my heart. Keep up your creativity and working hard. You'll go great places.

Lucas, thank you for the joy of raising such a sweet boy and for making me laugh daily. Our ten minutes every night is the highlight of my day. (And yes, I'll get you a truck.)

Sienna, thank you for filling that little piece of my heart that I didn't realize needed you. You make me smile every single day. I'm sorry I passed on my lion hair but it looks much better on you.

AJ, thank you for your support and joining me on these adventures. Thank you for your honest feedback, thoughtful criticism, and extensive proofreading. You are my rock and I'm so happy to be on this trip with you.

ABOUT THE AUTHOR

KAITLYN JAIN IS a world traveler and dedicated mom to her four young children. She has visited over twenty-five countries and nearly all fifty states, dragging her kids wherever she can. She loves seeing and trying new things and aims to instill compassion and love of travel in her children.

Kaitlyn has worked for fifteen years in corporate America. She serves as PTA President, loves baking and making homemade-baby-food-inspired applesauce, and hopes to coach her kids again soon.

Kaitlyn received her BA in Economics from Davidson College while playing Division I volleyball and earned her MBA from NYU Stern while carrying a baby. She has written for *Chicken Soup for the Soul*. She lives in Maryland with her husband, children, and playful Boston Terriers. *Passports and Pacifiers* is her first book.

www.kaitlynjain.com

Made in the USA
Middletown, DE
12 February 2021

33616122R00158